D1333719

DUDE,

WHERE'S MY

JESUS FISH?

A Compilation Highlighting the Blunt and Uncompromising Teachings of Arten and Pursah on A Course in Miracles

MIKE LEMIEUX

Giddy Up Mikey Press

Ashland, Oregon, U.S.A.

Contact Mikey: mikey@giddyupmikey.com

Portions from:

Gary R Renard

The Disappearance of the Universe Copyright October 2004

Your Immortal Reality Copyright August 2006

Hay House Inc

Carlsbad, CA

Foundation For Inner Peace

A Course in Miracles Third Edition Copyright 2007

Foundation For A Course in Miracles

Temecula, CA

ISBN 978-0-615-38184-8

Book cover design by four different contributors, it's a long story: Alexander Marchand, Robert Donaghey, Bruce Rawles, & Mike Lemieux all contributed.

Title page image designed by Alexander Marchand

Back cover photo taken by Patti Ann McAlister

This book is lovingly dedicated to my mom, Patti Ann McAlister, and her husband, Dougy aka 'West Coast Daddy' – my fellow *Seinfeld* and *Disappearance of the Universe* junkies – they're freakin' awesome! Great minds think alike….and so do ours!

Table of Contents

Foreword by Gary Renard

You gotta wonder about a guy who calls himself 'Giddy Up Mikey' and compiles a book titled *Dude, Where's My Jesus Fish?* What kinda guy does that? I'll tell you. The kind that would order out for vegan pizza if two ascended masters showed up on his couch! Just kidding.

Mikey's a great guy. Like me, Mikey is a Masshole from Massachusetts. We're both self-actualized jerks working on our own forgiveness lessons. We're also both adamant about the teachings found in *A Course in Miracles* and devote most of our time to studying and sharing this important message.

Mikey's also a personal friend who I've had the pleasure of spending some good times with. On top of that, he's made consistent and important contributions to the on-line study group that discusses my books, which is the biggest *A Course in Miracles* study group in the world. It wouldn't be the same without him.

What Mikey's done with this book is create a valuable tool for directly accessing *Course* concepts (as taught by Arten and Pursah) in a topic-based fashion. Additionally, he's added his rather colloquial insights which make this book a light, humorous read, a refreshing change from most *Course*-related materials. My first book, *The Disappearance of the Universe,* is frequently referred to as the 'can opener' that helps students open the rather heady *A Course in Miracles* book. *Dude, Where's My Jesus Fish?* is like a cheat sheet that helps you make the grade. If this book turns more folks onto *A Course in Miracles* – and I expect it will – then we have Mikey to thank for growing our beloved *Course* community and helping us all to get Home.

~ Gary Renard, the best-selling author of *The Disappearance of the Universe of the Universe*

Introduction

This book is intended for those already familiar with Gary Renard's books, and/or the self-study course called *A Course in Miracles*. It's not a substitute for either, but rather it is more like a supplement to Gary's first two books, *The Disappearance of the Universe* and *Your Immortal Reality,* which heavily reference the aforementioned *A Course in Miracles* aka the *Course*. That's not to say that if you have little or no familiarity with Gary's books, or the *Course,* that you cannot derive any benefit from reading this book, as it could very well serve as your introduction. However, it is geared a little more towards those who already have some familiarity with Gary's books and the *Course* and just appreciate the necessary repetition and reminders to *get* this stuff on a *deeper* level, while helping one to stay focused and motivated on the ambitious task at hand – to completely undo the ego by the means of *true* forgiveness.

An analogy I like to use about this book is that it's like watching the highlights of a sporting event on ESPN rather than watching the entire game – you get the gist of what went down, but not all the details. So, for those who may be reading this who are not already familiar with Gary Renard's books, or perhaps have struggled in the past to understand *A Course in Miracles*, I highly recommend that you read Gary's first book, *The Disappearance of the Universe – Straight Talk about Illusions, Past Lives, Religion, Sex, Politics, and the Miracles of Forgiveness*. It's the best thing since, well, sliced bread! And it's the greatest gift I have ever received – and I bought and paid for the book myself!

You can read excerpts of *Disappearance* at Gary's website and see if it's for you. (www.garyrenard.com) By the way, Gary is very proud of the fact, as he informs us on his podcasts, that he came up with that website name all by himself! Also, check out my recommended material section at the end of this book for 'all things' Gary Renard.

Gary's first two books are written in a dialogue format. Gary is the student, while his teachers, who are two ascended masters that go

X

by the names of Arten and Pursah, were two of Jesus' disciples two thousand years ago, Thaddaeus and Thomas, respectively. They refer to Jesus as *J*, as they did not know him as Jesus, but rather as Y'shua, and they say that a proper translation into Greek then into English would have been *Jeshua*, so they simply refer to him as *J* in order to cover both *Jesus* and *Jeshua*.[1]

Arten and Pursah promise in the first chapter of the spiritual masterpiece, *The Disappearance of the Universe*, that they will supply all the answers to life's biggest questions: 'You will find out what you really are; how you got here; exactly why you and all other people behave and feel the way that you do; why the universe keeps repeating the same patterns over and over again; why people get sick; the reason behind all failure, accidents, addictions, poverty, and natural disasters; the real cause of all of the violence, crime, war, and terrorism in the world; the only meaningful solution to all of these things; and how to apply it.'[2]

For those of you who are new to all this, well, to be perfectly blunt, I'm not here to blow sunshine up your ass as I'm not exactly a 'people pleaser' or a 'yes-man.' There are plenty of candy-coated spiritual teachings out there for you to choose from if that's what you want. I have no investment in people feeling warm and fuzzy about me, and have no political agenda, so, like Gary and his teachers, I'm free to just tell it straight up for those who are ready to hear it. As Pursah tells Gary in *Disappearance,* 'People need to be educated, but if you *really* tell them the truth, then you're bound to give up some popularity. But it's better to tell them the truth and have some people walk out on you than to tell them only what they want to hear and have them stay.'[3] So, that's what *I'm* all about and where *I'm* coming from.

Anyway, it's not my intention to be such a hard ass, but I wouldn't be doing anybody any favors by compromising on Arten and Pursah's, as well as J's teachings, and I see the *Course* the same exact way as they and Gary all do. And Jesus wouldn't be Jesus if He had compromised on these teachings. I have no interest, or desire, in making up my own thing,[4] or incorporating dualistic teachings into the *Course* and telling people that those teachings are saying the *same thing* as the *Course*. I'm a straight shooter so you're not going to get any bullshit from me, only a sincere desire to be truly helpful.

So, if you're one who is seeking an intellectual truth, that, when applied, will eventually lead you to an experiential truth, then you've come to the right place. The message in Gary's books is designed to help you save time, so I'm just passing along the message while reinforcing it for myself.

For all the newbies, now may be a good time for you to burn this book or run it through a shredder, or better yet, donate it to your local library or resell it on Amazon, because you don't know what the hell you're going to be getting yourself into here. This isn't 'fast food spirituality'[5] as this particular spiritual path separates the men from the boys – metaphorically speaking, of course. For those of you who have already set foot on this spiritual path, well, there's no turning back *now*!

Now, without further ado, here is a revised version of an article I wrote for my local newspaper, the Ashland *Daily Tidings*. It was printed in the March 7, 2009 edition. It explains what *The Disappearance of the Universe* is all about:

Of all the books I've read during my many years of feasting in the 'spiritual buffet line,'[6] nothing has explained the truth about God and our existence, and why we are seemingly here, any clearer to me than Gary Renard's *The Disappearance of the Universe*.

Disappearance addresses heavy subject matter, while cutting to the chase in no uncertain terms, and doing so in a very entertaining and humorous fashion. I highly recommend it, though it is not intended for the squeamish[7] nor the faint of heart, as the material is not sugarcoated.

Forgiveness is the theme of the spiritual path presented in *Disappearance*. Gary's teachers tell us, 'Forgiveness is where the rubber meets the road. Without forgiveness, metaphysics are useless.'[8] Of course, they are talking about forgiveness in the quantum sense, rather than what traditionally passes as forgiveness in this world. As Gary's teachers say, 'The kind of forgiveness J used, and that his *Course* is teaching, is not the same kind of forgiveness that Christianity and the world sometimes participate in. If it were, then it would be a waste of time.'[9]

Disappearance is the unofficial 'cliff notes' to *A Course in Miracles* – or as Gary would call it, 'street language'[10] for the *Course*. *A Course in Miracles* is a spiritual, purely non-dualistic, self-study course, which is often referred to in *Disappearance*. The *Course* is over thirteen hundred pages long, and consists of the *Text*, *Workbook for Students*, *Manual for Teachers*, and the most recent edition includes two pamphlets called *Psychotherapy: Purpose, Process and Practice* and *The Song of Prayer*.

Written in Shakespearean blank verse and loaded with subtly humorous rhetorical questions, while being holographic in nature,[11] the

Course is Jesus' teachings the way, I believe, they were intended to be – consistent and uncompromising, all about love and forgiveness, and absolutely nothing to do with sin, fear, guilt, sacrifice, and showing up to church on Sunday. As Gary's teachers put it, 'The *Course* is Jesus speaking as an artist correcting the Bible.'[12] And as J states in his *Course*, 'Those who seek controversy will find it. Yet those who seek clarification will find it as well.'[13]

The *Course* is all about the healing of the subconscious mind, which entails looking at your illusions, examining them, and eventually releasing them through the process of *true* forgiveness. As it states in the *Course*, 'No one can escape from illusions unless he looks at them, for not looking is the way they are protected.'[14]

The *Course* gives you the practical tools necessary in order to attain the objective of lasting inner peace and happiness, and ultimately enlightenment, regardless of what is going on in the world and with your own personal life's circumstances. Through the application of *true*, or *quantum* forgiveness, you're taking full responsibility for your life's experiences, including the experiences that are not seemingly your fault, because on the level of the unconscious mind, you made it all up.

With *quantum* forgiveness, you're not forgiving people because they really did something – you're forgiving them because they haven't really done anything. Whatever pushes your buttons and pisses you off on any given day is *symbolic* of what's in your own unconscious mind. Once you really get that the world is not being done *to* you, but rather *by* you, then what you are really doing by practicing *true* forgiveness is forgiving the symbolic contents of your own mind. So nobody is ever really a victim in this world. As the *Course* puts it, 'I am not the victim of the world I see.'[15] Indeed, you are the *maker* of it – not always easy to accept, but it is definitely the truth. As Gary's teachers ask, 'Are you going to get that you're *not* a victim and take responsibility for dreaming, or are you going to make it real and stay stuck here?'[16] And as J states in the *Course*, 'Beware of the temptation to perceive yourself unfairly treated.'[17]

This isn't the most glamorous of spiritual paths, because it's not about manifesting stuff; it's about undoing the muck buried in the subconscious mind. So it's not always pretty, dressed up with lipstick and powder, however, it does have teeth. As Gary's teachers say, 'The most striking evidence of this approach's validity will be that it works.'[18] And as the *Course* states, 'No one who learns from experience that one choice brings peace and joy while another brings chaos and disaster needs additional convincing.'[19] From my experience, I can assure you that *true* forgiveness does in fact work. It does, however, take practice to develop faith and trust in it, but once you start experiencing the benefits of doing this work, it encourages and inspires you to keep going, and eventually it does become easier.

Though the *Course* is presented in Christian terminology, it is very Eastern-like in its theology and practice, as it gets in touch with the power of the mind. I don't recommend taking it on without having read *Disappearance* first, as it will save you much time while helping you to really grasp the heart of the *Course*.

All spiritual paths lead to God in the end,[20] however, the *Course* does imply that this is a *faster* way. The *Course is* simple, however, it's *not* easy, as we all have this thing called the ego, and it would much rather you be right, than be happy and at peace. And as J asks us in the *Course,* 'Do you prefer that you be right or happy?'[21]

This path isn't about fixing up your life, it's about waking up from what you *think* is your life,[22] and as Gary's teachers would add to that, '...that's not just a minor distinction.'[23] Although it's not about fixing up your life, it *can*, however, be a fringe benefit[24] – and Mikey's *down* with fringe benefits! Anyway, sticking to this path requires faith, trust, discipline, patience, vigilance, perseverance, as well as the willingness to question every motive that you have and every value that you hold,[25] the ability to be objective with yourself, and the determination to face all of your fears. Oh, and did I mention faith and trust? Anyway, as Gary's teachers put it, 'Comfort is the goal, not necessarily the means.'[26] With all that said, however, it's not about giving anything up, as J puts it in the *Course,* 'This course does not attempt to take from you the little that you have.'[27] So, it's really about letting go of your *psychological attachment* to it all, as well as forgetting not to laugh.

Author's Notes

#1

In this book, there may be some things said that may make me seem a bit arrogant, or full of myself, or maybe just weird. It's done so intentionally. As the *Course* says, 'Into eternity, where all is one, there crept a tiny, mad idea, at which the son of God remembered not to laugh.'[1] So if something I say in here offends you or rubs you the wrong way, try to remember to use it as an opportunity to laugh, and *forgive*.

We tend to take things so seriously in this world, and we make it *all so real*, instead of seeing the humor in it. So, in order to encourage some laughter in my book, I'll be using an Internet slang term (LOL) at the end of a sentence that's not meant to be taken too seriously. For those of you not familiar with Internet slang, 'LOL' stands for 'Laughing Out Loud' which people generally use at the end of a statement that is intended to be taken humorously, tongue-in-cheek. Of course, feel free to laugh at anything I have written in here regardless of whether or not you see an 'LOL' at the end of a sentence. But if you see an 'LOL' at the end of a sentence, and you *don't* laugh, then there is something seriously wrong with you!

Oops, my bad, I was supposed to put an 'LOL' at the end of that last sentence. Anyway, the truth is that there is something very wrong with *all* of us. As Bill Murray humorously put it in the movie *Stripes*, 'There is something *wrong* with us, something very, very *wrong* with us, something seriously *wrong* with us!' What's *wrong* with us is that we're all insane, some much more than others. (LOL) This insanity is the result of appearing to be separate from our Source. It is arrogant of us to think that we can have an individual existence separate from God. While many even *thinking* the idea of you and God being one and the same is arrogant, the truth is that *real* humility is accepting what you *really* are – perfect spirit, one with God in Heaven.[2] And that's the long term goal of the *Course*, returning our seemingly separated minds to that awareness. Remember what J tells us in the

Course, 'The truth about you is so lofty that nothing unworthy of God is worthy of you.'[3] So, with all that said, my book will either inspire you to forgive, or give you an opportunity to forgive; either way you slice it, I am here only to be truly helpful.

#2

I love _A Course in Miracles_, I totally _get_ it, however, I don't like reading it, so I generally don't. I _have_ read through all 365 of the _Workbook_ lessons, as well as the _Manual for Teachers_, only so I can say I have. Quite honestly, it didn't really do it for me the way Arten and Pursah's words do, although J is the one I converse with regularly in my mind. I already understood _A Course in Miracles_ before I ever touched a _Course_ book; Arten and Pursah spell it all out so clearly with their 'blue collar' style, and I knew right off the bat, based on my experiences, that their message was 'dead on balls accurate,' to borrow a phrase from Marisa Tomei in the movie _My Cousin Vinny_.

So, I already understood Gary's books viscerally[1] which is why I was able to easily understand _them,_ and the _Course,_ intellectually, because I had already had many of the experiences that they spoke about. In a lot of ways, I was already applying the non-dualistic teachings of _A Course in Miracles_ before I ever knew anything about it! Arten and Pursah put my spiritual path into words, while tying up the 'loose ends' and simplifying it all for me.

Understanding this thought system came rather easily to me, as if I had studied it already in a past life. Going through the _Course_ book was actually unnecessary for me. In addition to having read through the _Workbook_ and _Manual for Teachers,_ I have read _parts_ of the _Text_ at a study group that I attend here in Southern Oregon, but I usually find myself either daydreaming, silently or not so silently laughing, or making funny faces at people during the reading time; certainly not due to a disrespect for the material, but rather because it's too complicated and intellectual for my simple mind. As J says in the _Course,_ 'Simplicity is very difficult for twisted minds.'[2] So, it appears my mind is just less twisted than most. (LOL)

Anyway, the more you undo the ego, the more you can handle simple, and then you may very well find that you'll have no use for complicated. As Gary's teachers put it, 'The ego wants and believes in complexity. The truth of the Holy Spirit is simple.'[3] And J says, 'The reason this course is simple is that truth is simple. Complexity is of the ego, and is nothing more than the ego's attempt to obscure the obvious.'[4]

Other than the humorous rhetorical questions, reading from the *Course* just doesn't do it for me. Art, poetry, and literature are not things that have ever really been of interest to me. So I've never been a culturally sophisticated type; the extent of my enjoyment in art has been limited to listening to loud and obnoxious rock n'roll! However, I am a big fan of Yanni's music, so I at least I have *that* going for me. Anyway, not getting heavily into the *Course* is certainly not a 'resistance'[5] thing on my part, it's just a matter of what works for me, and what I feel guided to do. I got exactly what I needed and what I've been waiting for all my life from Gary's teachers – it's like I found my home away from Home. And I wouldn't have been able to relate to the *Course* at all if it weren't for them. In fact, I wouldn't have touched the *Course* with a ten foot pole!

I've pretty much renounced everything else as far as spiritual teachings go that don't come from Arten and Pursah, via Gary, ever since *Disappearance* made its way into my life. Once you *really get* what's being said in Gary's books and *A Course in Miracles* on a deep enough level, you don't *need* anything else – the rest is overkill, and quite frankly, a waste of time – at least for me. However, I do recognize that I needed those other spiritual teachings to prepare me for what was being said in Gary's books and the *Course*. In fact, by the time I read *Disappearance* for the very first time, I was prepared so well that I was able to easily accept what was being said without fear or resistance as I had already gone through that phase of my spiritual path, which I'll get into a little bit in the first part of this book. It feels really good to no longer be a spiritual seeker with a bunch of unanswered questions; it's just a matter of 'keep on keeping on' along the path of *true* forgiveness from here on out.

When it comes down to it on this spiritual path, it doesn't matter how well you can quote from the *Course* or how well you understand it. What really matters is that you start to *grow up*[6] in the spiritual sense by taking responsibility for your life's experiences which means you practice *true* forgiveness. That's the bottom line; that *is A Course in Miracles!* If that is where your mind is at, then I can assure you that you are making spiritual progress regardless of how much or how little of the *Course* you have delved into. As Gary's teachers put it, 'The truth is an awareness – not a book.'[7] In addition, if you are working with the *Workbook* lessons, or just trying to master the forgiveness gig, and you feel you are not making progress or feel guilty about not doing it perfectly, don't beat yourself up about it. Be kind to yourself. If you could do this all perfectly right off the bat, then you wouldn't need to do this work in the first place – you'd already be enlightened. And none of us can just skip to the end.

There's nobody 'out there' judging you, so go at your own pace; *A Course in Miracles* is not a sprint – it's a marathon. Except in the end, as a crazy lady shouted in a *Seinfeld* episode, 'You're all winners!' Anyway, mastering forgiveness is no different than trying to master anything else. It takes practice[8] and elbow grease to become great at anything, and not just a little.[9] As Arten puts it, 'While the *Course* is *directed* toward experience, it takes the wise intellectual choices of a trained mind to bring about that experience.'[10] So, it's just a matter of how much you want it. Eventually, if you haven't already, you'll go from having a *little* willingness to having *abundant* willingness.[11]

Now, on the flip side, there are many people who think they understand the *Course* and what it's really saying, and yet they really don't; they don't even realize how unique[12] and radical it really is. Some confuse it as being part of the New Age movement – which it is *not*![13] The New Age stuff is conservative compared to what J is teaching in his *Course*. Most, if not all, of the New Age stuff out there is geared towards fixing up the world, making certain things happen in the world, making the world a better place, saving the rain forests, freeing Tibet, achieving world peace, manifesting abundance, and yada, yada, yada, while the *Course* is about waking you up from your *dream* that there *is* a world in the first place!

So, now you may be thinking, 'What makes *you* so damn special that you think *you* know what the correct interpretation of the *Course* is?' Well, to quote Bill Murray from the movie *Groundhog Day*, 'That's exactly what makes me so special!' (LOL) The New Age stuff certainly has its place, however, it should *never* be confused with the uncompromising and non-dualistic teachings presented in *A Course in Miracles*. Suffice it to say that the *Course*, when it's *really* understood, is beyond New Age thought and is well ahead of its time.[14]

Besides people trying to 'New Age' the *Course*, there are those who try to make a religion out of the *Course* and make it all about your behavior – God help us! My personal opinion on organized religion, as a result of my nine years of Catholic school, is that it's like a cult, albeit, a subtle one. The church just wants to control your mind, take your money, and make you feel guilty about anything that pleasures you. (LOL) And as Pursah tells Gary, 'Organized religion is politics.'[15] In other words, you get a little bit of truth with a 'huge, steaming pile of crap'[16] on top! But it does serve a useful purpose for many people, so I would never try to take that away from anybody. And Arten and Pursah make a very interesting point with this statement, 'The religion or spirituality you believe in does not determine how spiritually advanced you are in terms of your awareness. There are Christians who are among the very highest of attainers, and there are Christians who are babbling fools. This is true of *all* religions, philosophies, and spiritual forms, without exception.'[17]

From my personal observation, 'the babbling fools' theory certainly holds water with both the on-line and off-line *Course* community – that's for *damn* sure! (LOL) These are the folks who J might refer to as 'the self-accusing shrieks of sinners mad with guilt'[18] who may or may not understand the metaphysics of the *Course*, and go on to apply their understanding of it in a very misguided way, using it as a weapon, rather than using the *Course* for what it's meant for – practicing forgiveness. Now, I certainly don't make these comments here to pass judgment on anyone, but merely for the benefit of the *Course* novices who may come across these folks on the Internet *Course* forums and such. You may be impressed by their 'knowledge,' thinking that you're getting some divine guidance from them, however, most of the time all you're really getting is a boatload of the ego, not to mention their 'macho head games,' to borrow a phrase from a *Seinfeld* episode. (LOL) At the same time, Gary's teachers would tell you, 'Don't assume malice for what stupidity may be able to explain.'[19] (LOL)

Moving along now, for some folks, if not most, going through parts or all of the *Course* will be necessary. For other folks, applying what Gary's teachers have to say may be enough. And perhaps for others, there will be several *Workbook* lessons that really stand out for you, and you find yourself working with them over and over again. It's an individual thing – everybody's path is unique.[20] As Gary's teachers say, 'The ego is very complex and highly individualized.'[21] So, some folks will have to do the *Course,* literally, by the book, while others will feel very comfortable in improvising[22] while staying in alignment with the metaphysics of the *Course.*

There is no getting around the fact that in order to become a master, and to return to God, you'll have to undo all the walls of guilt buried in the mind. These walls are the blocks to the awareness of love's presence.[23] Gary's teachers, as well as J, say forgiveness is the *only* way to remove these blocks.[24] But as Gary's teachers also say, 'Everyone has certain phrases and ideas from the *Course* that work the best at reminding them of the truth.'[25] So, do what feels right for you as guided – not what *others* think you should do. Becoming comfortable with listening to that inner voice of wisdom can take practice in itself, and it takes wisdom to choose the right teacher.[26] So, do whatever it is that helps you to best facilitate that forgiveness process in your everyday life.

Reading Gary's books, as well as listening to his audio programs over and over again is what works best for *me*. That's what keeps me focused, motivated, inspired, and driven to do *my* forgiveness work. I know what Arten and Pursah say is true, so it's just a matter of my being able to master the art of *true forgiveness*. I haven't as of yet, Mikey still has issues. (LOL) I certainly don't claim to be enlightened, as I'm not exactly walking on water here, and furthermore, if you drove a nail through my wrist at this time it would *freakin'* hurt – so please don't! Now despite all that, I do think it is fair to say that I don't have any special *hate* relationships, although I do have a number of special *undesirable* ones. (LOL)

Anyway, I know I'm making spiritual progress because I find that I have a lot less things to forgive than I did, say, ten years ago, or even a year ago for that matter. There are many things that once pushed my buttons that I can now simply laugh at, or shrug at, so I know I'm getting closer to that place Gary's teachers describe where you are so happy it doesn't matter whether you are a master or not.[27] And that's the place where Mikey wants to be! Heaven can wait – I know it's inevitable, because we never really left in the first place. Giddy up!

#3

Towards the end of *The Disappearance of the Universe*, Arten tells Gary, 'People can choose however they want to use our book in the future.'[1] First time I read that, it struck a chord with me; at that moment I knew I would be using it somehow other than just for my own personal use. Now I'm using it to create my *own* book – not that I feel like a *real* author. On his podcasts and in his workshops, Gary has referred to himself as the 'alleged' author of *The Disappearance of the*

Universe and *Your Immortal Reality*. Well, since much of the material herein comes from his books, I guess that makes me an author twice removed! But how much can I possibly add when Arten and Pursah say it all, and with such clarity?

In this book, not only I do quote many times from Gary's books and *A Course in Miracles*, but you will find I repeat some of the *same* quotes and ideas. Well, as Arten puts it in *Disappearance*, 'Repetition is not only perfectly all right, it's mandatory;'[2] which is the main reason to justify *this* book's existence. Even though most of the material contained herein is not anything I came up with myself, and that you've probably already read in Gary's books or from the *Course*, there is no such thing as too much repetition. If you're not perfect at practicing forgiveness just yet, then you can't hear these ideas enough times. God knows I'm not perfect at practicing forgiveness yet. Well, God doesn't really know that, but that's another story.

Also, just so you'll know, some of the quotes I put in here are slightly paraphrased in order to maintain the proper context in which they were spoken. There are also some quotes that were said by more than one individual that I combined into one quote, several other quotes I changed from past tense to present tense, and a few of Gary's quotes I changed from being spoken in the first person to the second person, and some others from multiple pages that I combined into one quote where I felt it was appropriate to do so. I can assure you that any changes that I have made do not change the meaning of, nor compromise the integrity of, what Arten, Pursah, and Gary have to say in any way. If by some chance the meaning has been altered, it was an honest mistake made on my part and not done so deliberately to deceive.

One more thing, sometimes I have something to say in-between the quotes I'll be sharing; that verbiage will be labeled as 'Mikey's Note.'

#4

I'll soon be in the process of writing my second book which will likely be at least a good two or three years before it is ready, assuming I go through with it, that is. If I do, I'll get into more personal details about my own experiences, as you'll notice I'm a bit vague at times on certain aspects of my personal story in this book. At this time, I'm still toying around with the title for that second book. The potential titles

I've come up with so far are: *Autobiography of a Skinny White Guy,* *The Disappearance of Mikey, God is a Non-Idiot, Kiss My Ass and Forgive,* or perhaps a spoof of my own book and call it *Dude, Where's My Beavis Fish?* I don't really think I'll be using any of these titles, but you never know.

Acknowledgements

Thanks first and foremost to my mom, Patti Ann McAlister. Don't know where I'd be on my spiritual path, or even if I'd be on one, if it wasn't for her 'force-feeding' me books on spirituality for over ten years prior to my DU/ACIM days. But I suppose that's why I picked her as my mom.

I would also like to thank Doug McAlister, Bruce Rawles, Jonathan Joshua, Jean Roorda-de Fauw & Mikael de Fauw, Joan Bridgit Tyler, Jessica Bradshaw, Barrie Smeeth and Alfred Harrison, Terry & Dan Miller, Becky Hale, Kim Olson, Triskana & Paul West, Rosemary Volpato, Saskia Reilly, Rebecca R Riales, Nhien T Vuong, Linda J McNabb, Roberta Grace & Robert Donaghey, Gene & Helen Bogart, Doris Lora, and Cindy Lora-Renard for all your support during this process.

Special thank you to Dawn Sechrist Burkett for all your love and support this past year. I have much enjoyed our weekly marathon phone calls, and talking about all this stuff with you. I have met my match in passion for the teachings of Arten and Pursah, as Dawn has read *The Disappearance of the Universe* 24 times and *Your Immortal Reality* 19 times. You freakin' rock!

And of course a big thank you to Gary Renard aka 'The Garman' for putting himself out there, and bringing the teachings of Arten and Pursah into our lives. I don't know what the hell I would be doing with myself if he hadn't gotten his books out there. I had become stagnant, bored, restless, and uninspired in my spirituality. I asked Spirit for something new, and I got it. Gotta love this Gary character, he really sticks to the *Course!* Thanks for all you do buddy!

And I gotta give a 'shout out' to my DU/ACIM friends on Facebook – too many to list – you know who you are. Thanks for all the love and support. I'm sure we'll meet in person one day, and some I already have. Giddy up!

Two things are infinite: The universe and human stupidity.
And I'm not sure about the universe.

~ Albert Einstein

PART I

Life of Mikey

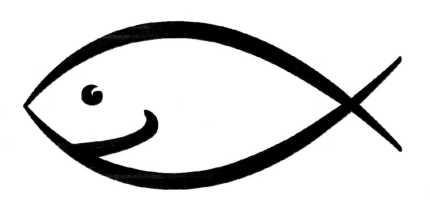

Chapter 1

Masshole Mike

**You've seen some of your guilt symbolized in different ways, now.
What would you say it's like? Oh, the words ugly, monstrous,
demonic, savage, ghastly, and tormented come to mind.[1]**

I was born Michael Robert Lemieux on August 26, 1974 on the
south coast of Massachusetts in the city of New Bedford. This was the
place I called home for the first thirty years of my life, though it never
really *felt* like home to me. I didn't mean to become a spiritual person,
it just sort of happened by 'accident.' Since moving to the West Coast
in 2004, I've met many folks who have also been on a spiritual
journey, some of whom have changed their names along the way,
because they felt that their birth name no longer suited them. Well,
I've never felt that way about *my* name, despite all the shifts and
changes as well as the several 'incarnations' I've had in this lifetime.
My first name, Michael, is Hebrew for 'One Who is God like,' and my
last name, Lemieux, is French for 'The Best.' Now, with a name
combination like that, you might think it would stroke my ego some.
However, I really just see it as a helluva a lot to live up to. Well, it's a
dirty job, but *somebody's* got to do it!

Despite both my parents being *non-practicing* Catholics and that
Catholicism wasn't part of my upbringing at home, I was baptized
Catholic, and spent nine years in a Catholic school from kindergarten
until my graduation from the eighth grade. I really had no business
being in a Catholic school, but you know how the saying goes,
'Everything happens for a reason.' It was as if my spirit guides told me
before I entered this incarnation, 'So, you want to attain enlightenment
in this upcoming lifetime? Well, we're gonna stick your little non-
conformist ass in a Catholic school for nine years and see if you can
forgive *that!*' To say I felt like a fish out of water in that school would
be a big understatement, not only because my family didn't practice

Catholicism, but because I was an underachiever amongst a class full of overachievers. I remember feeling very nervous, uncomfortable, and out of place quite often during my time there.

I recall the nun who taught our Religion class telling us that God and dogs don't get mad – they get *angry*. I didn't know what to make of that until I asked my parents about it shortly thereafter. My dad told me to spell *mad dog* backwards and I would find my answer. This same nun also told us that sex was dirty, filthy, and sinful. I remember thinking to myself, 'What the hell does that say about your parents?' They were trying to sell me Catholicism, but Mikey wasn't subscribing.

After graduation from the eighth grade in 1988, which felt more like making parole, I went on to a vocational high school for the next four years where I took up Architectural Drafting. Though it was such a relief to be out of the Catholic school system, I still didn't like school, and college was never a consideration. I had never really done particularly well in school, due as much to a lack of interest as a lack of confidence in my intellect, although math and numbers always came easy to me. All I really cared about was getting by – that was good enough for me. Towards the end of my junior year, a post-card arrived in the mail, an advertisement to join the United States Navy. I laughed at it. My mom half-kiddingly said to me, 'Why not?' Next thing I knew I was downtown at the recruiter's office getting more information. I had no direction in my life at that point and I knew I had to do *something*!

In September of 1992, three months after graduating from high-school, I got on an airplane for the first time in my life, flying out of Boston to San Diego, California for basic training. When I was picked up from the airport along with the other new recruits, we were immediately yelled at by the authorities; we were now property of the United States government, and they let us know it! During the eight week training, if our company commanders got pissed-off at us, they would exercise us non-stop for an extended period of time since they weren't allowed to hit us. I remember being crammed into the room where our bunks were, about eighty of us, doing pushups, sit-ups, leg lifts; resting position was standing up with our arms up in the air for a couple of minutes, then we were back on the floor for more pushups, sit-ups, and leg lifts. The floor was a pool of sweat. People were passing out. This was more intense than any high-school basketball practice I had gone through. We could barely walk the next morning. I joined the United States Navy – *what the hell I was thinking?*

I had signed up to be in the Navy for four years. However, eleven months later, after spending a short amount of time on a submarine, thanks to some guidance that seemed to come from some place else, I inadvertently found a loophole and got myself out of the Navy. So, in July of 1993, I was back in Massachusetts in the home I grew up in. Still having no direction in my life, I got a job delivering pizzas. I also went back to working for my uncle, cutting steel in his shop which I did during my high-school days.

Meanwhile, I had this girlfriend in Towson, Maryland, who I had met that spring while visiting my relatives next door to her. My submarine was stationed in Norfolk, Virginia, so I would often make the four hour drive up there on weekends when I was still in the Navy. But being back in Massachusetts, we were now four-hundred miles apart. After a few months of deciding whether we wanted to continue our relationship or not, considering the distance between us, she made arrangements for a place for us to live together in Bel Air, Maryland, about thirty miles north of Baltimore. I moved down there at the end of October. I recall telling my parents before I left that I could be back in six days, six weeks, or six months. I knew deep down this was not going to last, but it was an excuse to get out of New Bedford for at least a little while, so I was all for it. As far as how the relationship went, I can sum it up with a few short sentences from the late Rodney Dangerfield in the movie *Back to School*, 'I'm an earth sign. She's a water sign. Together we made mud.'

One evening in January of 1994, I had to call 911 after my girlfriend attempted suicide by overdosing on sleeping pills. She got the sense that I was about to leave the relationship, which I was, and she was very upset by this. A week later, I was back living in New Bedford with my parents, trying to figure out my life. I remember my old man shaking his head and saying to me, 'Michael, Michael, Michael – young, dumb, and full of....' well, you get the idea. Anyway, I've never been the womanizing type, so I felt a bit misunderstood.

My time in Maryland wasn't a total waste though. During my brief stay there, I read a book called *Fit For Life* by Harvey and Marilyn Diamond. This started me on my spiritual path without me even realizing it. During my senior year in high-school, and thereafter, I seemed to always feel tired and sluggish, and would often complain about it to my mom. She would tell me about this book every now and then, but at one point she just got annoyed with all my questions, and said to me, '*Read the book!*' So, I finally did 'read the book,' and I read the follow-up book, *Fit For Life II*, as well. I found the follow up book to be even better because it was more hard core and radical than the first one.

The two *Fit For Life* books were to my bodily life, as Gary's books now are to my spiritual life.[2] Applying the concepts worked tremendously in my life, and I had a lot more energy, my allergies cleared up, and my usual two to three colds per year totally disappeared. By the summer of 1995, I was a total vegan, eating mostly raw foods. I also stopped consuming alcohol, not that I had ever abused it, but it just no longer fit in with my new healthy lifestyle. It wasn't doing much for me at that point in time anyway, so I quit drinking before I was even legal – and life has been stone cold sober for Mikey ever since. I also recall telling my mom during this time of transitioning over to veganism that I had never tried pot in my life. With an almost disgusted look on her face she said to me, 'You're kidding? What do you mean you never tried pot?' That's my mom for you.

In the first year or so of changing my eating habits, my mom observed how arrogant I could be at times. She would get a little annoyed when I had my moments of being 'preachy,' or if I just had a smug look on my face when people were talking about their allergies or having the flu. I had become quite the health zealot, and it came with a little bit of attitude. Sometimes my attitude would rub some folks the wrong way. My mom would always respond to my sometimes uncompassionate attitude with, 'We're more than just physical bodies, you know.' She kept on suggesting I read this book by Louise Hay called *You Can Heal Your Life*. After months of much resistance, I finally read it, and I did get a lot out of it. I applied the material the best that I knew how to at the time. And I found myself starting to become less self-righteous and forthright, and more accepting and tolerant of other people's unhealthy eating habits. (LOL)

In 1994, I registered to go back to school, starting with the fall semester. Another thing I had learned while I was living away from home was that I didn't know 'jack shit.' I knew I had to get my butt back in school and learn something. So, I went to the local community college and entered into the Business Administration Transfer program with the intention of going on to the University of Massachusetts (Dartmouth) after earning my Associate's Degree, to get my Bachelor's degree in Accounting. Those two years went great; it was the first time in my life I actually *wanted* to be in school. After many years of being a total slacker, I was pretty much now an all "A" student. And not only that, it felt really good to no longer have my head up my rear end. I finally felt like I had some direction in my life; I still didn't really know where I was heading, but at least I felt like I was moving *towards* something.

In 1996, I graduated from Bristol Community College with *High Honors*, and then transferred to the university that fall as planned. However, between finishing up classes that summer that I had previously blown off, learning a new job as a bank teller, and being in the middle of my parents' separation process in a house filled with tension so thick that you *couldn't* cut it with a knife, I found myself feeling mentally drained and burnt-out. I lasted only four weeks that fall before I dropped out. Neither my mind nor my heart was into the college thing anymore. I decided to do what I really wanted to be doing all along, and that was to take the same self-study nutritional course that the authors of the *Fit For Life* books took prior to writing their best-sellers. So that's what I did while working at the bank. I successfully completed the nutritional course in less than two years but never did anything with it other than for personal benefit.

During the second half of the 1990s and early 2000s, I pretty much read any New Age book my mom suggested to me, usually after months of resistance on my part. I wasn't passionate about all this stuff like my mom was, but I certainly wasn't closed off to it either. I did enjoy listening to Wayne Dyer's audio programs and very much appreciated his inspiring and humorous stories. I also read the *Conversations with God* Books, *The Celestine Prophecy* series, a couple more of Louise Hay's books, and watched Shirley MacLaine's movie *Out on a Limb* numerous times. I also read other various metaphysical type books or parts of books my mom threw my way.

In the mean time, my work life was getting better. I grew tired of working as a bank teller, which was pretty much like being a glamorized cashier. But at the end of 1997, I started a new job within the company in the Boston area, working in a corporate office environment for the first time. It was a much better job for me, not only did it pay a lot more, but I no longer had to work with the public, and instead of being a bank teller, I got to do research work in order to correct errors *made* by bank tellers. Several years later, our bank underwent a big merger with another bank, and the job I had was now no longer mine – unless I was willing to relocate to New Jersey. Fortunately, I found another job within the newly merged organization doing money laundering investigations. So I did that up until the time I left for the West Coast.

However, in the late spring of 2002, my spiritual life came to a head when a very close friendship I'd had for two years with an older woman who lived out of state came to an abrupt end, or at least the end as we knew it. I didn't want to be in a romantic relationship with this woman, but at the same time I didn't want anyone else to have her either. One night she called me excited to tell me about a man she started dating. This did not sit well with me. In fact, my exact words to her in response to her 'good news' were, 'I don't like this.' The moment I said that, I knew there was something about *me* that was a tad askew, but I couldn't seem to control my words and emotions even though I *knew* I was in the wrong. It was very much like the experience Gary describes as having while visiting Cahokia where he says, 'I couldn't stop it if I wanted to.'[3] I recall having at least several similar experiences in the last year or so leading up to that time. Anyway, the plans she and I had for the summer, which included her teenage daughter, as they had become like my little adoptive family, were now out the window.

A year prior to this fallout, my mom had come to live with me as she was having some financial difficulties. It was an uncomfortable situation for me, as my grandmother (my *father's* mother) was my landlord, and my mom staying there with me didn't sit well with certain members of my dad's large family – not that it was really any of their business, but I allowed myself to feel uncomfortable about it nevertheless. And as close as my mom and I have been, I wasn't always a saint towards her, particularly during this time. In fact, I'm sorry to say that I even had my moments where I could be a downright jerk! Without going into details, yes, I did have some 'legitimate grievances,' but I wasn't exactly proud of my behavior towards my mom during this time. Anyway, she wound up moving out right around the same time as my fallout with my lady friend. So, between these two significant circumstances coming to a conclusion, where I got a good first hand look at my own ego during the time leading up to all this, I was left with the daunting task of analyzing this unprecedented turn of events that took place in my life. 'The dark night of the soul' had officially begun.

I didn't like this feeling I was having, and I knew I had to do something about my ego – it was out of control. In the prior two years leading up to this crossroads in my spiritual life, I found myself becoming an observer[4] of my life. It was a very strange experience for me. It was like Jesus or some kind of spirit guide was starting to show me, and make me aware of, the contents of my own unconscious mind. It wasn't a pretty sight. I wasn't doing anything special to bring the buried muck to the surface; it just started coming up on its own, from out of nowhere it seemed.

So, in that summer of 2002, I found myself questioning and analyzing *everything* about myself; from every motive that I had to every value that I held; examining[5] feelings of anger, resentment, guilt, jealousy, feelings of inferiority and superiority, and really just looking at all my fears, and questioning what I really wanted out of life. It totally sucked having to really look at all this crap, but at the same time I knew pretending these feelings didn't exist and continuing to gloss[6] them over wasn't going to do me any good either; that was no longer an option for me.

I now found myself spending my time trying to figure out what to do about all this unconscious stuff that was coming up to the surface. I had always thought my tendencies were just normal behavior, but I was now becoming aware that it was not. Not that I was an evil person by any means, but I was starting to see right through the ego thought system, and seeing it as being something that was totally unacceptable in my life. At the same time I felt so much resistance to do something about it. I thought maybe getting back into more Wayne Dyer material was the answer. Nope. I spent some time that summer listening to and reading his newer stuff, and then in October, my mom and I went to see him in New York City. It was cool meeting 'The Wayner' but I was starting to realize that I had outgrown his teachings and needed something that was really going to work for me in the long run. I needed something that packed more punch, something that had more than just a temporary, helpful impact. His stuff just wasn't helping me anymore as it did in the 1990s.

Also, during this time period, I decided it was time for me to start looking into where I wanted to relocate to. I knew I wasn't in Massachusetts for the long haul. I had always wanted to move to Florida because of the weather, even though I had never been down there. Part of the plans I had with my lady friend were to vacation along the Gulf Coast. Since we already had everything booked prior to our fallout, I decided to go alone, as I knew it was something I had to at least explore for myself. I added the rest of the Southeast to the itinerary; flying into Charlotte, North Carolina and driving down to the

Tampa/St. Petersburg area in Florida with several overnight stops along the way. I spent ten days at the Florida Gulf Coast, and with its soft, baby powder white sand, palm trees, bathtub-like gulf water, and stunning sunsets after late afternoon thunderstorms, I found it to be just absolutely gorgeous and breathtaking. However, it didn't feel like home to me, and I knew that would not be my relocation destination.

One evening during my stay at Madeira Beach in St. Petersburg, I had a pretty freaky 11:11 experience. I was already familiar with the symbol, 11:11, having had read Solara's book *11:11* in the 1990s so I understood what its significance was. I knew I was resisting moving forward with my spirituality. While I was eating dinner one evening while watching an exhibition football game around nine o'clock, the phone rang. This was kind of trippin' me out because I hadn't given the phone number of the condo I was staying at out to anybody. When I went to pick up the phone, I heard nothing but a dial tone. I went back to my chair, then a minute or so later the phone rang again. Again, I went to answer, nothing but a dial tone. So, I was already buggin' out, and as I was walking back to my chair, I happened to look over at the thermostat for the central air conditioning unit. The clock on the thermostat read *11:11* – again, it was nine at night when this happened. I knew immediately what that meant; it was time for me to *wake up*, which totally freaked me out. I called up my mom to tell her what had just transpired; it gave her goose bumps.

Back in 1997, my mom had lent me a twelve tape series she had had since the 1980s called *Pathways to Mastership* by a man named Jonathan Parker. My mom highly recommended them to me. Every once in a while I would play the first tape to see if I could get into it, but I couldn't. In addition to his monologue, he also has guided meditations on each of the tapes. So, I tried to do the first meditation, but I didn't feel like I was doing it right so I would just give up on it. In addition, I had no idea what this guy was talking about. He was talking about all this guilt, fear, and resentments we all have. Little did I know at the time that I was in total *denial* of what he was talking about.

I thought I was spiritually sophisticated at the time since I was a big Wayne Dyer buff, and considering all the other metaphysical literature I had read. I had always done my best to apply what I had learned but it *would* wear off. What I didn't know at the time was that the reason it would wear off was because the teachings didn't deal with the *unconscious* mind, only the *conscious* mind, and it's the *unconscious* mind that *really* runs us.[7] The mind is like an iceberg, most of it is underneath the surface; you can't see it.[8] And Jonathan's *Pathways to Mastership* series was addressing the *unconscious* part of the mind, the part of the mind you *can't* see, but I was now starting to become aware of it as it was rising to the surface in order for me to forgive and release it.

About six weeks after my 11:11 experience, and upon returning from New York City to see 'The Wayner,' I was feeling very restless about my spirituality and where I was going with it. I knew I needed to do something to start healing this crap, what the *Course* calls 'the secret sins and hidden hates'[9] we all have about ourselves. And I knew Wayne Dyer was not the answer for me anymore; it was now time for me to *grow up* [10] in the spiritual sense. One day I decided to poke around on the aforementioned Jonathan Parker's website just out of curiosity. I noticed that he was scheduled to do some week-long workshops in Sedona, Arizona in the spring and fall of 2003. That intrigued me. But I was hesitant to sign up for them. I mean I couldn't even finish listening to the first tape of that twelve tape series my mom had lent me. But a thought came to me that seemed to come from someplace else[11] and it said, 'You'll be ready by then.'

I had already started to get a sense of what the voice of the Holy Spirit was like, though I didn't think of it that way. Growing up, I was a huge fan of the NFL, and though I wasn't as big a fan in my adult life, I was still interested in it enough that the Holy Spirit could speak to me through it. In January of 2001, the Super Bowl took place between the New York Giants and the Baltimore Ravens. I grew up a die-hard Giants fan, so much so that to this day I could tell you the final score of every game they played from 1983 – 1990. I was obsessed as a boy and I gave a whole new meaning to being psychologically attached to outcome. If they lost on Sunday, I was depressed the entire week. Good thing they won a lot of games and a couple of Super Bowls during that time. Anyway, even though I was no longer the die-hard Giants fan I was as a kid, (at this point in time I was now a New York Jets fan) I still wanted them to win. Deep down, however, I knew they weren't going to, but I was in total denial of that feeling. Mikey just wanted his team to win and that was it. I remember 'talking trash' via e-mail with my uncle in Baltimore about how the Giants were going to dismantle his team. Well, that didn't happen. In fact, Baltimore kicked the crap out of the Giants. After the game, I was thinking to myself, 'Why the hell was I talking trash for? I knew they weren't going to win.'

The following year, the New England Patriots were in the Super Bowl playing the heavily favored St. Louis Rams. I grew up in New England but I never rooted for any of the Boston-based teams, in fact, I despised them, *especially* the Patriots. But I got that same feeling I had gotten the previous year – that feeling being that the team I would want to win wouldn't win – so I was *pissed!* I just *knew* the Patriots were going to win this thing despite the fact nobody outside of New England gave them a snowballs chance in hell of doing so, as they were fourteen-point underdogs. But this time, instead of being in denial about that feeling, I decided to do something about it. I came up with an idea. I asked myself how much I was willing to pay to see the Patriots lose. And my answer was that I was willing to pay $100 to see them lose.

So, I figured if I knew the Patriots were going to win this thing, then I may as well make some money off of it. If they lost the game, it would be fine because I would be happy that they lost, but if they won, I'd be happy too because that would mean I won money – either way Mikey was going to be happy. So I put down $100 on a sports betting website, and instead of taking the fourteen points, I went with the 'three and a half to one' odds instead. Well, sure enough, the Patriots won, on the very last play of the game no less, and I came out of it winning $350.

That started my trust in hearing the voice of the Holy Spirit, although I didn't really think of it specifically as the Holy Spirit at the time, but I knew now to trust it. In addition to that, during the game I found myself rooting for the Patriots, not just because they could win me money, but I felt in my heart I was ready to start forgiving Massachusetts, particularly New Bedford, for what it hadn't really done.

I wouldn't place another bet on the Super Bowl until six years later when I got that same feeling again. I would find myself placing money on the New York Giants to beat the Patriots in the big game. Ironically, I was rooting for the Patriots to complete their undefeated season and defeat the Giants, but the voice told me that the Giants were going to win, so I placed the bet on them and wound up winning some more money.

Getting back to Jonathan Parker, when I heard, 'You'll be ready then,' I just knew to trust it. So, in October of 2002, I signed up for Jonathan's two, one-week workshops that would take place the following April. By the end of the year, I found myself going back to try Jonathan's tapes again. This time I was ready to listen. I now realized I was unable to understand his teachings in the past because I had an abundance of unconscious resistance[12] to what he was talking about. He was addressing the part of the mind that all the popular New Age authors pretty much ignore. Anyway, I started listening to the first few tapes, and worked with them over and over again. He has these guided meditations on there that are designed to help remove the blocks in the unconscious mind. The two meditations I worked with over and over again were called *Fear and Fixation Removal*, and *Releasing Guilt and Resentment*. I worked with these tapes quite often in the months leading up to the workshops in Sedona. I was pleasantly surprised at not just how well they worked, but how quickly they worked too.

On the guilt and resentment meditation, Jonathan has you work through your memories, starting at the age of fifteen, working your way backwards each time you do the guided meditation, until you reach the year of your earliest memories. Then, he has you starting back up at the age of sixteen and going forward each year from there to present time. I was able to let go of, and heal, a lot of stuff going back to childhood, particularly stuff from my Catholic school days.

Also by working with these tapes, I was able to release what sometimes felt like down-right hatred I had towards two relatives who could push my buttons like nobody else; two people I thought I could never be at peace with in my mind, one of whom I thought of to be the biggest butt-wipe on the planet! But I knew this process was working because the anger I had towards these two individuals was no longer there. I had compassion in my heart for them instead, as I now understood why they were the way they were. They were hurting just like I was, and they were just mirroring back to me that particular aspect of *my* mind that needed healing.

Now, like Gary says in *Disappearance*, forgiveness doesn't mean you have to hang around with the people you are forgiving.[13] So, just because I was forgiving these people, didn't mean I would want to spend time with them. In fact, the ironic thing was that after I finished my forgiveness on them, they all of a sudden stopped showing up in my life. I rarely ever ran into either one of them afterwards, and when I did, it wasn't a big deal; the encounter didn't disturb my peace of mind. And not only that, people that *reminded* me of them stopped showing up in my life too. It was amazing! I was like, 'Holy shit, this stuff really works!' I was so giddy! So this was very encouraging for me.

In April of 2003, I went out to Sedona and did the two workshops just as the Holy Spirit suggested I would be ready to do. Sedona is known for its energy vortexes which help to bring unconscious stuff up to the surface which was why Jonathan liked to hold his workshops there. And from what I understand, the resident turnover rate in Sedona is pretty high – the vortexes may explain why. Now, please keep in mind, I'm not trying to spiritualize Sedona and make it important and real. I only mention this here as that was my experience of Sedona at the time – it was a pretty intense place on an energetic level.

So during my time in Sedona, I found more unconscious stuff coming to the surface of my mind that I wasn't previously aware of. I was able to release some of it, but not all of it, thanks to the guided meditations Jonathan led us through during the workshops. I would return to Sedona in September for two more one-week workshops, but it wasn't the same. I was feeling pretty burnt-out at the end of the first week, so I opted out of the second week and just explored more of Sedona instead.

Soon upon my return to Massachusetts from the April workshops in Sedona, my mom came up with some more reading material for me. She turned me on to a series of books by a man named Joshua David Stone. I got a lot out of his books – *Soul Psychology*, *Your Ascension Mission*, and *The Ascended Masters Light the Way* and read parts of his other books as well over the next year or so. This opened up a new world to me because he was talking about what the ultimate goal in all this was, which is to attain enlightenment, although he used the word *ascension*.

As much as I got out of Joshua's books though, they also left me confused and conflicted as he often seemed to contradict himself from book to book. And he really complicated the hell out of this ascension process. As exciting as this stuff was for me at the time, I also felt like I had to give stuff up,[14] so there was depression in this path too. But I didn't know any better, so I just continued to go along with it, feeling that it was the right thing for me at the time, and I just did the best I could with it.

My world was now being flipped upside down,[15] and I had no idea where all this was leading me to.[16] And I assure you it was no coincidence that my hairline started to recede around this time. (LOL) Granted, I released quite a bit of unconscious guilt through the guided meditations I had been doing, but at the same time, it was bringing up more unconscious guilt and fear that was once suppressed so it was a bit overwhelming for me. I was feeling even more fearful than

I otherwise would have if I *wasn't* doing this work.[17] I didn't want to talk to anybody. I would not return phone calls and would often go out of my way to avoid people, especially people I knew, as much as possible up until the time I left for the West Coast. I felt kind of paranoid actually, thinking that people could read my mind or something, so I became even more hermit-like than I already was. The only exception to this, of course, was my mom, who was on the same path as I, the only person I could talk to about all this stuff, which we did, just about every day.

In July, we found out about the annual *Wesak* event that Joshua conducted every spring in the Mount Shasta, California area. He held this event annually for about ten years before his passing in the summer of 2005. I decided to purchase tickets in advance for my mom and I, and then I surprised her with them. I then blurted out that maybe I would move there. Well, one week later, not only was I set on moving there within one year's time, but my mom said she was coming with me. My mom would never drive anywhere outside of a twenty mile radius from the area we lived in – I was shocked that she would be joining me in this great adventure of moving three-thousand miles away.

For me, it didn't make much sense from a practical point of view to make this move. I had a pretty good paying job with great benefits, and my grandmother was my land-lady so I had a nice grandson-rent-deal going on too – I had it made back east. But this move felt like the right thing to do, no doubt about it, even though I had my concerns about how I would make a living in a very small town in the middle of nowhere. Despite having no real plan, I just knew it was something I had to do. It was time for me to take that 'leap of faith' into the abyss, and it felt as right as placing that long-shot bet on the Super Bowl. As the saying goes, 'No balls, no glory.' I had done my forgiveness work on Massachusetts and just knew it was about time for me to leave; there was nothing else for me there. As Kramer put it in a *Seinfeld* episode where he made a decision that he was going to leave New York for Los Angeles, while pointing to his head, 'Up here, I'm already gone!'

Chapter 2

Go West Young Man

**Your time is at hand, but only if you're willing to follow
the Holy Spirit's thought system instead of trying
to lead the planet on a wild goose chase.[1]**

June 18, 2004, the day that I had been longing for my entire adult
life – I was leaving Massachusetts for good! The movers had arrived
three days earlier to pick up our stuff at our respective places. We
drove cross country in my jeep, and despite a few close calls, we made
it to Mount Shasta a week later in one piece. Once we were there and
got settled in, I remember waking up every single morning saying to
myself, 'What the hell I am doing here?'[2] I spent most mornings
watching reruns of *The Brady Bunch* and *Happy Days* followed by *The
Price is Right* – Bob Barker was showing up in my dreams at night for
crying out loud! One of my goals in this lifetime is to win a new a jeep
on the aforementioned game show, but that's another story.

Anyway, I didn't know what the hell to do with myself. There
was little going on as far as job opportunities go, so I didn't work for
my entire year in Mount Shasta. I was also feeling very land-locked, as
the closest beach was three hours away. I had lived on the coast back
east where the closest beach was only *ten minutes* away. Despite all
the free time I had on my hands, I hardly ever used any of it to
meditate, which of course I felt guilty about. But the other part of me
felt like I was supposed to be rewarded for all the spiritual work I had
done on myself. Little did I know at that time that my work was just
beginning.[3] But I was half-expecting a check from God in the mail, or
for the ascended master Saint Germain to come knocking on my door
to take me inside the mountain for a tour of the Lemurian world or
something, and tell me how freakin' awesome I am for coming this far.
Instead, I felt totally abandoned[4] from the guidance that led me there
in the first place – I was jonesin'! I felt as if they were saying to me,

'We got you this far – figure out the rest on your own!' So, I felt like I was getting shafted on this deal, not that I wanted to go back to New Bedford, in fact, the thought of that made me sick to my stomach.

In May, my mom and I visited the Mount Shasta area to look for a place to live. But we were also there for the aforementioned *Wesak* event – we were not impressed. For whatever reason, I felt awkward and uncomfortable at the event, and realized that I didn't feel a need to be there, nor *wanted* to be there! I told my mom that I had no use for this and that I wanted to leave, but she suggested we give it a chance – I felt myself growing even more impatient. Then, after a while, Joshua David Stone got up on the stage and talked a bit and then started leading us into a meditation, a *long* meditation. Somewhere along the way, he started going on and on about his umpteen million books, during what was supposed to be *a guided meditation! What's up with that?* My mom and I opened our eyes, gave each other a look, and then we got the hell out of there. What was supposed to be a three-day event lasted less than two hours for us. So by the time we moved to Shasta, Joshua's books weren't something we were interested in any more, even though it was *his* material that was our symbol of the Holy Spirit at the time that led us there in the first place.

During our first week in Shasta, my mom came across a couple of newly released books at one of the book stores in town by a local author named Aurelia Louise Jones, who channeled an ascended master named Adama. The books were titled *Telos*, and contained the teachings of the Lemurians, who apparently live at a higher vibrational frequency – the fifth dimension – beneath Mt. Shasta.

These *Telos* books became my path for the next two years or so, but again, it still felt like something I *had* to do rather than feeling really passionate about it, though I didn't necessarily realize that at the time. The teachings did emphasize the importance of facing your fears, so I knew these books had at least some accuracy to them. And I did feel more comfortable with the teachings presented in Aurelia's books than Joshua's. I went to her home a few times in late 2006 and early 2007 when she invited people over to experience her channeling the ascended master Adama. Like Joshua, Aurelia later become ill and passed away in the summer of 2009.

Other than having a few weird experiences while living in Mount Shasta, including another freaky 11:11 experience, it was pretty much ho-hum, and I was ready to leave. Also, from an energy perspective, it was pretty intense living there, as all my fears just seemed to smack me in the face. And coming from the crowded and congested Northeast, to living in a town of a population of less than four thousand people was just too weird for me. And not only that I didn't get to see any UFOs while I was living there!

Just prior to relocating to Mount Shasta, I had found out about Ashland, a pretty cool artsy, hippy town, which is located just over the California border in Southern Oregon. My mom had spotted an annual publication magazine about Ashland at one of the local bookstores. I remember going through it and saying, 'Wow, this is where I *really* want to move to.' But the plan was to move to Mount Shasta, so we stuck to the plan and signed a one year lease for a duplex in town.

During my last six months in Shasta, however, I found myself driving up to Ashland quite often and getting accustomed to the area. I found this to be a place where I could be myself without being perceived as weird, or at least not too weird; a drastic change from living in New Bedford, which is like the exact opposite of Ashland. So after the lease was up, I packed up my stuff, and headed eighty miles north over the border to Ashland, Oregon. Meanwhile, my mom was also heading eighty miles north over the border, but to the other side of the Cascade Mountains from where *I* was moving to. She was moving to the town of Klamath Falls. She met the love of her life on Match.com at the end of 2004, who had just moved to Klamath Falls around the same time we moved to Shasta. They got a place to live together and married a year later.

When I was living in Mount Shasta, I didn't feel inclined or inspired to get involved in the community or find a way to meet people. I just did what I did while I was living in Massachusetts – I lived like a hermit. The word *community* was a totally foreign concept to me during my days in Massachusetts. In fact, I don't think I really knew what the word meant. (LOL) This reminds me of a line from Jerry in a *Seinfeld* episode, 'All these years I'm living in a community, I had no idea.' But with this move to Ashland, I was feeling inspired to live a little bit differently. I became a volunteer at the metaphysical library in town, which I actually started doing several months before I even moved there. I also started going to a Sunday morning dance ritual called *Ecstatic Dance*. Through these two activities, I was getting involved and becoming part of a community for the first time in my life.

Also, in December of 2005, I was one of many who volunteered to be an extra in Neale Walsch's *Conversations with God* movie. I can actually be seen in the movie in one of the opening scenes, which was shot in the auditorium at Ashland High School. In that scene, the actor who plays Neale, Henry Czerny, is speaking to the audience. I show up in that scene, several times, with my hair down and wearing a long sleeve denim shirt, sitting behind and to the left of the heckler in the audience. I also do a very nice seat shift in that scene too! (LOL)

Anyway, I was feeling burnt-out with my spiritual life so this year and a half to two year period of meeting new people through volunteer work, dancing, potlucks, and parties was a fun break for me from my spiritual pursuits. But in the beginning of 2007, I was starting to feel a need to become a recluse again and refocus on my spirituality. I felt like I had some unfinished business to get on with. I needed something new, but I was totally clueless as to what to pursue next. I felt like I had most of the pieces in place but just had a missing link.

Around this time of seeking again, my mom told me about a book called *Sanctuary: The Path to Consciousness* by Stephen Lewis and Evan Slawson. I read it and it was ok but I wasn't excited about it. It felt like I had been there, done that, as far as energy goes. But they talked about this energetic healing technique they have where they put a picture of you on this energy healing tray in Nevada and it's supposed to like help heal you. I remember 'The Wayner' enthusiastically talking about this on one of his audio programs. I wasn't really sure if that was the new thing I was looking for, so I decided to think about it. In the mean time, I posted a message on a local spiritual community website, inquiring as to whether anybody had been on this healing program. After a week, I figured, 'What the hell, I'm gonna spend my tax refund on *something*.' So, I plopped down a thousand dollars to be on this program for the next fourteen months.

One week later, on a Friday evening, even though I wasn't feeling very social, I went to a dance in order to support a couple of people I knew who were putting on their very first dance event in the community. When I got there, a young woman by the name of Jean, who I had seen at other community events but never formally met, walked up to me and asked me if I was the one who posted the inquiry about the *Sanctuary* material. I said yes, and then she started telling me about this book called *The Disappearance of the Universe* by Gary Renard, and she told me that I needed to read it. She first started telling me about the ascended masters in the book, and then I found myself cringing inside because I was so burnt-out on that sort of talk. For the last several years prior to that point, I had read *the Life and Teachings of the Masters of the Far East* books by Baird T Spalding, *Unveiled Mysteries* and *The Magic Presence* by Godfre Ray King, the books of the aforementioned Joshua David Stone and Aurelia Louise Jones, *Doorway to Eternity* by Kiara Windrider, and various Internet articles by Patricia Cota-Robles on all that unworldly sounding stuff. So, I felt like I had my fill with all that.

Anyway, Jean went on to tell more about Gary's book, as well as his follow up book *Your Immortal Reality.* She said enough good things for me to at least look into it. Up until that point, no one outside of my mom had successfully gotten me to read something spiritual, so between that, and the ascended master talk, the odds weren't likely that I would be interested in this. So I was skeptical, not because I didn't believe in ascended masters, but I just didn't feel like going down that road again with all that 'airy fairy' talk you get in channeled material. Then I went home that evening and went on Gary's website and read the excerpts of *Disappearance.* Wow! Much to my surprise, this was very much different than anything else I had ever read – I was hooked immediately. I ordered both books on Amazon.com that evening. This was not your typical ascended master talk. *Thank God!*

On March 31, 2007, the books arrived in the mail. I started my first read *of The Disappearance of the Universe* the very next day – no foolin'! The more I got into it, the more excited I got about the way Arten and Pursah put everything. I kept saying to myself throughout my reading, 'Jesus Christ, it's about freakin' time somebody put it like this!' I was very much appreciative as to how clear, blunt, and straightforward their teachings were. Of course, the book had already been out for four years at that point, but it came to me when I was ready for it. I think plopping down that thousand dollars to the Sanctuary folks gave J the message I was serious about moving forward with my spirituality. Apparently, that was my invitation[5] for him to bring this, and the *Course* into my life. I had become stagnant with my spirituality, and this was exactly what I needed. Anyway, I can't possibly overstate how much of a breath of fresh air it was to read something on advanced spirituality that was put in actual, everyday plain English – what a concept!

The one thing that disturbed me, however, is that Arten and Pursah were saying that energy isn't real. Had I known that two weeks earlier, I wouldn't have spent a thousand dollars to be on that energy healing program in the first place. But what they were saying about energy made perfect sense, and Mikey now wanted his money back. (LOL) On the other hand, if I hadn't made that decision to be healed in the form of plopping down that money to be on that program, would Gary's books still have found their way into my life at that time?

Looking back on my spiritual path now prior to Gary's books, it reminds me of a *Seinfeld* episode where Jerry is suspicious that his new mechanic is trying to rip him off. George responds, 'Well, of course they're trying to screw you. What do you think? That's what they do. They can make up anything. Nobody knows. "By the way, you need a new Johnson rod in there." Oh, a Johnson rod. Yeah, well, you better put one of those on.' That's what my spiritual path had been like for a few years, 'Oh, I gotta have my crystal implants removed from my etheric body? Well, I better get that done.' (LOL)

Anyway, It seemed like there was this smorgasbord of stuff that needed to be done in order to have any chance of ascending; DNA activations, aura cleanses, channeling sessions with ascended masters, violet flame meditations, Tesla watches to protect yourself from radiation, purple plates to energize your food, visualizing white light going through every cell in your body, a subscription to *Sedona Journal*, putting your picture on an energizing tray in Las Vegas, and I'm sure I'm forgetting a few things too. It all sounds so comical now, but not only did I do all those things, but I paid *good money* to do all those things! (LOL)

These days, my spiritual path feels much more practical and down to earth. I have *A Course in Miracles* telling me that everything is for forgiveness, and nothing else matters – *halle-frickin-lujah, sanity restored!* So, now I can save my airfare and just forgive, and I'll get Home a thousand times faster.[6] Anyway, that missing link I referred to earlier is the forgiveness practice that Arten and Pursah emphasize in Gary's books where forgiveness becomes an *attitude*. I already knew of the importance of forgiveness, but the only way I knew how to do it prior to my reading of Gary's books was through guided meditations that tapped into the unconscious mind. Arten and Pursah presented a way for me to be able to forgive right on the spot, rather than waiting until I got home (assuming I was out when presented with a forgiveness opportunity) and do my meditation, which I didn't always feel like doing.

Well, perhaps naively I tried a lot of different things on my spiritual path prior to my introduction to Gary's books, but at least no one can say I didn't have an open mind. (LOL) *Now*, I don't have to have an open mind! I've got Arten and Pursah's words to keep me focused and motivated to do my forgiveness work, as well as my internal interactions with the great J-Dog going on in my mind, so what the hell else do I need? Anyway, I've never felt this driven and inspired with my spirituality before, so thanks to Gary's books, that's how it is for me now. It feels really good to no longer be complicating the hell out of my spirituality and feeling conflicted with what I've learned.

Shifting gears a little bit here, upon waking one morning in January of 2009, I had a Jesus sighting. After being into Gary's books and CDs, and the *Course* for nearly two years, I woke up one morning while it was still dark outside, and felt a presence in my room at the end of my bed – it was Jesus! A transparent, ghostly looking image of J with short hair appeared to me. His appearance lasted about five seconds. He was facing me with a look of laughter on his face. Then He turned to the side, I noticed He had a big ear. He then floated toward my bedroom wall where my picture of Him is hung. I was kind of in disbelief about it. I dismissed what had happened, and went right back to sleep. Later that same morning, I was reading *Your Immortal Reality* and this quote[7] from Pursah quoting the *Course* just jumped right off the page at me: 'When I said "I am with you always," I meant it literally. I am not absent to anyone in any situation. Because I am always with you, *you* are the way, the truth and the life.'[8] When I read that, I was like 'Whoa, He ain't kidding!' I immediately wrote that quote onto a 3x5 card and posted it underneath my picture of J.

On Christmas Eve day in 2009 as I was heading to my mom and step-dad's place, upon entering town, I hit a patch of ice, on a windy and curvy road. I was driving about 25 to 30 MPH when I hit the ice. My jeep started spinning out of control. I was looking all around, concerned about what I might hit, and hoping no cars were coming in either direction. The jeep continued spinning out of control for about four to six seconds, I couldn't stop it! I shouted out in my mind, 'Uh, I could use a little help here, J!' Instantly the jeep stopped spinning. I was very fortunate that there was no traffic on the road and that I didn't hit any of the nearby houses or end up in the lake.

Another cool experience I've had at least a half-dozen times or so since I've been indulging myself in Gary's material, is that I have found myself calling on Jesus or the Holy Spirit for help in a dream where I am feeling very fearful. When I remember to do so, I wake up from the dream immediately. I remember one dream in which I was about to get my head cut off in China for being part of a rescue operation of freeing children from prisons. I called on J for help and I woke up immediately.

On Easter Morning in 2010, I had a dream where there was this football game going on, and one of the players was severely hurt. He was bloody all over and his limbs were practically falling off. I was very scared for this person and was feeling very fearful. But then I remembered to use a forgiveness thought process in the dream and I said to this man, 'No, that's not you. You are Christ. Pure and Innocent. We are forgiven now.' The guy immediately popped up, smiled, and walked away. I see that as a cool symbol, if I keep calling on J to help me 'see' correctly in *this* dream, then I'll *wake up* from this dream as well.

Remembering to choose the strength of the Holy Spirit in the dream state has been a pretty cool experience for me. As Pursah puts it, 'At some point, the *Course's* thought system becomes so much a part of you that you'll choose the strength of Christ even when you're asleep at night, which means you'll often choose that same strength automatically after you lay your body aside. That should be a comforting thought for you, not only because it will make you less fearful of death, but because it confirms that even if you died today you'd still take your learning with you – even though you're not a master.'[9]

Chapter 3

Dude, Where's My Jesus Fish?

A wise fisherman cast his net into the sea. When he drew it up it was full of little fish. Among them he discovered a large, fine fish. He threw all the little fish back into the sea, and he chose the large fish. Anyone here with two good ears should listen.[1]

So, what inspired Mikey to do this book? Well, around Christmas time in 2007, my friend Jean, the same friend who had recommended Gary's books to me earlier that year, gave me the Enlightenment Cards, a 72 card deck set which feature quotes from *The Disappearance of the Universe*. When I finally got around to going through them all in June of 2008, I wasn't that impressed, although the cards *did* smell good. (LOL) Some of the quotes were satisfactory, but about half of them didn't do anything for me. My attitude was like, 'Uh, I can do a helluva better job at picking out quotes.'

So, I decided that I would make my own card set using quotes and passages that I had highlighted from both *Disappearance* and *Your Immortal Reality*. A couple of months later, once I got enough cards written out, as I hand printed them on 3x5 index cards, I started bringing them to the Wednesday evening *Course* group meeting that I attend. We always start our *Course* group meeting with each person picking out a card from the *A Course in Miracles* card set to read aloud; we added my card set to the mix. Everyone seemed to like them, particularly my buddy Bruce.

Then one day in early February of 2009, I was on my lunch break at work, doing my usual lunchtime walk while rockin' out to some Metallica on my iPod, and I was just in this blissful, peaceful, state. Then all of a sudden an inspired idea came to me. The idea was to start posting these quotes that I had been writing out, as a 'Quote of the Day' on *The Disappearance of the Universe* Yahoo group. I wasn't sure of the idea at first. I figured somebody else had already done that at some point. But when I researched the posting history of the group, I didn't see any such thing. So that evening, I posted my first quote.

After a while, my buddy Bruce, who loved seeing my daily quote on the Yahoo group, as much as reading them at our Wednesday night meetings, suggested that I make a book of the quotes I was posting. I was a bit resistant to the idea at first. In fact, I thought it was kind of tacky. My idea was that if I was ever going to write a book, it would be my own material and not someone else's. But after a couple more times of him hinting at me to do it, as well as my mom encouraging me to do so, I was like, 'What the hell, I don't have anything else better to do!' I get bored easily so if nothing else, this would give me something to do for a while. And upon further examination, I realized that Arten and Pursah really do say it *all* for me, and that people can't hear their words and ideas enough times. So this was looking to be a worthwhile venture indeed.

So in April of 2009, I got permission from both Gary and his publisher Hay House to use the material from his books. I then sent a letter to the Foundation for *A Course in Miracles* asking for permission to use quotes from the *Course*, but I was informed that I didn't need permission because the *Course* was now considered part of the public domain due to a court ruling a few years back. The only sections of the *Course* protected under copyright now are the *Preface*, the *Clarification of Terms*, and the *Psychotherapy* and *The Song of Prayer* supplements. I only needed permission to use material from those sections if I was planning on using substantial portions of it, which I wasn't.

Once I had the green light from the Holy Spirit to get moving on this project, the next thing I had to do was figure out a title for this thing. I was toying around with some ideas, something like *Pathway to Inner Peace and Enlightenment* and some nice sounding spiritual titles like that. I figured if it's about spirituality then it should be proper and serious. But in the summer of 2009, I saw a commercial on one of the local TV channels for a movie that had come out a number of years ago called *Dude, Where's My Car?* I had heard of the movie but I had totally forgotten about it. The movie, starring Ashton Kutcher and Sean William Scott, is about two potheads who wake up one morning after a night of partying with no recollection of what took place the night before. They spend the entire day looking for their car while encountering many angry people.

Not long after that day, and after hearing the commercial in the background several more times, I found myself looking all over my apartment for my iPod. I couldn't find it anywhere, and I unconsciously said to myself, 'Dude, where's my iPod?' At that moment I realized that what I had just said would make a great title for a spiritual book some day but I would need to find a replacement for the word *iPod* – *Jesus Fish* immediately came to mind. That sounded pretty cool to me but I wasn't serious about using that title at first.

Later on in the summer I started 'chatting' with a young woman on Facebook, a fellow *Course* student from the San Francisco Bay area. We soon began talking on the phone and got to know each other. One evening, I told her about my book and what I was going to call it. I told her I was thinking something along the lines of *Pathway to Inner Peace and Enlightenment*. She wasn't all that crazy about the title, and surprisingly, she suggested I title it something that matched more my personality. I say 'surprisingly' because this young woman had a little more of a serious demeanor than I, while I was more like the '*Course* Clown' in comparison. So, I kind of had the idea, but I guess I just needed to hear it from someone else first in order to go through with it. Thankfully, the Holy Spirit was coming through loud and clear through her. That's supposed to be my mom's job, but apparently she was out to lunch on that one.

So, I slept on it that evening, and when I woke up the next morning I was all excited, I was like 'Yeah, I'm gonna do it Mikey's way!' Soon thereafter, I also decided I wasn't gonna even bother to pretend to be professional and sophisticated about *any* of it – I was now determined to go with 100% facetiousness. The plan now was to have an irreverent book title, a silly book cover; and a picture of me on the back cover wearing a tie dye t-shirt, sunglasses, and a bandana. Hell yeah!

Once I was certain about my title, I had to come up with a subtitle. I wanted something self-explanatory, which I managed to do, but you may be wondering why it's so *bloody* long. Well, my step-dad reminded me of what Gary says on his *Secrets of the Immortal* audio program. Gary kiddingly suggested that if you're ever going to write a book to be sure it has a long sub-title, because it'll make it look like you did a lot. So kidding or not, I decided to take both Gary's and my step-dad's advice to heart so that I could try to make myself look good. And I even managed to make my sub-title a tad longer than the one Gary used for *The Disappearance of the Universe!*

Chapter 4

Meeting Gary Renard

It is impossible to overestimate your brother's value.[1]

In August of 2008, Gary came here to the Ashland, Oregon area to do a two day workshop in nearby Medford. Gary and I are both natives of Massachusetts so I thought it would be funny for us to get a picture taken together wearing matching t-shirts that say *Masshole*. *Masshole* is a term used by people from the other New England states in reference to people from Massachusetts, usually in regards to their driving habits. I use the term on myself, in jest. Anyway, I had e-mailed Gary about this idea ahead of time and he agreed to it. So, I designed a *Masshole* t-shirt on-line, and ordered a couple of shirts for us. After day two of the workshop we got our pictures taken together wearing them.

Another cool part of that weekend was at the potluck afterwards. Some of us were sitting around eating, including Gary, and at that point I decided to do my favorite impersonation of him. 'There you see. You see what Jesus did for *you*. You see how he suffered and sacrificed himself for *you*. You guilty little bastids.' Now of course the impersonation wouldn't be complete without saying bastards the Masshole way – *bastids!* So, that was fun to share. One person even suggested I play Gary on his next audio book. I'd be up for that. Hell, I'd probably do it for free too! (LOL) I eventually recorded myself doing the impersonation from my living room and posted it on my You Tube page.

At the end of February of 2009, I attended the *A Course in Miracles* three-day conference in San Francisco, which was the second time I saw 'The Gar-man.' I rode down with my buddy Bruce. Upon arriving on the first day of the conference, I got to meet Gary's 'mystery woman' at the time, and now wife, Cindy. While the four of us were standing around having a conversation, I happened to notice Gary wearing a t-shirt that read *Jesus Saves!* When I saw that I busted out laughing. I lifted up my sweatshirt and showed them what t-shirt *I* was wearing. Mine read *Beavis Saves!* I should have gotten a picture – oh well.

Bruce and I sat at the same table as Gary and Cindy, and Gary's booking agent at the time, Jan Cook, several times during meals throughout the weekend. Jan informed us that Gary's trip to Australia had been postponed from April to November, so he was available to come back to Ashland to do another presentation during that time. Bruce and I, of course, jumped on that.

So, two months after the conference in San Francisco, Gary was back in Ashland. At that point, I had been posting the 'Quote of the Day' on *The Disappearance of the Universe* Yahoo group for almost three months. I walked up to Gary to say hello before he got up on stage. He gave me a big hug. He told me how appreciative of me he was for my posting the 'Quote of the Day' on the Yahoo group, for my *Disappearance of the Universe* blog, and especially for the newspaper article that I had recently written about his books. He then said to me, 'Mike, you're freakin' awesome!' Although, *freakin'* wasn't really Gary's f-word of choice that day, and we're not talking about forgiveness here. (LOL) Anyway, I said back to him, 'I'm just your mirror, bro!'

In mid July, I decided to take a little road trip down to Lake Tahoe as Gary would be speaking in nearby Truckee, California. I had never been to the area before so I figured it was a good excuse to check it out. Since Gary and Cindy had just gotten back from their honeymoon in Hawaii, I wore a Hawaiian dolphin shirt in their honor. I got to talk with Gary and Cindy a bit before the workshop, and even more so at dinner afterwards. We talked about all kinds of different stuff. At one point I said to Gary, 'You know, I've heard all your jokes at least a half-dozen times, but they're all still funny!' His response was, 'Well, that's because you're getting them on a deeper level.' (LOL) I went to another one of Gary's talks three months later (another excuse for a road trip) in San Rafael, California, which is about twenty miles north of San Francisco. So, I had seen Gary in four different towns in 2009.

Gary and Cindy came to Ashland to do a workshop here in July of 2010. They were in town for four days so me and my peeps had a great time hanging out with them throughout the weekend. I then took a road trip up to the Portland area two weeks later to catch them there as well. I always enjoy going to Gary's talks – the only *Course* teacher

I'm interested in listening to, quite frankly, as I see the *Course* the same exact way as he does. And it's always fun to say hello to him and to connect with other people that show up for his events, which is a totally different experience for me considering I've never been much of a 'people person.'

Anyway, what I love about Gary as a spiritual teacher is that he is authentic, sincere, and funny. He doesn't present himself as being perfect, better than, or holier than thou. In fact, in his workshops, one of the first things he'll tell you is that he is a recovering jerk. (LOL)

Gary doesn't claim to be a master nor has he ever suggested that he is perfect at practicing forgiveness. He's just going through his crap like the rest of us. But most importantly about Gary, he doesn't mislead people because he doesn't compromise on the integrity of the *Course*. He's not concerned about being a popularizer. He just puts the truth out there for those who are ready to hear it. He doesn't water down the message in order to suit a larger audience. And he's not afraid to use humor either, although I'm not quite certain everyone catches on to his dry sarcasm at times, and they wind up taking some of it all too seriously instead. As Gary's podcast buddy Gene Bogart once put it regarding Gary's workshops, 'You get the raw truth mixed in with a few jokes.'[2]

Speaking of Gene Bogart, there's been this running joke on the Gary Renard podcasts, as well as on Gary's tele-conference calls. It all started on the podcast[3] where Gary was talking from Oahu while on his honeymoon with Cindy. First, Gary humorously shouts out to Gene, 'I love my baby!' And Gene's like, 'Uh, oh.' Gary goes on to mention that Cindy is turning a lot of heads while walking around on the resort in her little bikini, and immediately Gene Bogart inserted a 'boingoingoingoing' sound. I nearly busted a gut holding in my laugh listening to it for the first time on my iPod while sitting at my desk at work.

After listening to the aforementioned podcast, I sent Gene aka G-Bo an e-mail and let him know how amused I was by that sound effect he inserted. I told him that I do my own verbal version of it which was inspired by Beavis from the cartoon *Beavis and Butthead* that aired on MTV in the 1990s. Beavis would make this 'boingoingoingoing' sound whenever he saw a pretty girl walk by, or if he saw one while watching TV. Anyway, Gene dedicated a 'boingoingoingoing' sound to me on a few podcasts[4] afterwards, so that was pretty cool! Gene also hooked me up with an 'assistant' role on Gary's tele-conference calls, so it's been fun being a part of that as well.

With all that said, I want to close out this part of the book by addressing some possible misperceptions some of the people in the *Course* community may have had about me. I make no secret that I'm huge fan of Gary Renard's books, and that they are the *only* books I'm interested in these days; not just books about *A Course in Miracles*, but books in spirituality altogether. Within the first three years of reading his books, I read *The Disappearance of the Universe* twelve times and *Your Immortal Reality* nine times, which says a lot considering I don't really like to read. And I've also listened to Gary's audio programs and podcasts too many times to count. Gene Bogart once called me 'the king of repetition.' To say I'm very passionate about the material would be an understatement, and that passion is often demonstrated in my Internet postings, e-mail exchanges, and in my face to face encounters with people in the *Course* community. As I like to say, 'This is wicked awesome stuff!'

Now, some people may have gotten the impression that I'm like a Gary Renard groupie or some kind of a Gary worshipper. I have even been called a 'Gary disciple' and a 'Renardite,' so it seems some people think I have Gary up on a pedestal or something. Well, I love Gary and all, but quite frankly, I'm too self-centered and have too much of ego to put *anybody* up on a pedestal! (LOL) Just ask my mom, she'll tell you! (LOL) If anything, Gary should have *me* up on a pedestal! (LOL) Seriously though, my mom used to say to me when I was younger when I had my moments of getting caught up in my self-centeredness, '*It's not all about you!*' Well, *The Disappearance of the Universe* and *A Course in Miracles* teach that the dream isn't being dreamed by somebody else,[5] and that there's nobody out there.[6] So *now* it really is all about me – *and it's about time!* (LOL)

Part II

A Course in Miracles
and
The Spiritual Community

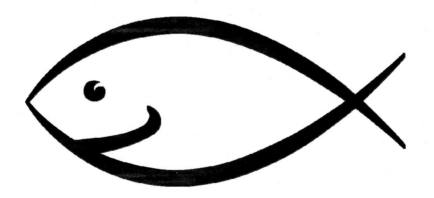

Chapter 5

Arten and Pursah's Keys to Understanding
A Course in Miracles

**Without its practical method of forgiveness, the *Course*
would be nothing but a beautiful and useless book.**[1]

This chapter will consist of quotes from Arten and Pursah that I
feel are important keys to understanding *A Course in Miracles;* what
it's about, and what it's *not* about. These quotes address, among other
things, trouble areas and pitfalls that *Course* students often run into.
The topics addressed include, but are not limited to: why the *Course*
seemingly contradicts itself; what should and should not be taken
literally; why Christian terminology is used in the *Course*; the use of
judgment and common sense; the proper use of denial; and, falling into
the trap of over-analyzing and nitpicking the *Course*.

As previously stated earlier in this book, I'm not as heavily into
the *Course* itself as I am into Gary's books and audio programs. With
that said, however, I have a great appreciation and respect for the lofty
goal the *Course* has to offer, and am *very* adamant about not
comprising on the integrity of its message. Because once you have
compromise, you no longer have *A Course in Miracles* – you have
something else instead. And it is not my function to mislead or confuse
anybody – you just get the straight up truth from Mikey! And though
I am very adamant about not compromising on the integrity of the
Course, I know better not to become psychologically attached to
having people see it *my* way, even though it *is* the *right* way. (LOL)

Introduction to *A Course in Miracles*

*This is a course in miracles. It is a required course. Only the time
you take it is voluntary. Free will does not mean that you can establish
the curriculum. It means only that you can elect what you want to take*

at a given time. *The course does not aim at teaching the meaning of
love, for that is beyond what can be taught. It does aim, however, at
removing the blocks to the awareness of love's presence, which is your
natural inheritance. The opposite of love is fear, but what is all-
encompassing can have no opposite.*

This course can therefore be summed up very simply in this way:

Nothing real can be threatened.
Nothing unreal exists.

Herein lies the peace of God.[2]

DU108 (Arten)

The *Course* is required because it expresses the truth. I'm sorry if
that sounds arrogant. It doesn't mean that the *Course* is the only way
for anyone to ever find the truth. The truth is an awareness – not a
book. But you can't find this awareness alone. Can a sick mind heal
itself? On the level of the world, the answer is no. You need help. You
need the miracle.

DU106 (Arten)

There are some people who will play down the importance of
understanding what the *Course* means. They'll quote the first few
lessons of the *Workbook* out of context. They'll say that since the
Course is making a *metaphysical* statement that everything is
meaningless, then the *Course* doesn't mean anything either! Let's be
very emphatic about something. The *Course* certainly *does* have
meaning on the level where it meets you, and it is very important for
you to understand it – or else it will be useless to you. That's because
the *Course* is about reinterpreting the world and what you call your
life. It's about giving up the meaning that *you* have given the world
and switching over to the Holy Spirit's meaning for the world. This is
absolutely necessary in order for the Holy Spirit to help you gently
awaken from your dream.

DU162 (Arten)

We've never said that *A Course in Miracles* is the only way to
God, and we've never said that our words are the only way to *A
Course in Miracles*. Ours is one approach. It's for some people – not

for everyone. Having said that, let me remind you that we've come here to help you save time. If you really want to know God, then we want you to find the way to your experience of the absolute truth as soon as possible. The *Course* teaches that 'the miracle minimizes the need for time.'[3] Our goal is to help you understand the miracle.

The Miracle and the Holy Instant

DU103 (Arten)

A miracle, according to the *Course,* is a shift in perception[4] over to the *Holy Spirit's* way of thinking, and not merely a modification of your own thoughts, forms, or circumstances. The *Course* says that the miracle can progress you much farther and faster along your spiritual path than would have otherwise been possible. For example, the *Text* says, 'The miracle is the only device at your immediate disposal for controlling time.'[5] And, 'The miracle substitutes for learning that might have taken thousands of years.'[6]

DU115 (Gary & Pursah)

A miracle, according to the *Course,* has nothing to do with the level of the physical. It's a shift in perception that takes place in the mind. Then you're dealing with the cause. As the *Course* says, 'This is a course in cause and not effect.'[7] And, 'Therefore, seek not to change the world, but choose to change your mind about the world.'[8]

Mikey's Note: Yes, if you spend your time trying to change the world, or change others *in* the world, you're going to find that you'll be spending a lot of time being upset, angry, and frustrated because you'll be psychologically attached to things happening a certain way. And if you seem to get something or someone to change for the better, it doesn't matter, because as Gary's teachers point out, 'If you solve one problem in the universe of time and space, then what you get is another problem.'[9] By changing the way you look at everything, you're coming from a position of strength, being at cause, rather than a position of weakness, and thus being at the mercy of the effect.

DU221 & 222 (Pursah)

The holy instant is simply that instant when you choose the Holy Spirit as your Teacher instead of the ego. This happens anytime you choose forgiveness – thus acting in both you and your forgivee's best interest. Of course, the forgivee is really you; it just doesn't look that way. What you're really accomplishing is the forgiveness of the symbolic contents of your own mind.

DU255 (Pursah)

Whenever you think forgiveness thoughts, it means you've chosen J or the Holy Spirit as your Teacher, which *is* the holy instant. When you remember to do that and forgive – in the *quantum* rather than the Newtonian sense – and you see your brothers and sisters as innocent like *you* are, then that *is* the miracle.

YIR102 (Gary & Pursah)

What does forgiveness do, then? J has your answer, brother. 'The miracle (forgiveness) does nothing. All it does is to undo. And thus it cancels out the interference to what has been done. It does not add, but merely takes away.'[10] And when the ego is undone, the truth will be all that's left.

DU157, 158, & 283 (Arten & Gary)

One of the goals of the *Course* is to train your mind so that the time will come when instead of judging automatically, you will forgive automatically. The benefits to your mind from such a habit are immeasurable and unimaginable to you. It's like one of the miracles principles early in the *Text* where it says, 'Miracles are habits, and should be involuntary.'[11] You get so used to thinking the thought system of the Holy Spirit that His true forgiveness becomes second nature to you.

Mikey's Note: Here's another quote from the *Course* about the holy instant that I would like to share here, 'The holy instant is the opposite of the ego's fixed belief in salvation through vengeance for the past. In the holy instant it is understood that the past is gone, and with its passing the drive for vengeance has been uprooted and has disappeared. The stillness and the peace of *now* enfold you in perfect gentleness. Everything is gone except the truth.'[12]

This reminds me of what Jerry tells George in a *Seinfeld* episode, 'If every instinct you have is wrong, then the opposite would have to be right.' George goes on to do the exact opposite of what he would normally do in a given situation, and everything turns to gold; the only episode where things worked out for Georgie boy!

Level Confusion

One big issue that some *Course* students have encountered, according to Gary and his teachers, is that over the years there have been a number of people who gave up on *A Course in Miracles* because they incorrectly thought the *Course* was contradicting itself. Arten and Pursah point out, however, the reason the *Course* seems to contradict itself is because it is speaking on two different levels. Jesus, as you know is the voice of the *Course*, speaks to us on both the level of the world, as well as the level of absolute truth, and does so interchangeably throughout the *Course*.

The key to understanding the *Course* in regards to the matter of different levels is that anything that expresses the absolute truth, the level of oneness, the level of non-duality, should be taken literally. On the other hand, Jesus also speaks to us in the *Course* on the level of the world, the level of form, the level of duality. The reason being is that He is meeting us where we think we are, and where our experience is, which is in the world. If he spoke to us just on the level of absolute truth, we wouldn't get very far due to the very complex nature of the ego.

DU92 (Pursah)

The parts of the *Course* that express non-duality *should* be taken literally, but the parts of it that seem to express duality should be taken as *metaphor*. There is no conflict in that, but without getting it, you'll incorrectly think the *Course* is contradicting itself. In the end, everything except for God is metaphor.

Mikey's Note: Here are a couple of examples of statements in the *Course* that should be taken literally, as it expresses the absolute truth:

There is no life outside of Heaven. Where God created life, there life must be.[13]

There is no separation of God and His creation.[14]

Here are a couple of examples of statements in the *Course* that should be taken as metaphor, as J is speaking to us where we think we are, which is in the world:

God wills you be in Heaven.[15]

God turns to you for help to save the world.[16]

Now, without understanding that not everything in the *Course* should be taken literally, one may incorrectly see the *Course* as contradicting itself with its mix of metaphorical and literal statements. However, if you properly make the distinctions of what should be taken literally, and what should be taken as metaphor, you'll understand that the *Course* is speaking on two different levels, and that it is indeed, not contradicting itself.

So when something like 'God wills you be in Heaven' or 'God turns to you for help to save the world' is read in the *Course*, those statements should be taken as a metaphor as the Holy Spirit wanting us to choose His voice rather than that of the ego. God doesn't will anything for anybody, or turn to us to save the world since that would imply God recognizes our seeming separation, and that we are lacking in some say. But God only recognizes *what* we really are *where* we really are.

DU128 & YIR160 & 161 (Gary & Pursah)

The *Course* is purely non-dualistic, meaning that of the two *seeming* worlds, the world of God and the world of man, only the world of God is true and He doesn't interact with the false world – but the Holy Spirit is here to guide you home. The message of the *Course* should always be viewed in the light of pure non-dualism, even when metaphor is used to describe the separated world and those who believe in it.

Christian Terminology

Now moving on to the use of the Christian terminology in the *Course*, some people may be turned off by it, and others may see the *Course* as being a continuation of Christianity like it's the *Third Testament* or something. But *A Course in Miracles* should not be confused with Christianity. The foundation[17] of Christianity is based on Jesus suffering and sacrificing himself for other people's 'sins,' and despite Jesus supposedly doing this, Christianity goes on to give you a million reasons why you're still a guilty sinner anyway, and gives you a God that loves you one day, but seeks vengeance on you the next day, apparently all depending on what kind of mood He's in.[18] All the while the devil is just waiting for you to slip up so you can spend all of eternity burning in Hell – now that's nine years of Catholic school talking! So suffice it to say that Christianity doesn't make any sense.

It's certainly not my intention to put down anybody's beliefs, and I have no interest, nor desire to 'convert' Christians to this way of thinking, only to clarify what the *Course* is *really* saying for those who want to learn it. Like Arten says, 'We don't mean to be disrespectful, but we have to make certain controversial statements because there's not exactly an oversupply of people in your society who are willing to point these things out.'[19] And then he goes on to say, 'We're not saying there isn't some good in Christianity or that Christian people are not sometimes the salt of the earth. But their religion is a mixed bag, because the world that is a projection of the mind that made it is such a mixed bag. If the mind is going to be healed, then it needs something that is *not* a mixed bag.'[20]

Now, the thought system of *A Course in Miracles*, on the other hand, is consistent in its message, as it is all about love and forgiveness, and gives us a God that is perfect Love and sees us all as being innocent no matter what we dream up here in the illusion of time and space. In the mean time, our memory of God, the Holy Spirit, is with us to help us return our awareness to our natural state of peace and bliss while we appear to be here, and ultimately, returning our awareness to where we *really* are – one with God in Heaven. The terminology may be the same but that's where the similarities of Christianity and *A Course in Miracles* end, as *A Course in Miracles* is the *correction* of Christianity, while being more Buddhist-like, than anything, in its approach.

DU97 (Pursah)

Jesus is using Biblical, metaphorical language in the *Course* in order to correct Christianity.

DU44, 319, & YIR2 (Pursah & Gary)

When J used the word *He* to describe God 2,000 years ago, he was speaking metaphorically in the language of scripture. And in the *Course*, J is speaking as an artist correcting the Bible that was allegedly based on his teachings. That's why he uses Biblical language. He had to use metaphor to communicate with people, but *you* make everything real. J knew that God cannot be limited by gender, and neither can people – because they're not really people. How can you really be a person if you're not a body? In fact, you could just as easily substitute the word *She* for *He*, but that would not be any more accurate than using *He*. You would just be replacing one mistake with another.

Mikey's Note: So when Jesus uses the word *He* to describe God, he's not suggesting that God is some old white guy with a long gray beard sitting on a throne up in Heaven while judging the hell out of us. Who among us that went to Catholic school doesn't have this image of God ingrained in his or her mind?

This reminds me of an episode of *Beavis and Butthead* titled *The Final Judgment of Beavis*. Beavis has this dream that he dies, and is greeted by St. Peter at Heaven's gate. St. Peter has this laundry list of things Beavis did wrong in his life, and lets Beavis know about each one of them. And then St. Peter gets to the last one and says, '....and then on the third day of the fourth month of your twelfth year, you touched yourself in an impure manner.' And Beavis was like, 'You saw that? No way, I had the covers over me!' So, suffice it to say, Beavis wasn't allowed into Heaven. Anyway, technically speaking, the correct pronoun used in place of God and the Holy Spirit would be *It*.[21]

DU5 (Pursah)

There is no concept of male or female in Heaven. The only true reality is God or pure spirit, which in Heaven, are synonymous, and God and pure spirit have no form.

Judgment and Common Sense

DU116 (Arten)

When the *Course* talks about not judging your brother, what it means is that you don't *condemn* him. Obviously, you have to make judgments just to cross the street. The *Course* isn't talking about abandoning that kind of judgment. Without it, you couldn't get out of bed in the morning. One thing the *Course* has nothing against is common sense.

DU111, 114, & YIR177 (Arten & Pursah)

You should never allow yourself to be harmed physically, or seek out danger or suffer in order to prove a point. You can still live a relatively normal earthly existence while being awakened slowly and gently from your dream. The crucifixion was an extreme teaching lesson. It is *not* necessary for you to go through it in order to learn from it. Remember, the *Course* is done at the level of the mind. If you're a woman and a man is trying to rape you, kick him in the balls.

Mikey's Note: Yes, so please use common sense and discernment in your everyday life. Yes, it is your job to save the world, as the world can't be saved without you – since the world is just a projection of *your own mind.* But remember, you saving the world is *always* done so at the level of the mind, and *never* at the level of the physical. Forgiveness can always be applied after the fact if you ever find yourself in a situation that calls for you to physically protect yourself from any harm. As J says in the *Course*, 'I do not call for martyrs but for teachers.'[22]

YIR43 (Pursah)

The teachings of the *Course* are *always* applied at the level of the mind, and *never* at the level of form or the physical. That's why J says in the *Course*, 'This is a course in cause and not effect.'[23]

DU218 (Gary & Arten)

Just because you're forgiving someone, that doesn't mean you have to hang around with them. Forgiveness isn't about being a do-gooder, not that there's anything wrong with doing good deeds if it turns you on. The *Course* is about being a right *thinker.* Forgiveness has to do with what you think. What you do isn't the important thing, even though it is a *result* of what you think. It's what you think that will either keep you dreaming or help get you home, not what you do.

Mikey's Note: For example, you don't have to give money to every homeless person you see out on the street in order to consider yourself to be a spiritual person. If that feels right for you, then go for it. But it's best not to do such things out of feelings of guilt. And regardless of whether you give them money or not, the important thing is to be watchful of your mind to make sure that you are not *condemning* them; you want to see them as they *really* are – as innocent.

On his audio program, *Fearless Love,* Gary quotes J in a special message given to the scribe of the *Course*, Helen Schucman, 'If you cannot turn down the requests of others, then you have not yet overcome ego centricity.' So, in other words, don't do things for people out of guilt. It's perfectly all right to say no if a request is made of you that doesn't feel right for you – you won't go to hell! (LOL)

Denial

Now, some folks new to the *Course* might think that practicing the true forgiveness that the *Course* talks about is a form of denial. Well, in a sense it is – but in a different way from what the world commonly views as denial. Here's what Gary's teachers have to say about that:

DU113 & 114 (Pursah)

The thought system of love and the thought system of fear are *both* forms of denial. One of them, the Holy Spirit's teaching, leads to Heaven by uncovering and reversing the ego's denial of the truth. As the *Course* says about the peace that results from the Holy Spirit's teaching, 'It denies the ability of anything not of God to affect you. This is the proper use of denial.'[24] Of the forgiveness that leads to peace, the *Course* says, 'Forgiveness then, is an illusion, but because of its purpose, which is the Holy Spirit's, it has one difference. Unlike all other illusions it leads away from error and not towards it.'[25]

DU166, 167, & 193 (Pursah)

The Holy Spirit's dynamic of forgiveness undoes the ego at *both* the conscious and unconscious levels. The Atonement principle undoes denial and projection at the level of your mind by forgiving what you perceive, and the Holy Spirit undoes the denial and projection at the metaphysical level of your mind at the same time – as well as undoing the whole idea of separation right along with you.

You must practice forgiveness on the level where your experience is. Yes, you have to understand the metaphysics of the *Course* in order to understand what you're doing. But your *forgiveness* is done here, which means you should be practical – and respectful of other people and their experience. In other words, when you're living your everyday life, be kind. Your job isn't to correct others. Just help the Holy Spirit clean up *your* wrong mind by switching to your right mind, and then leave the rest to Him. And when we say you should be kind to others, it doesn't mean you should be in denial about the ego thought system. But don't try to change others; change your own mind instead.

DU132 & 133 (Arten)

The memory of what you are *is* both the answer to the separation and the principle of the Atonement rolled into one. As the *Course* teaches about the Holy Spirit, 'He came into being with the separation as a protection, inspiring the Atonement principle at the same time. Before that there was no need for healing, for no one was comfortless.'[26] As the *Text* explains, the Holy Spirit has always taught the Atonement, 'He tells you to return your whole mind to God, because it has never left Him. If it has never left Him, you need only perceive it as it is to be returned. The full awareness of the Atonement, then, is the recognition that *the separation never occurred.*'[27]

Nitpicking the Course

Another stumbling block that some *Course* students may run into is getting caught up in nitpicking and overanalyzing the *Course*.

DU329 (Pursah)

Let me caution you about something. Don't nitpick the *Course* to death. All the details of the *Course's* teachings should be put within the context of its larger teachings on forgiveness.

YIR73 (Arten)

The mind will go to such lengths to avoid what the *Course* is saying and delay the clarification of it that people will read the *Text* and interpret it, usually incorrectly. They'll ignore the definitive statements of the *Course*, and start nitpicking and focusing on individual words or phrases that, when taken out of context, seem to support their interpretation. Yet everything the *Course* says *must* be put within the context of the *Course's* larger teaching, which shows up unmistakably in those definitive statements.

Mikey's Note: I would add that you don't need to sit there dissecting and analyzing every sentence in the *Course* – don't get so caught up in the trees that you can't see the forest. If you don't understand what a particular sentence or paragraph is saying, it's not something to get all frustrated about and/or beat yourself up over – just move on.

Nitpicking the *Course* is the ego's way of looking for excuses to not do the necessary forgiveness work that's required in order to attain the goal of the *Course*. If you read a sentence in the *Course* that doesn't make sense to you, most of the time, it'll clear itself right up after reading a little bit more. And if doesn't seem to, then just remember what Pursah says about all the details being put within the context of its larger teachings on forgiveness – that'll save you much time and grief. And always remember, the first four letters of the word *analyze* spell *anal* – and I don't generally believe in coincidences. (See chapter 13 for more about definitive statements.)

Gotta love the following two quotes from J in the *Course* in regards to the ego's many questions:

'There is no need to further clarify what no one in the world can understand.'[28]

'The ego will demand many answers that this course does not give. It does not recognize as questions the mere form of a question to which an answer is impossible. The ego may ask, "How did the impossible occur?", "To what did the impossible happen?", and may ask this in many forms. Yet there is no answer; only an experience. Seek only this, and do not let theology delay you.'[29]

Course Study Groups

DU106 (Pursah)

Study groups are not mentioned at all in the *Course;* they should be viewed primarily as a social phenomenon. They are not always the best sources of information either, but if they are given to the Holy Spirit and used for forgiveness, then you can be certain He'll be happy to participate with you.

DU121 (Arten)

Study groups are not about joining with individuals on the level of the world, but for the sake of forgiveness that becomes possible through the relationships and the examination of your own ego. In study groups, churches, or anywhere else in this world, it appears that there are multiple teachers and learners. But there is really only one Teacher of the *Course* – and only one student.

Mikey's Note: As far as I'm concerned, *Course* groups are not about the *Course*. Sitting around in a circle and taking turns reading from the *Course* book doesn't do anything for me. In fact, it usually bores the hell out of me. If I want to spend two hours reading from the *Course*, well, I don't need people to do that, I can just stay home and do that on my own. For me, *Course* groups are all about sharing experiences, being with people of like-mind and enjoying their company, and *especially* for practicing forgiveness on those whose company you *don't* necessarily enjoy. (LOL)

For me, it's not about seeing how many pages of the *Course* the group can plow through during any given session. Also, anybody new to Gary's books and the *Course* should be studying it on their own, and not relying on people from *Course* groups to teach them. One reason for that being is that you are not likely to find total agreement on what the *Course* is saying amongst the people in the group, so you'll just end up confused and thinking we're all a bunch of idiots. But what I love about Gary's books is that Arten and Pursah spell it all out for you on what the *Course* is *really* saying. So, like I said in my *Introduction*, I highly recommend the 'newbies' read that first.

YIR150 (Arten)

Dividing is what the ego does. Everything in the world separates, even if only through death, because everything here is symbolic of the thought of separation. Don't fear that. It will always happen as long as there appears to be any kind of form. There has never been a church or spiritual organization that didn't undergo some kind of a split, usually sooner rather than later. Your job is to forgive it. Do the *Course*. If there appear to be divisions on the level of form within the *Course* community, understand that the way out of it is *not* on the level of form, it's through the *forgiveness* of the level of form. And *that's* done at the level of the mind, which has *nothing* to do with the level of form.

Random stuff to keep in mind when studying the *Course*

On disc four of *The Secrets of the Immortal* audio series, Gary advises that you can replace the word *but* with *only* if that helps you to understand a particular section better. For example, here are a couple of lines from the *Course* with the word *but* in it:

For time but seems to go in one direction. We but undertake a journey that is over.[30]

So, if you replaced the word *but* with *only*, it would go like this:

For time only seems to go in one direction. We only undertake a journey that is over.

For me personally, when I actually *do* some reading from the *Course,* I find this suggestion to be very helpful. Another thing Gary also mentions to keep in mind that may be helpful while reading the *Course* is that J generally uses the word *make* or *made* in association with the ego – while using the word *create* in association with God or Spirit.

DU150 (Pursah)

A Course in Miracles has been given by J in order to show you *how* to return to the Kingdom of Heaven.

DU231 (Pursah)

The *Course* teaches that your sole responsibility is to accept the Atonement for yourself.[31]

DU108 (Arten)

The *Course* does not claim to be superior to any other spiritual path, yet at the same time it doesn't make any secret about the fact that it is ultimately, absolutely necessary for you to learn it.

DU127 & 128 (Pursah)

The reason for understanding the *Course* is not merely for an intellectual comprehension! That plus a dollar will get you a cup of coffee. The reason it will be extraordinarily helpful for you to understand J's *Course* is so you can better *apply* it to the problems and situations that confront you in your alleged daily existence.

Mikey's Note: I don't drink coffee, but I would imagine that the price for a 'cup of joe' has gone up since Pursah made this statement back in 1993. Of course, you could do what Kramer did in that *Seinfeld* episode where he spilled hot coffee on himself when sneaking it into a movie theatre, then decided to sue the coffee company because the coffee was too hot. He wound up getting free coffee for life.

DU98 & 105 (Arten & Pursah)

When people begin studying the *Course*, they always mistakenly think they are being asked to sacrifice something. As the *Manual for Teachers* points out, 'It seems as if things are being taken away, and it is rarely understood initially that their lack of value is merely being recognized.'[32] Additionally, one who already has a personal relationship with J or the Holy Spirit should by all means continue to develop it. Eventually you will find the experience to be beyond this world, because where you join with J or the Holy Spirit, at the level of the mind, is also beyond this world. At first people always think of J as helping them *in* the world, but the *Course* will teach you to outgrow that.

Mikey's Note: It was such a relief for me when I read this for the first time that this path wasn't about sacrificing or giving anything up. Everything I had read up until that point on the subject of ascension and enlightenment implied that you had to give stuff up. At the same time, some of these same teachings, as well as other teachings, were spiritualizing abundance, making it important and real. I'm so grateful for Arten and Pursah for their clarity on everything. *Their way* actually makes perfect sense to me, as they put everything in its proper perspective.

DU334 & 335 (Pursah)

The *Course* is set up so you can live what you thought was your life and gradually attain your salvation at the same time. Go at your own pace. That way you won't feel like anything is being taken away from you, and you can realize *for yourself* that the world has no value. For example, you should remember what the *Manual for Teachers* says about almost all of the *Course's* students, 'By far the majority are given a slowly evolving training program, in which as many previous mistakes as possible are corrected. Relationships in particular must be properly perceived, and all dark cornerstones of unforgiveness removed. Otherwise, the old thought system still has a basis for return.'[33]

DU362 (Pursah)

No matter what your preferences are, the *Course* isn't about changing your behavior. If your behavior changes, then so be it. If it doesn't, don't worry about it. You might not even want it to. The important thing is to understand your total innocence.

YIR49 & DU167 (Arten & Pursah)

God did *not* send the Holy Spirit to rescue you. The Holy Spirit could be said to be your memory of your true home with God, which is the right part of your mind. The ego is the wrong part of your mind. At first people think that the *Course* is talking to them as a person, because that's what they think they are. But the 'you' that the *Course* is addressing is actually your seemingly separated mind that needs to choose to listen to the right teacher instead of the wrong one. The *Course* is addressed to the part of your mind that needs to choose between the ego and the Holy Spirit.

DU93 (Arten)

Since the Holy Spirit is your Inner Teacher, you should always expect to be a student as long as you appear to be in a body. This is a lifelong spiritual path for people who are serious about wanting to break free from the world and go home. That doesn't mean you always have to take things seriously. If anything, the *Course* is saying that the world *cannot* be taken seriously.

YIR64 (Gary)

People think it's the beliefs they have in their conscious mind that runs them, and that they can control their mind by changing their thoughts from negative to positive ones. That's not true when it comes to the big picture. It will only have a temporarily helpful impact. What *really* runs us are the beliefs we have that are *unconscious* to us, the things we *can't* see. *A Course in Miracles* presents a way to actually heal and remove the things that are hidden in the deep canyons of the unconscious mind. Very few spiritual teachings do anything on that level.

DU100 (Arten and Pursah)

There are over 20,000 different kinds of organized Christian churches in the world today, each with its own particular interpretation of Christianity. So, if you have over twenty thousand churches that don't really understand J's message – and I assure you they don't – and if you have them all disagreeing about what J's message is supposed to mean, and in the meantime the world hasn't changed – not *really* – then do you honestly believe it will serve humanity if you end up with twenty thousand different interpretations of *A Course in Miracles*?

Mikey's Note: Gotta love Arten and Pursah's bluntness and rhetorical questions. Anyway, according to WikiAnswers.com, which references the year 2000 version of the *World Christian Encyclopedia*, there are actually 33,820 different denominations of Christianity – holy crap, Batman! Talk about screwing up a spiritual message! So that means there are at least 33,819 denominations of Christianity that misunderstand Jesus' message from two thousand years ago – and that's being kind. That was the reason why Arten and Pursah appeared to Gary in the first place – they wanted to set the record straight about Jesus and his message from two thousand years ago, and didn't want

A Course in Miracles to turn into what Jesus' original message has become through organized religion – distorted and twisted!

DU91 (Arten)

If J meant for his *Course* to be subject to your interpretation rather than his instruction, then why give it in the first place? Why not just let you make up your own version of everything, which is exactly what you've been doing throughout your seemingly separate existence? The truth is that if you really understand *A Course in Miracles*, which is rare, then there *is* only one possible interpretation. If you change it, which is typical, then it is no longer *A Course in Miracles*.

Mkey's Note: So, you're either in alignment with J and the Holy Spirit's interpretation of the *Course* or you're not. And if you're not, then you're not really *getting* it. But it doesn't mean you can't eventually *get* it – so don't give up, just keep working at it. But that's what I love about Gary's books – Arten and Pursah just spell it all out for you – so you don't necessarily have to plow through 1300 pages of Shakespearean blank verse and Christian terminology to figure it out. Thank God!

I know I wouldn't have likely understood the *Course* if it wasn't for Arten and Pursah spelling it all out for me, I probably would have thought the *Course* was contradicting itself had I tried to attempt it on my own. As Gary's teachers go on to say in regards to those who not yet fully understand what the *Course* is really saying, '…it's not because of a lack of intelligence, but because of an abundance of conscious and unconscious resistance to the truth.'[34]

YIR118 (Pursah)

The *Course* is saying the same thing all the way through. From the *Text*, to the *Workbook*, and through the *Manual*, the *Course* is a purely non-dualistic teaching. It's consistent. And if that's true, and it certainly is, then it means there's only one authentic way to interpret it.

DU92 (Pursah)

Everybody is trying to find and express *their* truth. Their so-called truth is actually designed to keep them stuck where they are. What J is teaching in his *Course* is that the truth is *not* different for everyone. It is *not* relative. He's saying the truth is the truth whether you understand and agree with it or not. The truth is not subject to your interpretation, and neither is his *Course*. He's the Teacher, and you're the student. If that's not the case, then why do the *Course?*

DU103 & 104 (Arten)

In order for you to learn to save time, it would be very helpful if you approached the *Course* like the original thought system that it is, rather than seeing it as a continuation of Christianity, which it isn't. Please don't call it the *Third Testament*. It's not. It's the *Course*. You get J without the religion.

DU114 (Pursah)

The kind of forgiveness J used, and that his *Course* is teaching, is not the same kind of forgiveness that Christianity and the world sometimes participate in. If it were, then it would be a waste of time.

DU223 (Gary & Arten)

Some *Course* students seem to think God created the good parts of the world and not the bad, and that the *Course* is trying to get people to give up their bad perceptions, but keep the good ones. Let's be very clear about this; God did not even create *part* of the world. The *Course* says that there is no world! How could God have created *part* of it if there isn't any? It's not the Holy Spirit's intention to do *anything* except wake you up from *your* dream that there *is* a world! That's true whether it seems to be temporarily good or bad.

DU378 (Pursah)

A Course in Miracles is a presentation of the absolute truth, which can be summed in just two words, but only accepted by a mind that has been prepared for it. Two thousand years from now, 'God Is' will still be the absolute truth, and God will still be perfect Love. The *real* truth *doesn't* change. To accept it however, requires the kind of mind training the *Course* gives you. Some people may not choose to be prepared in this lifetime. They want the meaning of God and the world to be open to their own ideas. That's fine if that's what they want for now. But as J asks you in his *Course*, 'Would God have left the meaning of the world to your interpretation?'[35]

YIR43 (Arten)

There can be no separation from God. Only God exists, and all else is false. The *Course* is completely uncompromising on that, for those who care to see it.

DU376 (Arten)

It will take time for the principles of *A Course in Miracles* to be understood by society, and the overwhelming majority of people will continue to believe as they always have. They'll continue to live in denial. They will try to bring God into the world and spiritualize the universe, thinking there is some kind of compassionate intelligence behind what is really a murderous thought. They will see death as a part of a 'circle of life,' when it is really just a symbol of the great mistake.

DU225 (Pursah)

The purpose of the *Course* is peace, not to scare the hell out of you. The more prepared you are, and the better you do your forgiveness work, the less scary your journey with the *Course* will ultimately be.

DU118 (Arten)

The *Course* is not a movement; there are more than enough of those. You don't have to take over the world. It doesn't matter whether the *Course* is popular or not. J knows what he's doing. Those who are ready for the *Course* will find it. His *Course* is unique. It gives an individual a chance to learn that he or she is not an individual, and that they are never alone. It gives you the opportunity to commune with the Holy Spirit and ultimately, God. It accelerates your return to God by helping the Holy Spirit heal you.

Mikey's Note: To reemphasize for clarification purposes, when J, or Arten and Pursah make statements about the Holy Spirit helping to heal you, 'you' always refers to your seemingly separated mind; they're never talking about the body.

DU195 & 196 (Pursah)

It should be pointed out that people who are not as successful in the world have a tendency to get more out of the *Course* than highly successful people. Some of the people who appear to have it made in the world, and who are relatively satisfied with their lot in life, are actually falling into a trap. The ego sucks them into thinking that the world is a good place. What's really happening is that they're living one of the few lifetimes where good karma is called for in the script, so they have a good time.

DU151 (Arten)

Remember this with certainty. Whenever you are prepared to choose the Holy Spirit as your Teacher, J will be there with you. If you are not prepared, he will still be there with you. For as he tells you in the *Text*, 'If you want to be like me I will help you, knowing that we are alike. If you want to be different, I will wait until you change your mind. I can teach you, but only you can choose to listen to my teaching.'[36]

The perfect segue into the next chapter

DU200 (Arten)

You think the *Course* is part of the New Age movement, but it's not. Don't limit it. Yes, it's good that some people are more open-minded and ready for new ideas. Remember, the *Course* is unique because it's J explaining what he really wants to say. Remember that this is his *only Course*. There are other things that have come out since the *Course* was published that people have said came from him. Yet they don't really teach the same thing as the *Course*. I ask you, would J contradict himself? I don't say that to put anybody down. Obviously, we are not angry at people who we disagree with. We say these things merely for your clarification.

Chapter 6

Arten and Pursah's Take
on Other Teachings

Most of what the world thinks of as the wisdom of the ages is actually full of it. The 'divine intelligence of the universe' is a phrase that's entirely worthy of having the plug pulled on it.[1]

For those of you who may be still partaking in the 'New Age buffet line,' this chapter may rub you the wrong way – and Jimmy crack corn and *I* don't care! (LOL) In this chapter, I have some quotes to share from Arten and Pursah regarding what they have to say about other teachings, including a couple of lengthy excerpts from chapter nine of Gary's second book, *Your Immortal Reality*. Now, I certainly don't put these quotes and passages here to put any teachers or their followers down. A lot of these teachings I had gone through in the earlier phases of my spiritual path, and they were all very helpful concepts to me at the time. I know I couldn't have handled *Disappearance* ten years ago had it been out then, as the message would have been too threatening to my ego. I needed the other softer, gentler, teachings to get me to open my mind, change my old ways of looking at things, and get me heading in the right direction. So all my learning prior to Gary's material served a useful purpose in my life, and I'm very thankful for that.

With all that said, however, a lot of what is out there is not the same thing that is being taught in Gary Renard's books and in *A Course in Miracles*. So, I'm not trying to be an arrogant jerk here, or as Gary once said, 'I don't mean to poop in anybody's Cheerios.'[2] I'm just trying to reiterate the point that Gary's teachers make in his books on what it takes to heal the mind and become a master. As an idealist, I very much appreciated Arten and Pursah's blunt take on the other teachings out there for my own clarity, and feel very strongly that they are worth reprinting here. What Arten and Pursah are teaching, and what J is teaching in his *Course*, is not cupcake spirituality. And there are very few teachings out there that are in alignment with the *real* message of *A Course in Miracles;* and Arten and Pursah came to help us save time.

Now, there's certainly nothing wrong with learning all the different teachings that are out there. However, if you just stay stuck in that, the problem will be that you'll just sort of become like a 'jack of all trades but a master of none.' For me, I came to a point on my spiritual path where I outgrew the New Age teachings and needed something that packed more punch; something that would really work for me in the long run. I needed a teaching that could help me build my house upon the rock instead of on the sand. So, you'll eventually have to go beyond these more popular types of teachings in order to obtain the lofty goal the *Course* has to offer – to become a master like our brother J.

Anyone who is really serious about attaining the goal of the *Course* is going to find, just as I have, that teachings that once served them well will become useless to them now. Of course, as I already stated, I needed those previous teachings to help me get to that point. To go from my awareness at the age of eighteen to reading *The Disappearance of the Universe* fifteen years later without all those other teachings in between would have been too far of a stretch for me. From my experience, the Holy Spirit always guides us to what we are ready for, even if the teachings are not total truth. Not everyone is ready for the Truth. In fact, very few are, including many people who consider themselves to be *Course* students – just sayin'.

With all that being said, this chapter is mostly geared towards the problems of the New Age teachings that are out there. Like I said, they were all very helpful, as well as necessary, teachings for me at one time, but ultimately they will lead to a dead end. I know, otherwise I'd still be listening to Wayne Dyer, Neale Walsch, and the like. What's being said in Gary's books doesn't fit in with the Marianne Williamsons and the Echkart Tolles of the world – it's totally different. And just so we're clear, I certainly don't mean any disrespect to any of the aforementioned teachers. They are all helping people where they are at, and that's a wonderful thing. But what I *am* saying is that *A Course in Miracles* and the teachings presented in Gary Renard's books are *not* the same thing in a different package. And applying the thought system presented in the *Course* and Gary's books is what's going to get people Home. The popular New Age teachings will only have a temporary, helpful impact, as they pretty much only address the conscious part of the mind. So, it's just a matter of what you are ready for.

YIR10 (Pursah)

Most spiritual students spend almost all of their time in the phase of *gathering information*. This is encouraged by the belief that the more spiritual information they put in their heads, the more enlightened they'll be. So they jump around from one thing to another, reading dozens of books on different spiritual subjects, what we have referred to as the 'spiritual buffet line.' Now there's nothing wrong with learning information. Indeed, it gives people a necessary background. The problem is that people make a false idol out of gathering information, and it doesn't lead anywhere. It's a trick, a carrot and a stick. That's why what's really important isn't what you know, but what you *do* with what you know. What really matters in terms of quickening your spiritual development is the phase of *application*.

Contrasting Other Teachings

DU17 (Arten)

It will appear to you that we are making judgments, a lot of them. There's a good reason for that. The only possible way to teach the thought system of *A Course in Miracles*, is by contrasting the Holy Spirit's thinking with the thinking of the world. His judgment is sound, and leads to God. Your judgment is poor, and leads you back here, again and again.

Mikey's Note: As the *Course* states, 'Contrast and differences are necessary teaching aids, for by them you learn what to avoid and what to seek.'[3] And, 'The Holy Spirit must teach through comparisons, and uses opposites to point to truth.'[4]

DU20 (Arten)

There are teachers who will try to tell you that life is not a classroom and that you're not here to learn lessons, but simply to experience the truth that is already within you. They are mistaken.

Your life is very much a classroom, and if you *don't* learn your lessons then you will *not* experience the truth that is within you.

DU16 (Arten)

There's a big problem holding people back that the popular New Age authors didn't tell them about. Perhaps the most overlooked error of all religions and philosophies, including the New Age models, is the failure to understand that although doing things like thinking positively, being 'in the now,' saying prayers, affirmations, denying negative thoughts, and listening to famous speakers may have a temporarily helpful impact, they *cannot* release that which is locked in the deep canyons of your unconscious mind.

YIR82 & 83 (Pursah)

The idea of thinking that God would have to make this world in order to experience duality so He could appreciate and enjoy Himself, is the equivalent of the idea that in order to experience and enjoy sex you would have to also experience getting shot in the gut. No. Pain is the result of the guilt that came from thinking you separated yourself from God, and you *don't* have to experience pain in order to experience the pleasure of reality. But you do have to forgive pain and suffering and give it up in order to *return* to reality. J couldn't be any more clear about that in his *Course*, and he *is* the one you should listen to:

'From the ego came sin and guilt and death, in opposition to life and innocence, and to the Will of God Himself. Where can such opposition lie but in the sick minds of the insane, dedicated to madness and set against the peace of Heaven? One thing is sure; God, Who created neither sin nor death, wills not that you be bound by them. He knows of neither sin nor its results. The shrouded figures in the funeral procession march not in honor of their Creator, Whose Will it is they live. They are not following His Will; they are opposing it.'[5]

DU406 (Pursah)

Salvation is not a critical mass thing. People cannot be enlightened by the thinking of others, or simply by being in their presence. But they *can* be pointed in the right direction.

Mikey's Note: Gary adds on his *Secrets of the Immortal* audio program that there is no such thing as vicarious salvation; being around an enlightened being will not rub off on you. You can, however, be pointed in the right direction, but you have to do your own work, there's no getting around that. As the *Course* says, 'My salvation comes from me.'[6] And, 'The sole responsibility of the miracle worker is to accept the Atonement for himself.'[7] So, it's a choice that only *you* can make.

YIR184 (Pursah)

Many famous teachers teach that people are born innocent, with a clean slate, and then are messed up by the world. *It's not true.* People are born with the ego intact. It then plays itself out. If the ego weren't already there, then they never would have come here in the first place. Still, every lifetime is an opportunity to undo the ego and break the cycle of birth and death.

DU126 & 127 (Arten)

In the 1990s, one of the most popular spiritual books ever written has God Himself saying that He created fear! This is an inaccuracy so major we cannot stress too much how completely false it is. God does not create anything that is not the perfect oneness of Heaven. As J puts it very early in his *Course* when describing *anything* that doesn't reflect the thought system of the Holy Spirit, 'Everything else is your own nightmare, and does not exist.'[8] And later on, 'You are at home in God, dreaming of exile but perfectly capable of awakening to reality.'[9]

Mikey's Note: I read the first three *Conversations with God* books back in the 1990s. There were some helpful ideas in them for me at the time, but I found myself moving on rather quickly to the next item in the 'spiritual buffet line.'

DU10 (Arten)

As far as the Gnostic sects are concerned, they were right in believing that God did not create this excuse for a world, but they made the same error that almost everybody else does: They made the mis-created world psychologically real for themselves. They saw it as an evil to be despised. J, on the other hand, viewed the world as the Holy Spirit sees it: a perfect opportunity for forgiveness and salvation.

New Age Myths

In the rest of this chapter, I want to share what Arten and Pursah have to say about certain New Age topics that so many people are crazy over. Arten and Pursah are very blunt in putting these many popular *New Age* concepts in their proper perspective – as well as putting the entire universe in its place! How can anybody not love these guys? They really hold back no punches! In this section, we'll review what Arten and Pursah have to say about many of the hot topics in the spiritual community, including but not limited to, energy, consciousness, body-mind-spirit, and being in the now.

Energy

DU104 (Arten)

Energy cannot seemingly be destroyed on the level of form because it is not *really* energy, it is thought. Or more accurately, it is mis-thought, which *will* eventually be changed over to the eternal. In the meantime, there is a very simple criteria that the *Course* gives you to distinguish between the real and the unreal, 'Whatever is true is eternal, and cannot change or be changed. Spirit is therefore unalterable because it is already perfect, but the mind can elect what it chooses to serve. The only limit put on its choice is that it cannot serve two masters.'[10]

So the fact that energy *can* be changed means that by its very nature it is untrue. It is not our intention to deflate the enthusiasm of your New Age buddies who are so ga-ga over energy. But energy is nothing. It's a waste of time, a trick, just another device for building your house upon the sand instead of on the rock. Sure, it may be a helpful idea for some people to be interested in the unseen instead of the seen. But we came to help you save time. The good news isn't that *energy* can be changed, the good news is that the mind that made it can be changed.

DU129 (Arten)

Try to remember that energy is not spirit – spirit being your *unalterable*, true reality. Energy, which changes and can be measured, exists within the domain of perception.

Mikey's Note: I used to be pretty obsessed about energy myself. Arten and Pursah really cleared this whole thing up for me. They really simplify the whole process of what it takes to attain enlightenment, while some other authors whose books I read prior to this point really complicated the hell out of it – making DNA and every single cell in the body so *real*! Energy really *is* nothing! Just practice true forgiveness and the rest will take care of itself. What a relief!

YIR54 & 55 (Pursah)

One of the most important things is not to make the universe of time and space real. You're innocent because it's *not* real. Don't spiritualize the universe. Don't spiritualize matter or energy. Energy looks like matter to you sometimes only because of the way you perceive it and perceive yourself.

Consciousness

DU129 (Arten)

Consciousness is yet another thing you foolishly value highly. In order to have consciousness you have to have separation. You've got to have more than one thing. You have to have something else to be conscious *of*. This is the beginning of the split mind. As the *Course* teaches in no uncertain terms, 'Consciousness, the level of perception, was the first split introduced into the mind after the separation, making the mind a perceiver rather than a creator. Consciousness is correctly identified as the domain of the ego.'[11]

DU131 & 214 (Arten)

Consciousness is not of God. In Heaven, you don't have to think at all. In fact, you are thought *by* God.

Mikey's Note: So since consciousness is not of God, that means, the popular term, 'Christ-Consciousness' is actually an oxy-moron. Christ is of God, while consciousness represents separation *from* God.

DU387 (Gary)

Consciousness, even though it's an unreal state, does continue after the seeming death of the body. When you completely awaken from the dream, consciousness disappears and you experience your oneness with God and All Creation.

Evolution and Reincarnation

DU145 & 146 (Gary & Pursah)

Since everything happened all at once, then doesn't that mean evolution is also an illusion, kind of a smokescreen? Congratulations to the one who knows that. Your generation worships evolution, thinking that you're on the way to creating some kind of new, hot consciousness. You value evolution almost as much as you value energy. What is called evolution was merely the ego separating all at once by seemingly dividing and sub-dividing cells over and over again in order to make bodies and brains that appear to be more *complex* – and thus more impressive. Yet *all* bodies are the same in their unreality.

Mikey's Note: Yes, everything is happening and has happened all at once, though that is not our experience. Arten notes that Albert Einstein said that the past, present, and future all occur simultaneously. Arten also mentions that Einstein still had to learn that it actually never happened at all.[12]

DU328 (Gary & Pursah)

Some people believe reincarnation leads to the evolvement of the soul. True? Your soul is *already* perfect, or otherwise it wouldn't be a soul; it would just be something you're mistaking for a soul – like your mind, which people do mistake for the soul, or a projection of your mind, which includes bodily-shaped ghostly images that people think are souls.

Evolution is something that appears to happen on the level of form, but it's just a dream. Once your mind has learned all its forgiveness lessons, then it awakens to spirit or soul, and everything else is gone except Heaven. Most people think of their soul as being an individual thing because they can't help but think of themselves as individuals. When that false belief is gone, then you know that there is really only *one* soul – which is our unlimited oneness as spirit.

DU179 (Pursah)

We should emphasize something about the subject of reincarnation. We talk about it as though it actually happens. Yet just like everything else, it's only a dream. Yes, it appears that you incarnate into a body, and your experience is that you are a body – but as we like to point out, the *Course* says that what you are seeing is not true.[13]

DU387 (Gary & Arten)

Reincarnation is only something that appears to happen; you're just dreaming that you're going from one body to the next. Also, it doesn't really matter what one's personal belief is about it, as long as you forgive. The *Course* says, 'All that must be recognized, however, is that birth was not the beginning and death is not the end. Yet even this much is not required of the beginner. He need merely accept the idea that what he knows is not necessarily all there is to learn. His journey has begun.'[14]

YIR96 (Pursah)

The reason the *Course* says that reincarnation isn't true[15] is because it's an illusion. It *appears* to happen, but you never really go into a body, it just looks that way. It's an optical illusion. The *Course* teaches that the body doesn't even exist. So how could you really be going into one? As the *Course* says, 'The body does not exist except as a learning device for the mind. This learning device is not subject to errors of its own, because it cannot create. It is obvious, then, that inducing the mind to give up its miscreations is the only application of creative ability that is truly meaningful.'[16]

Body-Mind-Spirit

DU76 (Pursah & Gary)

Today, many believe in the existence of a trilogy – body, mind, and spirit. The 'balance' of all three is important in your philosophy. But the seemingly separated mind which makes and uses bodies, must choose *between* the changeless and eternal reality of spirit – which *is* God and His Kingdom – or the unreal and ever-changing universe of bodies – which includes *anything* that can be perceived, whether you appear to be in a body or not.

Giving equal value to body, mind, and spirit actually *contributes* to you coming back here over and over again as a body, rather than being free. But this doesn't mean that you should neglect your body. We're speaking of another way of looking at it.

Mikey's Note: This means using the practical forms of judgment when it comes to the body. We are still going to bathe it, dress it, feed it, and exercise it, as well as looking both ways before crossing the street. This reminds me of a quote from the *Course* that many people misinterpret, 'I need do nothing!'[17] Well, it's true that we need do nothing on the level of the world in order to attain enlightenment, but we are still going to be doing things in this world as long as we appear to be in a body.

The point of the statement, 'I need do nothing,' is that your salvation is dependent on what's going on in your mind, while you go about living your daily life. What you do in the world doesn't matter, no matter *what* it is – nothing you do on the level of the world will help get you home because the *Course* is *not* about your behavior. Resurrection is of the mind, and has nothing to do with the body.[18] But once again, it's not about giving anything up physically.

Also, anything in the *Course* that seems to contradict 'I need do nothing' and suggests you need to do something should *always* be applied at the level of the mind. What you *do* is make the choice to listen to the Holy Spirit instead of the ego, which means you apply forgiveness; that's the only thing you need to *do* in order to attain the goal of the *Course*. This is actually a very pro-active spiritual path, but it's always done at the level of the mind. If you feel inspired to do something in the world after you forgive, then go for it. And 'while you're doing it, you can continue to practice forgiveness at the same time.'[19]

DU293 (Arten)

You may hear from those seeking balance: the balancing of body, mind, and spirit, or balancing dual forces like yin and yang, or balancing 'the force' itself. Balancing illusions is not forgiving them.

Karma

DU116 (Pursah)

Karma is just an effect. We're going to change the cause of *everything* by changing the mind. The effect on the level of the physical is not something to be concerned about, because it isn't real.

The *real* things you should be interested in are inner peace and returning to Heaven.

Mikey's Note: In other words, karma is the result of the unconscious guilt in the mind. Once the guilt has been healed and removed by the Holy Spirit as a result of your practice of true forgiveness, then the so called karma no longer exists. Therefore, whatever 'bad' things you think you have done in the past are only 'karmic' if you have yet to truly forgive yourself for dreaming them.

Co-creating with God

DU41 (Gary & Arten)

I've been taught that I'm a co-creator with God. Is that true? Not on this level. The only place where you are really a co-creator with God is in Heaven, where you would not be aware of being any different from Him or any way separate from Him. So then how could you *not* be a co-creator with Him? But there is a way here on earth to practice the thought system of the Holy Spirit like J did, which *reflects* the laws of Heaven, and *that* is your way home.

YIR96 (Gary)

The body doesn't exist and can't create, and all the mind can do is choose spirit instead of the ego and its projections, a projection being anything that appears to be separate from anything, and that would include the body. There's nothing meaningful in the concept of being a 'co-creator' with God on the level of the world, because J is saying that the *only* meaningful thing the mind can do that involves any kind of creative ability is to give up whatever appears to be separate. That doesn't mean you give it up physically, which would just make it real to the mind; you give it up by not believing in it, and choose perfect spirit as your identity instead.

Making the Ego Your Friend

YIR54 (Arten)

There are teachers who will tell you to make friends with your ego or make peace with your ego as a way of dealing with it. All that will do is keep it in place. If you practice true forgiveness, which is the only way out, then the ego isn't interested in being your colleague. As

J says, 'What if you looked within and saw no sin? This "fearful" question is one the ego never asks. And you who ask it now are threatening the ego's whole defensive system too seriously for it to bother to pretend it is your friend.'[20] Your job is not to keep the ego in place; your job is to undo it through the dynamic of right-minded thinking. As the *Course* says, 'Salvation is undoing.'[21]

Mikey's Note: Here's another quote from the *Course* about the ego, 'The ego is capable of suspiciousness at best and viciousness at worst. That is its range.'[22]

DU170 (Pursah)

Remember, the ego already hates you. If it gets vicious, so what? It would have eventually, anyway. The weird thing is that now when you think about it, you realize that whatever it is that hates you is not really on the outside, it's on the inside – right along with you. The murderous thought system of the ego can no longer be denied and projected. Your only way out is to undo it.

YIR54 (Arten)

People will have unconscious resistance to practicing true forgiveness because the ego senses this is its end, and would rather kill you than have you kill *it*.

Abundance

DU26 & 27 (Pursah)

You have no idea how uninspired it is that people, including your spiritual leaders, are always trying to spiritualize abundance in the world. How much success or money you get has nothing whatsoever to do with how spiritually enlightened you are. Stop trying to spiritualize money. There's nothing wrong with money or success, but there's nothing spiritual about them either.

Mikey's Note: Abundance is about a *feeling*. You could have millions of dollars and still not feel financially secure and feel like that it's not enough; or you could be afraid of losing it all, or even feel guilty for having too much. Also, it's very possible that you don't have much in comparison to others but feel totally abundant and provided for. As an example that Gary shared on one of his podcasts,[23] the problem isn't when the landlord comes knocking at your door and you don't have the rent money. The problem is how you *feel* when the landlord comes knocking at the door and you don't have the rent money.

DU249 (Pursah)

Money won't buy you happiness, but it *will* buy you food, shelter, clothing, methods of communication, and a lot of other things that aren't bad. There's nothing wrong with making it big either, but why make it real? It's fun to know the truth! You don't have to take everything so damn seriously. Why would you be envious of those who don't know the truth?

I Am That

DU293 (Arten)

Another thing you should remember is not to be distracted by teachings that may serve others and help them feel temporarily better, but are not part of the path you've chosen. There will be those who tell you that when you have a problem, person, or object to deal with you can say, 'I am that,' and it will disappear. Becoming one with something in your projection only makes it real for you, and will not undo the guilt in your mind that you *can't* see. Only true forgiveness can do that. There will also be those who tell you that observing and being aware of your emotions will free you from your compulsions. Yes, observing your feelings can lessen their impact, however, it is still not the same as forgiving them. Only the true forgiveness of your relationships, and thus the healing of the unconscious guilt in your mind, can really free you from your compulsions or anything else.

Being in the Now

YIR27 (Gary & Arten)

What about being in the now? Where the practice of 'be here now' will get you is here. Sure, it will relax you, but it won't get you home. One aspect of that kind of a system is to watch your judgments. But watching your judgments is not forgiving them. And the now that is experienced is *not* the eternal always of Heaven, which can only be consistently experienced when the ego has been completely undone by the Holy Spirit. That requires that you do your part to forgive, and the

Holy Spirit takes care of the part of the job you can't see, deep within your unconscious mind.

YIR192 – 195 (Arten)

What we're about to say isn't meant to be anything but helpful. It's said with the understanding that everyone is completely innocent, and that they're doing their best to further whatever philosophy or method they sincerely believe in. That having been said, there are many spiritual teachers who are diluting the message of *A Course in Miracles* by teaching methods they claim are in agreement with the *Course* when they actually are not. This confuses the student by diverting attention from what the *Course* is teaching to something different, which the teachers of apparently don't even understand are different, or else they wouldn't be presenting them as though they're the same by quoting the *Course* out of context to support their teachings.

One good example is the teaching that one should be *in the now*. Keep in mind that we're not saying there's anything *wrong* with the idea that there may be some good in focusing on the now rather than the past or the future. The quality of life would be improved. The problem is that doing so *cannot* remove the unconscious guilt over the original separation from God that is still hidden in the deep recesses of the mind. Because of that, it makes each experience of being in the now *temporary* by definition, because it fails to remove the blocks that prevent that experience from being permanent. All of which is to say that there's not just a minor difference between the approach of *The Power of Now* and the real power of *A Course in Miracles*. It's the difference between being temporarily in the now of an illusion, or being permanently in the *presence* of reality.

It's absolutely essential to remember that unless and until *all* unconscious guilt is removed from the mind, you cannot stay in the endless present on a permanent basis. It's impossible. Any attempt to remain in the now is doomed to failure without doing the work of true forgiveness.

Until you've completely forgiven that which you made and projected outside of yourself, you are not forgiven in your own unconscious mind, and until you are, the cycle of birth and death cannot be broken. Being in the now does *not* heal your unconscious guilt and undo the ego. True forgiveness, on the other hand, removes the blocks to the awareness of love's presence which is your natural state of being, undoing the ego completely and making it possible to remain in the eternal 'always' simply because that's all that's left.

Remember that any attempt at eternity is a nonstarter as long as there's any unconscious guilt in the mind, period. That guilt *must* be healed *before* you can permanently stay free of the past or future. And the way to undo it is not to ignore it, which is exactly what's going on when you shut off and deny the past or future. It's when you *forgive* the past and your concerns about the future that they are undone, and the endless present becomes truly available to you. That forgiveness always takes place now. Remember, we said that there's no difference between forgiving the original separation at the time it appeared to happen, and forgiving it right now, for they are one and the same.

The now is meaningless as long as guilt exists in the mind. But when you're free, you open up to the endless present and your oneness with God. And to add one point, with all due respect, you don't undo the separation from God by ignoring Him. How can you undo the sense of separation from your Source without acknowledging your Source? Whatever reason you make up for not doing so, the real reason is guilt and the resulting fear of Him.

Calibrating Energy

<u>YIR196 – 198 (Arten)</u>

Once again, we mean this only to be helpful. We have nothing but respect for the person we're about to discuss. He's an early student of the *Course* who's a doctor, and because of that he has a tendency to put things in scientific terms. This can be very impressive to the uninitiated. One of the things he does is use kinesiology, which is muscle testing, to test the truthfulness of statements. Because of this doctor's research, some people mistakenly believe that he has perfected this method. However, because all he's really doing is using illusions to measure illusions, his tests are flawed by definition. He's using the body to test for the truth! As the *Course* clearly teaches, anything that can change or be changed is not real. How then, can students of the *Course* put their faith in it?

The doctor we're discussing developed it into a method of testing the truthfulness of statements, making kind of a lie-detector test out of it. There's a bigger problem with that than just the fact that nothing on the level of form can ever be completely reliable, and things that are true can be mistakenly called untrue. The hidden ego hook is that now the student's attention is being put on the wrong place, focused on an illusory test of an illusory thing in an illusory world, instead of where the attention should be, which is the decision in the mind to forgive the world and leave the *entire* system behind. T*hat's* the focus of *A Course in Miracles.*

This doctor calibrates different teachings at various levels from 1 to 1,000. But enlightenment *has* no levels; you're either whole or you're not. So not only do things like tests and calibrations distract the student from bringing illusions to the truth instead of giving truth to their illusions, but on top of it, testing in that manner can possibly steer a student away from something that may be helpful if the student tests something and comes up with the wrong result.

Remember that the illusion wants to keep you stuck here. And in some cases, because of encouraging comparisons, categorizing teachings into numbers, and making it all real, the focus is now on the illusion, which is an *effect*, instead of on the mind, which is *cause*. Then before you know it, some people are testing other people's statements, calling people liars…in a nice, polite, enlightened way, of course, and all it really leads to is a lot of wasted time that could have been spent undoing the ego instead of unwittingly glorifying it.

Another problem with calibrations is that if you make a simple, true metaphysical statement, such as 'God is Love,' then it will calibrate near 1,000. It won't get anybody home, but it will calibrate near or at 1,000. If you *really* want to get people home much more quickly, then you have to talk about the ego and describe it, let people know what they're up against, and teach them to undo it. But just because you're talking about the ego, the teaching will calibrate lower!

YIR198 (Gary)

So if you just talk about all sweetness and light, you'll calibrate near 1,000, and you'll stay stuck here for many, many more lifetimes than if you expose the ego, understand it, forgive it, and undo it. But obviously to do that, you have to learn about the ego, and whatever teacher is doing you the service of showing you what will actually get you home much faster will calibrate lower, and the more general teacher who won't get you home anywhere near as fast will calibrate higher.

Mikey's Note: I read this book that they are referring to, *Power vs Force*, when it first came out. Of course, I thought it was pretty cool back in my pre-initiated days, but I know now that it is nothing to get giddy over – just another distraction for people. Anyway, one more quote to wrap up this chapter.

YIR97 & 98 (Pursah)

We've never said the *Course* is the only way home. We *have* implied that it's the fastest, and J makes a lot of statements about saving time in the *Course*. Some may scoff at that, but if they do, it's because they don't *really* get what the *Course* is saying. Still the *Course* isn't the only way, as J points out, 'Their readiness will bring the lesson to them in some form which they can understand and recognize.'[24] Maybe there are some people who think there are other teachers in the world today who can get them home faster than J can. They are mistaken, but because the *Course* is not for everybody at the same time,[25] then it doesn't really matter.

Chapter 7

A Course in Miracles –Teaching, Borrowing, and Compromising

Forgive those who want to take the easy way and pretend the *Course* is saying the same thing as everything else, and move on to what the *Course* is teaching.[1]

This chapter is sort of like a continuation of the previous chapter except most of the quotes herein are geared more towards Gary as a *messenger* and *teacher* of the *Course*. There are also more quotes from Arten and Pursah comparing their teaching method as to that of others. I include these quotes here as a reminder as to where Gary is coming from when he is teaching the *Course* in his workshops and audio programs. I feel strongly that they pertain to me as well in my alleged teaching role, as I am as adamant as Arten and Purusah, as well as Gary, on not compromising on the integrity of the *Course*.

So, I thought I'd post these quotes here for those who may think of Arten and Pursah as being arrogant, when they are really just trying to make things very clear for everybody. They are really just looking out for our own best interests. As they tell Gary in their first visit to him, 'If we gave you everything you think you want, you'd be looking for something else a month later.'[2]

DU156 (Pursah)

We're teaching a purist, non-dualistic interpretation of the truth – the way the *Course* was meant to be understood. As time goes on, there will be more who teach the *Course* in this manner, although we're not as polite as most of them will be. Right now there's a tendency for people to borrow from the *Course* and then do their own thing. There will be many more purists in the future. And the reason we're not as polite as the rest of them is because you are our messenger, and it's about time somebody put the universe in its place.

DU127 (Pursah)

We need you to pass along some of the things people *don't* want to hear – the vital things that are being ignored by so many. It's a dirty job Gary, but somebody has to do it. We're not calling on you to judge or attack other teachers or argue with people, because forgiveness and arguing are mutually exclusive, and forgiveness is *always* the way.

But the world isn't all sweetness and light, and when it comes to your writing, staying in line with everyone else isn't what's needed from you. By having you emphasize that the *Course* is a self-study discipline, people are more likely to check it out for themselves and give the ideas a chance. Don't hold anything back. Anybody can write what people already believe, but if you're going to pass along our words then what is needed is a willingness to say some things that people *don't* already believe.

DU96 (Pursah)

The *Course* is spreading at a much faster pace than Christianity did. A hundred years from now, a significant percentage of the world's population will accept that the *Course* is really J speaking the Word of God. What good will *that* do if people don't apply it? That's why we want you to be clear about what the *Course* is saying.

That's not as easy as you might think. Since the *Course* became available to people in 1975, there has been an explosion of channeled writings, techniques from *Course* imitators, and various teachings, many of whose followers say are the same as or just like the *Course*. But to the well-trained eye, these other teachings are missing the most important parts of the *Course* – the parts that make it what it is. While you do not want to attack other teachers, that does *not* mean that a commitment to the integrity of the message of the *Course* should not be voiced.

It's all right to agree to disagree with other teachers. There are vital features of *A Course in Miracles* that make it original and represent a quantum leap forward in spiritual thought. Some of those features are virtually ignored by the overwhelming majority of *Course* students, teachers, and interpreters. As with J's teachings of 2,000 years ago, the world is attempting to do its usual job of obliterating the truth by incorporating parts of it into its illusions and covering over the real message of the Holy Spirit. We won't leave out the ideas you don't like. If you resist them or don't want to accept them after you hear them then that's your decision, but at least it won't be because you weren't told.

YIR38 & 39 (Pursah)

Right now there are a lot of *Course* teachers who play fast and loose with the *Course's* message. If you point out to them that what they're teaching isn't the same as what the *Course* is saying, then they'll call you a '*Course* fundamentalist!' Apparently a *Course* fundamentalist is anyone who thinks you should go by what the *Course* actually teaches. You'll go a long way towards ending all that silliness. Your public teachings, along with your books, will force other *Course* teachers to get more accurate about what the *Course* is teaching. Your message is so clear that other teachers won't be able to get away from it, and they'll have to adapt or else look like they don't know the *Course* very well.

DU369 & 370 (Pursah)

Always remember to let other people have their beliefs. It's not necessary for you to get others to agree with what you think, and it's not necessary for people, whether they study the *Course* or not, to agree with the things you'll be reporting in your book. Just put the truth out there and leave the rest of it up to the Holy Spirit. Everybody learns and accepts exactly what they're supposed to learn exactly when they should. You couldn't change that if you wanted to – and you shouldn't want to. It's just a dream! Yes, say what you think, but don't make others wrong. Don't disagree with them; just say what you know is true in a nice way. Then back off; never confront.

YIR43 (Pursah)

It's imperative that you stick to the message of the *Course*. Don't compromise on it. *A Course in Miracles* is purely non-dualistic. We don't want the same thing to happen to the message of the *Course* that happened to J's message 2,000 years ago. That's one of the main reasons we're back: to help keep people focused, including you. We want you to tell it straight, and if someone criticizes you or your message, then after you forgive them, tell them that they are in error. You have the right to *not* remain silent.

Mikey's Note: As part of the forgiveness process, you'll be given guidance as to what you should say or do, or what *not* to say or do in any given situation, and that includes when discussing the *Course* with others. And always remember that earlier quote that 'forgiveness and arguing are mutually exclusive, and forgiveness is always the way.'

Now, you may be thinking that the advice that Gary's teachers gave him in the last two passages were contradictory, but I don't see it that way. The first one, about allowing the beliefs of others, to me means that you don't go out of your way to make others wrong about what they believe in. The second one I take to mean that when other people, especially *Course* people, 'attack' Gary for what he is teaching, is that it is perfectly ok for him to speak up on what the *Course* is really saying, and not to compromise on it in any way in order to please others.

YIR135 & 147 (Pursah)

Helping people stay focused isn't as easy as you might think. For example, the most popular teacher *of A Course in Miracles*, at least before you came along, has repeatedly put people's focus on fixing up the dream instead of waking up from it. For those who contend that the *Course* says you should do certain things in the world, there's an early quote that says, 'Listen to my voice, learn to undo error, and do something (act) to correct it.'[3] Well, what you *do* is give it to the Holy Spirit, who is in the mind. It's *never* about doing anything in the world. Never! If you're inspired to do something after you forgive, fine. But that's never the *focus* of the *Course*. To teach people otherwise is completely inaccurate.

YIR109 (Arten)

J's message is as clear as can be. He never compromised on it, and neither should you. If you give the ego an inch, it will take a mile. That's why we're happy to see that you stick to the *Course* and don't change the message. You have respect for the material. That's excellent, because one of the reasons we appear to you is to help prevent J's message from getting distorted the way it did 2,000 years ago. If enough people were to alter the meaning of the teaching, or even the words themselves, then after a century or two, you wouldn't even be able to recognize the *Course*.

DU91 (Arten)

The *Manual for Teachers* is the easiest part in the *Course*, except almost everyone forgets that to be a teacher of God means you practice forgiveness. As the *Course* says, 'To teach is to demonstrate.'[4] Most students seem to believe that their teaching has to fit the traditional teacher-student format, but there is very little about the *Course* that is traditional. They would be a lot better off trying to learn the *Course* rather than trying to teach it.

Mikey's Note: Yes, there are many people out there who would be much better off trying to learn and understand what J is actually teaching in His *Course,* getting in the necessary repetition in order to understand this stuff on a deeper level, rather than trying to teach it themselves, not to mention actually applying it – what a concept! (LOL) But that doesn't really matter, all that matters is that I do *my* job, which is to forgive. That would apply to whoever is reading this too.

DU194 & 195 (Pursah)

The *Course* doesn't need women teachers to teach other women how to be better women. What the *Course* needs is women teachers who are willing to teach other women that they are *not* women – because they are not bodies. That would make a unique contribution if the point were made in no uncertain terms.

DU92 & 143 (Pursah & Arten)

The *Course* is about the healing of your unconscious guilt by the Holy Spirit and your return to Heaven through the dynamic of forgiveness. Despite the fact that *A Course in Miracles* is very much *about* the healing of this unconscious guilt, most of the teachers of the *Course* never even mention it.

YIR80 (Pursah)

Given that the *Course* is the only teaching that not only addresses but completely explains the issue of unconscious guilt, it shows you how vital it is to make this teaching more available to people. Right now most of the people who teach the *Course* don't even understand it. And the ones who quote from it without teaching it certainly don't understand it. They take lines from it out of context to support what *they're* teaching. But what the *Course* is teaching is that you can undo the ego that's in your mind, have the Holy Spirit heal all of your unconscious guilt, and be free. The fastest way to do that is to change the way you look at other people, events, and situations. It also teaches you how to do that. Be grateful that you're one of the people who is privileged to spread this message. But don't stop there. The most important part of the *Course* isn't what it means. The most important part of doing the *Course* is applying it to your life.

YIR81 (Arten)

There are some people who have been studying *A Course in Miracles* for a long time who consider themselves to be very intelligent. They think they know what the *Course* means. In some cases, maybe they do; and in other cases, maybe they don't. Yet what's important is that you take your understanding of the *Course*, *whatever it is*, and apply it. The intellectual who uses his understanding of the *Course* to prove himself to be intellectually superior to others isn't really doing the *Course.*

I would contend to you that a person whom the world would judge as being mentally challenged, someone who has very little intelligence, who is going through life seeing people with love and non-judgment, is making more spiritual progress in this lifetime than the intellectual who goes through life making himself right and others wrong about what *A Course in Miracles* means.

Mikey's Note: A good example of this would be from my favorite movie of all time, *Radio, a*bout a mentally handicapped man who is seeing everybody with love and non-judgment. If you haven't already seen it, I highly recommend this movie. Actually, I highly recommend this movie even if you *have* already seen it. I think I've seen it about twenty times!

YIR55 (Pursah)

Make no mistake: There's a difference in levels between *A Course in Miracles* and other teachings. The rest of them are moving things around in a universe that isn't really there. That's like moving the furniture around in a burning house. Yes, it might look nicer for a little while, but it's denying the real problem. *A Course in Miracles*, on the other hand, is the undoing of all of it, and the return to the only thing that is real.

DU168 (Arten)

Fear, sin, rage, guilt, jealousy, anger, pain, worry, resentment, revenge, loathing, envy, and all other negative emotions are versions of the same illusion. That's why the *Course* taught very clearly, before all the borrowers came along, that, 'Fear and love are the only emotions of which you are capable.'[5]

People who borrow from the *Course* instead of teaching it generally make one of two mistakes. Either they try to make up a secular version of the *Course*, which doesn't work because when you leave out God, you're ignoring the one real problem – the seeming separation from Him – or they make up a version that includes God, but is a dualistic system. This *also* fails to solve the one real problem because of the very nature of duality. How can you undo the separation from God by believing that God created and acknowledges separation? Thus they end up wasting a lot of time by reinforcing the seeming separation rather than correcting it.

YIR198 & 199 (Arten)

Don't be discouraged by those who borrow from the *Course* instead of teaching it. There are even people who teach the *Course* exclusively who fail to understand it. They'll think that the *Course* is open to their interpretation. Yet if it were, it would be useless. What makes the *Course* unique is that what it says is *not* open to interpretation. It says there is no world and only God is real. The way to awaken from the dream of death is through total, uncompromising forgiveness of people because they haven't really done anything, which is how to forgive yourself. Any other interpretation is folly.

Yet you have *Course* teachers who are right there, making the Holy Spirit out to be like a real person acting on your behalf out in a world that the *Course* says doesn't even exist, quickly taking the student's attention away from where it should be, on the cause instead of on the effect, and delaying the student's progress. Then on top of that, it's a slippery slope from making the world real to eventually ending up like Pat Robertson (Televangelist and founder of the Christian Coalition) and telling everybody exactly how they should behave in that illusory world, or else.

Don't ever fall into that trap. Respect what the *Course* says. Honor the memory of Helen and Bill by telling people the truth about how it came and what it says. Don't compromise, don't sell out, and don't worry about what people think. If they were that smart, they wouldn't think they were here in the first place.

We're *not* saying the *Course* is the only way. What we *are* saying is that if you're going to do the *Course*, then do it. Don't do something else and *call* it the *Course*. *A Course in Miracles* was given to save people time if they choose to. If they don't, then it doesn't matter, because time isn't real. But it's up to you how long you want to stay trapped in the cycle of birth and death.

YIR215 (Pursah)

People will ask you where you fit in to the spiritual community. Tell them the truth. Given what you're teaching, you *don't* fit in. You're not saying the same thing as the others, so don't even try to fit in; just be yourself. Don't worry about fitting in with the other teachers or the mainstream spiritual types who think they're so progressive when they're actually very conservative.

Chapter 8

Those Who Seek Controversy...

**If a blind person leads a blind person, both
of them will fall into a hole.**[1]

Over the last several years, Gary has been the center of
controversy within the *Course* community, from being accused of
plagiarizing *Pursah's Gospel of Thomas* to people accusing him of
making up the existence of Arten and Pursah all together. Being
known as a '*Disappearance of the Universe* junkie,' people have asked
me for my opinion on this stuff, and though I don't have all that much
to say about it specifically, I will share what I *do* have to say.

First, to address the 'stolen' gospel issue, the only thing I really
have to say about the accusation itself is that, in my personal opinion,
Pursah's gospel is the *least* important part of Gary's second book *Your
Immortal Reality*. So as far as I'm concerned it's a non-issue. I have
read *Your Immortal Reality* nine times – seven times I skipped right
over the aforementioned gospel, and the two times that I *did* read it,
with exception of a few of the sayings, it didn't really do anything for
me. None of the sayings in the gospel are going to help anybody get
home. And Pursah herself puts it this way regarding the gospel, '*The
Gospel of Thomas* is not the Holy Grail of spirituality. It will not bring
you salvation and it will not train your mind to think along the lines
necessary for you to *attain* your salvation.'[2] So that's about all I have
to say about that.

Now, there are some alleged *Course* students, as well as some
alleged *Course* teachers out there who try to discredit the teachings
presented in Gary's books because they have a hard time getting past
the idea of two ascended masters materializing in Gary's living room
to present these advanced teachings of spirituality to him. Well, if
these same people spent more time applying Jesus' teachings on
forgiveness in the *Course*, and less time questioning the validity of

Gary's teachers, they would realize that it doesn't really matter in the first place. The bottom line is that Arten and Pursah's teachings – when applied – *work.* And that's *all that matters!* And not only do they work, they will also save most people much time on understanding and correctly applying the *Course* than if they attempted to do the *Course* on their own *without* their aid. If Gary *did* make up Arten and Pursah – and by no means am I suggesting that, as I take his word at face value – then he's a freakin' genius! And Gary would be the first to tell you that he's not *that* smart! (LOL) Like I said, the teachings are valid because they work, and that's *all that matters!*

Some people just want to try to bring Gary down. Why? Beats the hell out of *me!* Perhaps they feel threatened by the fact that he doesn't try to make up his own version of the *Course* and just sticks to what Jesus is actually *teaching* in his *Course.* As Pursah puts it in *Your Immortal Reality*, 'The seekers of controversy, and those who champion them, accomplish one thing and one thing only. They manage to distract potentially good students who otherwise would *do* the *Course*, get them to focus on the trees instead of the forest, and thus delay their experience of the truth. If that's the desired vocation of these people, then they're welcome to it. But the truth is still there to be found by anyone who seeks clarification and is willing to use the technology of forgiveness. They will also find the experience that goes along with it, which is the goal of the *Course.*'[3] Anyway, we are all really Christ, but I swear some people are disguised as *ass clowns!* (LOL)

Now on the flip side, I've observed some people being offended by Gary's rebuttals; particularly the one in response to the 'stolen gospel.' Well, how Gary responds to it is not important. *It doesn't matter!* It doesn't matter if Gary, or anyone else for that matter who you consider to be a *Course* 'guru,' appears to be practicing forgiveness or not. It's none of our business. That's between them and the Holy Spirit. It doesn't matter if these *Course* teachers appear to be a saint, an asshole, or somewhere in between on the level of form. The *Course* is about going within and getting in touch with your own inner guidance, the Holy Spirit. The ego always looks for excuses not to do your own forgiveness work. Seeing a *Course* 'teacher' appearing not to be practicing forgiveness is another excuse the ego will use to not practice forgiveness yourself. My parents would always say to me as a child when I was worrying about what other people were doing, 'Michael take care of Michael.' In other words, don't be concerned if others are practicing forgiveness or not; take care of your *own* business.

As a student of A *Course in Miracles*, the only thing that matters from *my* perspective is that *I* forgive whatever disturbs my peace of mind or gets in my face on any given day. And from *your* perspective as a student of *A Course in Miracles*, the only thing that matters is that *you* forgive whatever disturbs *your* peace of mind or gets in *your* face on any given day – that's the bottom line, *and nothing else matters!* If you think anything else matters, then you are missing the entire point of the *Course completely* – which is that *everything* is your own projection, *everything* is coming from *you,* and *everything* is for forgiveness! As the *Course* puts it, 'The *sole* responsibility of the miracle worker is to accept the Atonement for himself.'[4]

DU117 (Pursah)

J doesn't except his *Course* to live its life without controversy, whether in the *Course* community or outside of it. However, as he says in the *Introduction* to the *Clarification of Terms*, which are words you could apply to any aspect of the *Course,* 'All terms are potentially controversial, and those who seek controversy will find it. Yet those who seek clarification will find it as well. They must, however, be willing to overlook controversy, recognizing that it is a defense against truth in the form of a delaying maneuver.'[5]

Mikey's Note: This same statement can obviously be applied to what Arten and Pursah are teaching as well, which is the same thing that J is teaching in His *Course*, except put it in the everyday, human vernacular. So, if you want to get caught up in the controversy and stay stuck in it, so be it, that's *your* business; do whatever the hell you want, it doesn't matter to me, *I'm* going Home!

Once again, I don't say all this to pass judgment on anyone, I'm just suggesting that there *is* a better way. We're all innocent no matter what, but the question is, do you want to get *in touch* with that innocence?

Anyway, from my experience, I know the teachings presented in Gary's books are legit regardless of what you make of Gary, his teachers, and the controversy surrounding it all. Everything else is much ado about nothing! So, if you're ready to go beyond controversy and do the necessary forgiveness work it takes to undo the ego and go Home, then I leave you with this simple saying from *Pursah's Gospel of Thomas*, 'Congratulations to the person who has forgiven and has found life.'[6]

PART III

The Quotes

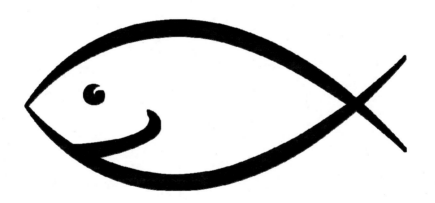

Chapter 9

Jesus, Jeshua, Y'shua, J, or how 'bout J-Dog?

It was never J's intention to start a religion. Whether then or now, the world needs another religion like it needs a bigger hole in the ozone layer.[1]

DU361 (Arten)

J didn't come to the world in order to start some religion so people could make other people wrong for having bodies and wanting to use them. He taught forgiveness, and still does, in order to teach people the total insignificance of the body – and lead them to their true Identity as Christ.

DU13 & 33 (Arten & Pursah)

Most people who approach true spiritual mastery are not interested in being leaders. At the same time, there are people who are highly visible when, rather than being true masters of spirituality and metaphysics, they are merely exhibiting the symptoms of an extroverted personality. J was the ultimate follower in the sense that he eventually listened only to the Holy Spirit.

DU15 (Arten)

It's not J that some of the New Age people don't like. It's the behavior-oriented, Biblical version of J who's been shoved down their throats all their lives that they can't stand. Christianity is so conflicted it openly promotes teachings that are diametrically opposed to one another. How is one supposed to deal with that? People will eventually have to stop blaming J for some of the ludicrous things Christianity has done and continues to do in his name. He has no more to do with these things than God has to do with this world.

DU98 (Arten)

The J of the *Course* is not the same version of J in Christianity, and the two thought systems are not compatible. For Christianity, their suffering image of J the body is extra special. He is different than you in the sense that he alone is God's only begotten Son. But the J of the *Course* informs you that because you and he are one, then you are equally God's only begotten Son or Christ – not any different than him – and furthermore, you can eventually experience this. As J states in the *Course*, 'There is nothing about me that you cannot attain. I have nothing that does not come from God. The difference between us now is that I have nothing else. This leaves me in a state which is only potential in you.'[2]

Mikey's Note: I like the analogy of that of an ice sculpture. You have this big block of ice and let's say you want to carve out a butterfly. Well, the butterfly is already in that block of ice. It's just a matter of chipping away the excess so that the only thing left is the butterfly. Same thing with us – what we really are, perfect Spirit, perfect Love, is already within us – it's just a matter of chipping away the excess, which, of course, is the ego. And forgiveness is the ice pick!

As J says in the *Course*, 'Where could your peace arise *but* from forgiveness? The Christ in you looks only on the truth, and sees no condemnation that could need forgiveness. He is at peace *because* He sees no sin. Identify with Him, and what has He that you have not?'[3]

DU73 (Pursah)

Conservative is not exactly the word you would use to describe J, who was the radical of radicals – not in temperament but in his teachings.

DU48 & 49 (Pursah)

J never cursed a tree and killed it, never got angry and knocked over the tables in the temple, but he *did* heal a few people who were already dead. Also, his body died on the cross, but he did not suffer as you would imagine. As for his way of being, words cannot do him justice. To be in his presence was an experience so unique it gave you a feeling of wonder. His peace and unalterable love were so total that sometimes people couldn't stand it and they had to look away. His attitude was so calm and sure it made you want to know how he did it. The people that spent time with him were inspired by his complete faith in God.

DU50 & YIR156 (Pursah & Arten)

One of the things about J that's rarely mentioned is that he had an excellent sense of humor. He was quite irreverent. He liked to laugh and bring out the joy in others. Many people today would be surprised at the irreverent humor he would occasionally display.

DU41 (Arten)

J's Love, like God's, was total, impersonal, non-selective and all-embracing. He treated everyone equally, from rabbi to prostitute. He was not a body. He was no longer a human being. He had passed through the eye of the needle. He had reclaimed his place with God as pure spirit. This is pure non-dualism: an attitude that, along with the Holy Spirit, will lead you to what you are. You and J are the same thing. We all are. There *is* nothing else.

DU44 (Pursah)

J treated each body the same – as though it didn't exist. He was then able to look completely past it to the true light of unchangeable and immortal spirit that is the one reality of us all.

DU214 (Arten)

The ego assigns specific, different identities. Both its 'love' and hate are directed at specific individuals. The Holy Spirit, however, thinks of everyone as being the same and totally abstract. Thus, like J, His Love is non-specific and all-encompassing.

DU18 (Arten)

One of the fundamental differences between the teachings of J and the teachings of the world is this: The teachings of the world are the product of a split, unconscious mind. Once you have that, you have compromise; and once you have compromise, you no longer have the truth.

DU28 & 29 (Pursah)

J was a savior all right, but not the kind who promoted vicarious salvation. He wanted to teach us how to play our part in saving ourselves. When he said that he was the way, the truth, and the life, he meant we should follow his *example*, not believe in him personally. You shouldn't glorify his body. *He* didn't believe in his own body, why should you?

DU41 (Arten)

When J made statements like, 'Of myself I can do nothing,' and 'I and the Father are one,' he wasn't claiming any kind of specialness for himself. In fact, he was *giving up* any specialness, individuality, or authorship and accepting his true strength – the power of God.

DU49 (Pursah)

J considered himself to be totally *dependent* on God, yet this dependence was not weakness, as the world usually views dependence. Rather, the result was a state of unbelievable psychological strength. Things that would scare the stuffing out of strong people meant nothing to him, because they *were* nothing to him. Fear was not a part of him. His attitude was the same as if you were having a dream last night asleep in your bed, except you were totally aware of the fact that you were dreaming. And because you knew you were dreaming, you also knew that absolutely nothing in the dream could possibly hurt you, because none of it was true; you realized you were merely observing symbolic images, including people, who weren't really there.

Mikey's Note: I find this quote of the psychological strength and being totally dependent on God to be very inspiring. I can almost taste it! This *really* is all a dream!

YIR18 (Gary)

J completely forgave the world. His love and forgiveness were total and all-encompassing. He knew that if you partially forgive the world, then you will be partially forgiven, which is to remain divided. But if you completely forgive the world, then you will be completely forgiven.

DU219 & 220 (Gary)

I turn the tables on the ego by using the same stuff the ego made to undo it. In order for that to happen, I have to bring my illusions to the truth instead of giving truth to my illusions. The *Course* says that J's a savior because he saw the false without accepting it as true.[4] If I do that, then not only will I be a Savior like him, but my mind will be healed by the Holy Spirit at the same time.

YIR105 (Arten)

A lot of the time in the movies, J has been portrayed as a suffering, angst ridden figure. That's not what he was like at all. He was a peaceful figure with a gentle smile. His eyes were clear and loving. There was no fear in him because he knew that there *was* nothing to fear. Nothing the world could do to him could affect him. He was not a body. He did not think of himself as being special. He was not the passion; he was a symbol of compassion.

DU63 (Pursah)

The difference between your mistakes and the mistakes of enlightened Beings rests in their ability to practice true forgiveness. They realize that if the mistakes of others should be forgiven immediately, then so should theirs. They also know it doesn't really matter what they do, but few people are ready to accept that. Most carry their mistakes and their guilt with them for eons, but there is no need for that.

DU43 (Pursah)

What you are experiencing here *is* destruction. But J knew the way out. That's why he said, 'Be of good cheer, for I have overcome the world.' If he wasn't a man who had lessons to learn like you, then why would he have to overcome the world in the first place?

Mikey's Note: J states in the *Course,* 'In this world you need not have tribulation because I have overcome the world. That is why you should be of good cheer.'[5] In other words, we can all transcend the world too, and be like our buddy J-Dog! He's not special, and he's the first one to tell us that.

DU217 & 218 (Arten)

The ego wants J 'the wonder-body' to be much different than you and very special, which is a very clever way of keeping everyone different and special. The Holy Spirit knows you're really the same.

As it says in the *Course*, 'The name of *Jesus* is the name of one who was a man but saw the face of Christ in all his brothers and remembered God. So he became identified with *Christ,* a man no longer, but at one with God.'[6] That's what He wants for you.

Chapter 10

Forgiveness as a Way of Life

Forgiveness is where it's at for the rest of your life if you're smart.[1]

Before I get into any of the quotes on forgiveness from Gary's books, there are several quotes from the *Course* on forgiveness that I'd like to share here first:

What is Forgiveness?

Forgiveness recognizes what you thought your brother did to you has not occurred. It does not pardon sins and make them real. It sees there was no sin. And in that view are all your sins forgiven.[2]

Forgiveness is the key to happiness.

Here is the answer to your search for peace. Here is the key to meaning in a world that seems to make no sense. Here is the way to safety in apparent dangers that appear to threaten you at every turn, and bring uncertainty to all your hopes of ever finding quietness and peace. Here are all questions answered; here the end of all uncertainty ensured at last.[3]

Forgiveness offers everything I want.

What could you want forgiveness cannot give? Do you want peace? Forgiveness offers it. Do you want happiness, a quiet mind, a certainty of purpose, and a sense of worth and beauty that transcends the world? Do you want care and safety, and the warmth of sure protection always? Do you want a quietness that cannot be disturbed, a gentleness that never can be hurt, a deep abiding comfort, and a rest so perfect it can never be upset?[4]

All this forgiveness offers you, and more. It sparkles on your eyes as you awake, and gives you joy with which to meet the day. It soothes your forehead while you sleep, and rest upon your eyelids so you see no dreams of fear and evil, malice and attack. And when you wake again, it offers you another day of happiness and peace. All this forgiveness offers you, and more.[5]

Forgiveness is my function as the light of the world.

It is your forgiveness that will bring the world of darkness to the light. It is your forgiveness that lets you recognize the light in which you see. Forgiveness is the demonstration that you are the light of the world. Through your forgiveness does the truth about yourself return to your memory. Therefore, in your forgiveness lies your salvation.[6]

The Only Purpose

The real world is the state of mind in which the only purpose of the world is seen to be forgiveness. Fear is not its goal, for the escape from guilt becomes its aim. The value of forgiveness is perceived and takes the place of idols, which are sought no longer, for their 'gifts' are not held dear.[7]

Mikey's Note: According to the *Concordance of A Course in Miracles*, the words *Forgive(s), Forgiveness, Forgiven, and Forgiving,* show up in the *Course* a total of 835 times. And to think there are *Course* students out there that don't realize how important forgiveness is – it's *everything!* The practice of true forgiveness *is A Course in Miracles*.[8] No one's going to attain the goal of the *Course* without the application of *true* forgiveness. As J states in the *Course*, 'You who want peace can find it only by complete forgiveness.'[9] And, 'The way to God is through forgiveness here. There is no other way.'[10] One more quote from the *Course* on forgiveness:

'Forgiveness is the only road that leads out of disaster, past all suffering, and finally away from death. How could there be another way, when this one is the plan of God Himself? And why would you oppose it, quarrel with it, seek to find a thousand ways in which it must be wrong; a thousand other possibilities? Is it not wiser to be glad you hold the answer to your problems in your hand? Is it not more intelligent to thank the One Who gives salvation, and accept His gift with gratitude? And is it not a kindness to yourself to hear His Voice and learn the simple lessons He would teach, instead of trying to dismiss His words, and substitute your own in place of His? His words will work.'[11]

Alrighty then, now on to the forgiveness quotes from Gary's books, starting with my very favorite:

DU343 (Pursah)

We came here to give people a spiritual message, a message that not everyone is ready for yet, and this is it: When you are ready to accept that the *only* thing that really matters in your illusory lifetime is the successful completion of your lessons of true forgiveness, then you will be truly wise indeed.

DU218 (Arten)

Forgiveness isn't about being a do-gooder, not that there's anything wrong with doing good deeds if it turns you on. The *Course* is about being a right *thinker*. A lot of Christians ask nowadays, 'What would Jesus do?' There's only one correct answer to that question, and it would always be the same. He'd forgive.

DU234 (Pursah)

Forgiveness is where the rubber meets the road. Without forgiveness, metaphysics are useless. That's why the *Course* is practical. In the end, there are really only two things you can do. As the *Course* teaches, 'He who would not forgive must judge, for he must justify his failure to forgive.'[12]

DU218 (Arten)

It might help you to remember that *you're* the one whom forgiveness helps. You don't always have to care personally about the person you're forgiving. Your job is simply to correct your misperceptions, and it isn't against the rules to know that you can't help but benefit because of it.

DU221 (Pursah)

True forgiveness is the real purpose of life, but you've got to choose it in order to make it yours. Remember, practicing real forgiveness can't help but lead you home.

DU183 (Gary)

It's not contradictory to say there's nobody out there and then turn around and say the only way home is to forgive what's out there, because you're only forgiving what *appears* to be out there – which is symbolic of what's in your own mind.

DU192 (Arten)

True forgiveness can change the world, for the world is merely a symbol of the collective or the one ego mind. To put it even more emphatically, forgiveness is the *only* thing that can *really* change the world, and that isn't even the purpose of forgiveness! The real benefits of true forgiveness go to the forgiver.

DU242 (Pursah)

Forgiveness doesn't mean you have to give up anything on the level of form. Your psychological attachment to things is one of the ways your ego clings to the body and the world. That *will* need to be forgiven. It masks your unconscious resistance to the truth that there is no world. Most people don't want to hear that their dreams and passions are really false idols – a substitute for God and Heaven. You've even chosen a place they call paradise! Hear this: There's nothing wrong with your dream if you understand it and forgive it. Forgive – and then do what you and the Holy Spirit choose to. And have fun!

DU218 (Arten)

Forgiveness has to do with what you think. What you do isn't the important thing, even though it is a *result* of what you think. It's what you think that will either keep you dreaming or help get you home, not what you do.

DU234 (Pursah)

What you do is a result of what you think. That doesn't mean you're always going to behave perfectly. Indeed, when the *Course* talks about a teacher of God becoming perfect here, it is referring to perfect *forgiveness*, not perfect behavior. True peace will come from true forgiveness. And violence – which is the acting out of one's own self-hatred *seen* as being outside of oneself – will *never* come as a result of the thought system of the Holy Spirit, who teaches only love and forgiveness.

DU277 (Gary)

In regards to this spiritual path, I have to do my part and choose forgiveness. Vicarious salvation that is magically brought to me by an outside force or figure can not work. Nobody else can wake up from the dream for me. Indeed, there *is* no one else to wake up from the dream. That's why the *Course* says, 'My salvation comes from me.'[13] It is up to me to change my mind about the world and choose the miracle.

Mikey's Note: *You* have to make the decision to practice forgiveness. That's why J says your salvation comes from you. Here's what J has to say in the *Course* about the statement, 'My salvation comes from me.'

'All temptation is nothing more than some form of the basic temptation not to believe the idea for today. Salvation seems to come from anywhere except from you. So, too, does the source of guilt. You see neither guilt nor salvation as in your own mind and nowhere else. When you realize that all guilt is solely an invention of your mind, you also realize that guilt and salvation must be in the same place. In understanding this you are saved.

The seeming cost of accepting today's idea is this: it means that nothing outside yourself can save you; nothing outside yourself can give you peace. But it also means that nothing outside yourself can hurt you, or disturb your peace or upset you in any way. Today's idea places you in charge of the universe, where you belong because of what you are. This is not a role that can be partially accepted. And you must surely begin to see that accepting it is salvation.'[14]

DU78 (Pursah)

The result of practicing true forgiveness will leave you with the potential to attain the very same peace of God as J. Right now, you believe that certain things have to happen in the world in order for you to be happy. As you gain the peace of God, it will eventually result in the ability to reclaim your natural state of joy *regardless* of what appears to be happening in the world.

DU360 (Arten)

The illusory universe is a place of tension and release. That's duality. With the *Course*, the tension is released by forgiveness, but until someone is very proficient at it, they shouldn't be expected to give up most earthly desires. That's something that comes naturally with the maturity of a mind that is advanced in the ways of true forgiveness.

DU127 & 128 (Pursah)

Forgiveness and arguing are mutually exclusive, and forgiveness is *always* the way. It is the application of true forgiveness, along with J or the Holy Spirit, that will lead you to genuine happiness, peace, and eventually Heaven.

DU234 & 235 (Pursah)

Forgiveness will never result in violence, but judgment will always result in some kind of negative effect on the level of form, even if the effect is just on your own health. Violence is the ultimate and illogical extension of fear, judgment, and anger. The delusional thought system of the ego will always lead to some form of violence and murder eventually, because it requires that people see their enemy – or the perceived cause of their problem – as being outside of them.

YIR14 (Pursah)

Everyone's been enormously famous and seemingly important in some lifetimes, and all have been the dregs of the earth in others. That's duality. What matters is doing your forgiveness work right now. That's the way out.

DU196 (Arten)

As you forgive, you may find yourself to be more at a loss for words than you used to be. Don't worry about that. This isn't about looking smart; it's about being healed by the Holy Spirit. This process is already accelerating within you. As the *Course* says, ' …you are no longer wholly insane.'[15]

Mikey's Note: Well, that's a relief – I'm only *partially* insane now! Anyway, this reminds me of a *Seinfeld* episode where George wants to stay in a relationship with a woman he doesn't even like because a mutual friend of theirs told her that he would just end up hurting her. To prove this person wrong, George tells Jerry that he will *marry* this woman if he has to. Jerry's response, 'You know George, they are doing wonderful things in mental institutions these days.'

YIR21 (Pursah)

The truth is not in the dream, but it *can* be heard in the dream. And when you start to know the truth, which will be communicated to you by the Holy Spirit in many different ways, you start to relax. You awaken slowly and gently through a cocoon process called forgiveness. Just as a caterpillar goes through a cocoon process to be prepared for a higher and less restricted form of life, you become prepared for a higher form of life by changing your perception of the world. As a result of this, your dream becomes happier. But that happiness is not dependent on what appears to happen in the dream. It's an inner peace that can be there for you *regardless* of what appears to be happening in the dream. And then, when you finally wake up, you see that you never really left home, which is your perfect oneness with God. You were actually home all the while, but it was out of your awareness.

YIR37 (Pursah)

Forgiveness is always a gift you're giving to yourself, not the person you think you're forgiving. You're the one who receives the benefits, in both practical and metaphysical terms. True, you're acting as a reminder of the truth to the other person. All thought has effects on some level, and it's good for the other person, too. Not that the other person is really there. We're talking about a seemingly split-off aspect of your own mind.

DU251 (Pursah)

It's been said that life is just one thing after another. Life with the *Course* should also just be one thing after another, except that when one of the things calls for forgiveness, you do it. Once again, you don't have to try to be loving. If you forgive, then love is revealed naturally, because that is what you *are*.

DU174 (Arten)

The *Course* teaches that you don't have to change anybody's mind and you don't have to change your world. All you have to do is change *your* mind *about* the world. For example, don't worry about world peace. The best way for you to help bring world peace is to practice forgiveness yourself, and share the experience with people. When the people of the world finally seek real inner peace by understanding and correctly applying the law of forgiveness, then the seemingly outer peace *must* follow. But that's not the focus of J's *Course*; the focus is on changing your mind about your dream.

Mikey's Note: As J says in the *Course*, 'There is no point in trying to change the world. It is incapable of change because it is merely an effect. But there is indeed a point in changing your thoughts about the world. Here you are changing the cause. The effect will change automatically.'[16]

DU235 (Pursah)

You don't have to wait until your experience of enlightenment before you enjoy the benefits of forgiveness. As the *Course* tells you, 'A tranquil mind is not a little gift.'[17]

YIR128 (Arten)

You can't wake up from a dream as long as you're stuck in it. Awareness of dreaming breaks the hold. And the more you forgive, the more you become aware that you're just dreaming.

DU289 & 290 (Arten)

Don't let anyone tell you forgiveness isn't practical on the level of form. Indeed, it can make all the difference in the world. Choosing true forgiveness and the Holy Spirit as your Teacher is *not* a part of the ego's script – it's a decision *you* have to make in order to be *free* of the ego's script.

YIR48 (Gary)

As a response to the false condition of separation, real forgiveness denies what *isn't* true and accepts what *is* true. As J puts it in his *Course*, 'It denies the ability of anything not of God to affect you.'[18]

DU378 (Arten)

Everyone will have their own particular forgiveness lessons, and as they go along and forgive with the Holy Spirit, and put everything they do more and more under His control, they will reach the immediate *and* eventually the long term goal of the *Course*. As J tells everyone in the *Manual*, 'To follow the Holy Spirit's guidance is to let yourself be absolved of guilt.'[19]

DU264 (Pursah)

Look to the Holy Spirit to attain your salvation while you are still seemingly in the body. If you don't, you're not going to find enlightenment somewhere on the other side afterwards. In other words, you have to forgive and make your progress *now*. Heaven is not a reward that is bestowed on you by an outside force for good behavior or clever metaphysical musings. The symbols that give you your opportunities for enlightenment are all around you – if you accept the Holy Spirit as your Teacher in forgiveness.

YIR139 (Pursah)

It's through your own choice for the Holy Spirit and His thought system instead of the ego's that your mind is returned to peace. That has to happen *first* in order for you to go home. You can't skip your forgiveness homework. Everybody wants to skip to the end and be enlightened now, but it doesn't work that way. If peace is the condition of the Kingdom, then the mind must be at peace in order to fit in. And in order for the mind to *be* at peace, you have to forgive. It's as simple as that.

Mikey's Note: Yes, there are some people out there, or more accurately stated, there are some people who appear to be out there who just want to try to skip to the end and not do the necessary forgiveness work it takes to *get* to the end. You can't be afraid to get your hands dirty on this path. You have to be willing to look at all your crap; your anger, your resentments, your guilt, your need to be right, your impatience, your self-loathing, your fears, your feelings of inferiority and superiority, and all your motives in life. It takes *work* on the level of the mind to undo all that; and where I come from, you're either working hard or hardly working!

YIR206 (Pursah)

It's by forgiving the world that you will awaken, and realize that you never left Heaven, and have remained exactly as God created you, which is perfect spirit. As J puts it, reminding us again that his themes in the *Course* are simple and consistent, 'You are as God created you. All else but this one thing is folly to believe. In this one thought is everyone set free. In this one truth are all illusions gone. In this one fact is sinlessness proclaimed to be forever part of everything, the central core of its existence and its guarantee of immortality.'[20]

But always remember the forgiveness that leads to this experience must be done at the level of cause and not effect, as J points out very early in the *Text*, 'You must change your mind, not your behavior, and this *is* a matter of willingness. You do not need guidance except at the mind level. Correction belongs only at the level where change is possible. Change does not mean anything at the symptom level, where it cannot work.'[21]

DU237 (Gary & Pursah)

Practicing forgiveness will cause you to gradually wake up from the dream. If you woke up all at once I assure you it wouldn't be pleasant. You have to be prepared for a different form of life. Even in this life, where people think they are bodies, change is not really welcome – even if people want to pretend it is.

DU253 (Pursah)

When you really get that there's nobody out there but Christ, then you can give the other person the gift of forgiveness and innocence. Then, as the *Course* teaches you, that's how you'll think of yourself, 'To give this gift is how to make it yours.'[22] Then after you forgive, trust J, who is also the Holy Sprit. Also, try to remember that it doesn't matter if you can see results or not. If you work with J or the Holy Spirit and practice forgiveness, then you *always* have an impact. As the *Course* says, 'A miracle is never lost. It may touch many people you have not even met, and produce undreamed of changes in situations of which you are not even aware.'[23]

Mikey's Note: Three more quotes from the *Course* to close out this chapter:

'How willing are you to forgive your brother? How much do you desire peace instead of endless strife and misery and pain? These questions are the same, in different form. Forgiveness is your peace, for herein lies the end of separation and the dream of danger and destruction, sin and death; of madness and of murder, grief and loss.

This is the "sacrifice" salvation asks, and gladly offers peace instead of this.'[24]

'The real world is attained simply by the complete forgiveness of the old, the world you see without forgiveness. The great Transformer of perception will undertake with you the careful searching of the mind that made this world, and uncover to you the seeming reasons for your making it. In the light of the real reason that He brings, as you follow Him, He will show you that there is no reason here at all.'[25]

'No one who learns to forgive can fail to remember God. Forgiveness, then, is all that need be taught, because it is all that need be learned. All blocks to the remembrance of God are forms of unforgiveness, and nothing else.'[26]

Chapter 11

Forgiving What Gets in Your Face

**No matter what tricks the ego throws your way,
just forgive and let live.**[1]

YIR10 (Pursah)

At some point, the serious spiritual student and teacher will have to take everything he or she has learned and actually apply it to every person, situation, or event that comes up in front of their face on any given day. That applies to *everything*. And usually it's not a mystery. Whatever is happening in your life, that's the lesson that the Holy Spirit wants you to apply the teachings to, and the Holy Spirit's great instrument of salvation is *true* forgiveness.

YIR97, 98, 136, & 137 (Pursah)

A successful relationship is one where you are forgiving, or have forgiven, the other person. That's what it takes to transform it into a holy relationship, and that's *all* it takes, whether it's professional or personal, it doesn't matter who it is or what it looks like. Even if the relationship appears to be a bad one and things are terrible on the level of form, it doesn't matter. As J puts it in the *Course*, 'Those who are to meet will meet, because together they have the potential for a holy relationship. They are ready for each other.'[2] And, 'The holiest of all the spots on earth is where an ancient hatred has become a present love.'[3]

DU171 (Arten)

You will *never* be able to find your way out and experience your own innocence and Divinity until you learn how to forgive everything you see around you. Until then, real escape is impossible. You think people who want to escape the world are weak; actually, they have the right idea. They just don't know how to do it right.

DU201 & 202 (Pursah)

Whenever you're tempted to judge someone, whether you're driving down the street, working with people, socializing, watching television, or reading something on your computer, if you feel the addiction of judgment assert itself, remember J's words from the section in the *Text* called *The Self Accused*, 'Learn this, and learn it well, for it is here delay of happiness is shortened by a span of time you cannot realize. You never hate your brother for his sins, but only for your own. Whatever form his sins appear to take, it but obscures the fact that you believe them to be yours, and therefore meriting a "just" attack.'[4] You judge only yourself, and you forgive only yourself.

DU200 & 201 (Pursah)

Don't just hide out and study. Interact with people. Experience them and forgive them when you should. Consider it to be an opportunity. Illusions must be forgiven on the level where they are experienced. That means living a normal life and interacting with society. Remember, the *Course* wasn't given to a solitary person on a mountaintop somewhere. It was given in New York City – the epitome of complexity.

Mikey's Note: From my experience, you don't even have to walk out your door to get your forgiveness opportunities, so you certainly won't be avoiding them by hiding out. Just turn on your computer, I'm sure you'll find some opportunities on the Internet or in your e-mail inbox. (LOL)

DU240 (Gary)

These are the major components of forgiveness: I remember I'm dreaming, I forgive both my projected images and myself for dreaming them, and I trust the Holy Spirit and choose His strength. My dream that the separation from God is real is the cause of the problem, and the Holy Spirit's forgiveness is the solution.

DU235 & 236 (Pursah)

A component of practicing forgiveness when you're confronted by an opportunity would be to *remember that you're dreaming*. You authored the dream and made the figures in it act out for you, so you could see your unconscious guilt outside yourself. If you remember you're dreaming, then there's nothing out there but your own projection. Once you believe that – and belief only comes from practice and experience – then there's no need for what you're seeing and now forgiving to have any impact on you.

As the *Course* puts it, 'The miracle establishes you dream a dream, and that its content is not true. This is a crucial step in dealing with illusions. No one is afraid of them when he perceives he made them up. The fear was held in place because he did not see that he was author of the dream, and not a figure in the dream.'[5]

DU236 (Pursah)

Another component of forgiveness would be to *forgive both your projected images and yourself for dreaming them*. The *Course* tells you to forgive your brother for what he *hasn't* done. That would be true forgiveness because, as the *Course* also says, you're not making the error real. You're not giving truth to your illusions; you're bringing your illusions to the truth. Now it's time to forgive yourself for dreaming this whole mess in the first place. If nothing's happened – and if the *Course* teaches *anything*, it's that nothing's happened – then you're innocent. Thus as you forgive your brothers and sisters, your mind realizes simultaneously that *you* are forgiven.

Mikey's Note: As Pursah adds, 'When you forgive others, it's really you yourself who is being forgiven.'[6] And as the *Course* says, 'As you see him, you will see yourself.'[7]

DU238 (Pursah)

The final major component of the attitude of forgiveness: *Trust the Holy Spirit and choose His strength*. The peace of the Holy Spirit will be given to you if you do your job. He will heal the larger, unconscious mind that is hidden from you, and give you His peace at the same time. This peace may not always come right away, and sometimes it will. Sometimes it may surprise you in the form of something happening that would usually upset you – except this time it doesn't.

YIR176, 177, & DU224 (Arten)

An additional component of forgiveness would be that after you forgive, if you feel some kind of action is required, then *always* ask the

Holy Spirit if there's anything you should do. Remember, the Holy Spirit doesn't do anything in the world, *ever*. But He *can* inspire you as to what you should do. And even though the Holy Spirit doesn't do anything in the world, His interpretation of the level of form can help you see more clearly what you should do here. That's just a fringe benefit of choosing Him as your Teacher, not the main reason, which is salvation.

DU241 (Pursah)

It's just as important to forgive the little things as the apparently big things. Anything that disturbs your peace of mind is disturbing your peace of mind, and that's *not* the peace of God. You have to be willing to forgive everything equally. That's why the *Course* says that miracles are all the same.[8] Eventually, you'll see the equality of the things that aren't important to you and the things that are important to you.

YIR97 & 98 (Pursah)

When you meet people in this lifetime whom you've had dealings and special hate interests with before in other lifetimes, it's because you're orbiting each other, just as planets orbit the sun. Because the unconscious mind has retained the memory of them, you'll have conflict, sometimes right away and sometimes later in the relationship. In some lifetimes you'll be the victim, and in others, the victimizer. The question is, what are you going to use it for this time, freedom or bondage? Are you going to get that you are *not* a victim and take responsibility for dreaming, or are you going to make it real and stay stuck here?

Mikey's Note: I love this forgiveness thought process of asking myself when I find my peace of mind being disturbed by *something*, or *someone*, 'Am I going to take responsibility for my dream, or am I going to make it real and stay stuck in it?' That stops my ego right in its tracks, usually.

DU248 (Pursah)

People always resist the truth; the ego wants what it made to be real. Forgive those who think you're a moron for not buying into the system, and stick to your principles. Don't forget, the *Course* isn't saying you can't be successful in the world, but it *is* saying you shouldn't believe it's true. Your real success is with God, because with

Him you can't ever lose. However, if you stick around psycho planet long enough, then eventually you *have* to lose!

DU199 (Pursah)

To forgive means to *give ahead of time.* In other words, your attitude is that you're ready to forgive, no matter *what* it is that comes up in your awareness. At first, that seems like a tall order. Yet I promise you the day will come when you'll be capable of laughing at anything the ego throws at you – just like J could. The day will come when you'll be ready to be like J and leave the script, and serve as a light for others to follow out of the dream.

YIR27 (Arten)

Repetition is important not just in learning right minded ideas, but in practicing forgiveness. Sometimes it may look like you're forgiving the same thing over and over again. You forgive the people you work with. Then you go back the next day, and they're still there. But even if it looks like you're forgiving the same thing, that's an illusion too. What's really happening is that more unconscious guilt is coming to the surface of your mind, and it's a chance for you to release and be rid of it by continuing to forgive.

DU221 & 222 (Pursah)

The holy instant is simply that instant when you choose the Holy Spirit as your Teacher instead of the ego. This happens anytime you choose forgiveness – thus acting in both you and your forgivee's best interest. Of course, the forgivee is really you; it just doesn't look that way. What you're really accomplishing is the forgiveness of the symbolic contents of your own mind.

YIR37 (Pursah)

Forgiveness is always a gift you're giving to yourself, not the person you think you're forgiving. You're the one who receives the benefits, in both practical and metaphysical terms. True, you're acting as a reminder of the truth to the other person. All thought has effects on some level, and it's good for the other person, too. Not that the other person is really there. We're talking about a seemingly split-off aspect of your own mind.

DU245 (Pursah)

You demonstrate that you mean you want the peace of God *not* with your words, but by your forgiveness. If you really want to pull the plug on psycho planet then you need to do your forgiveness homework, which means you practice the *Course's* true forgiveness on whatever comes up in front of your face on any given day. Those are the lessons the Holy Spirit would have you learn. You won't always do them perfectly, or even well. Sometimes you'll have to do them later. No problem; a memory is just as real an image as any other image. They're all the same. Forgive them and be free.

DU178 (Gary & Arten)

God doesn't have to forgive you; you need to forgive yourself by forgiving others instead of attacking them. Even if it's just a mental judgment and you don't say or do anything, an attack thought is still an attack thought. That's why you have to monitor your thoughts. Whether you attack *or* forgive, you do it to yourself because these people aren't real anyway – they're just symbols of what's in your mind. The world doesn't need God's forgiveness; people need to forgive themselves by forgiving the images they see. The *Course* couldn't be any more clear about that.

'God does not forgive because He has never condemned. And there must be condemnation before forgiveness is necessary. Forgiveness is the great need of this world, but that is because it is a world of illusions. Those who forgive are thus releasing themselves from illusions, while those who withhold forgiveness are binding themselves to them. As you condemn only yourself, so do you forgive only yourself.

Yet although God does not forgive, His Love is nevertheless the basis of forgiveness. Fear condemns and love forgives. Forgiveness thus undoes what fear has produced, returning the mind to the awareness of God. For this reason, forgiveness can truly be called salvation. It is the means by which illusions disappear.'[9]

Mikey's Note: Several months prior to my first reading of *The Disappearance of the Universe*, I was bouncing around some ideas in my head about God and forgiveness. It wasn't something I read in particular that made me think of this, the thoughts just seemed to come to me from someplace else. Anyway, I was thinking about God and forgiveness, and what God's role is with it. After a few minutes of pondering, I came to the conclusion that if God forgives us, that would imply that God originally condemned us. Then I was like, 'I don't think God would do that!'

So a few months later, when I started my first read of *The Disappearance of the Universe*, I read early in the book that 'God did not create the world.' I had to think about that one; I hadn't gotten that memo any place else before! Then later on in the book, Arten quotes from the *Course,* 'God does not forgive, because He has never condemned......' When I read that, I had that 'ah-ha' moment, and I instantly put that idea together with the thoughts I had a few months prior to reading *Disappearance* about God and forgiveness, which I had totally forgotten about, until that moment. I then put that together with the idea that God did not create the world, and it instantly made perfect sense to me that God indeed did *not* create the world and has nothing to do with it.

YIR53 (Arten)

True forgiveness means you don't judge and condemn another. There's not really any sin and guilt out there, because nothing has happened except in a dream, and dreams are not real. So J counsels you in his *Course* not to make the ideas of sin and guilt real in the people, events, and situations you see in the world, 'Call it not sin but madness, for such it was and so it still remains. Invest it not with guilt, for guilt implies it was accomplished in reality. And above all, *be not afraid of it.* When you seem to see some twisted form of the original error rising to frighten you, say only, "God is not fear, but Love," and it will disappear.'[10]

YIR134 (Pursah)

No matter what the forgiveness opportunity may look like, what you're *really* forgiving is always the instant of separation from God. And the purpose is always to be free of the false universe and return to the real Universe, Heaven, by forgiving what's right in front of your face. It's not about whether or not you come back for another lifetime in the future, and it's not about history.

YIR118 (Pursah)

In the *Text*, J says, 'Appearances can but deceive the mind that wants to be deceived. And you can make a simple choice that will forever place you far beyond deception.'[11] That simple choice is forgiveness, and it's applied the same way to everything, up to and including death.

YIR39 (Pursah)

The reason some of your forgiveness lessons are so hard is because your unconscious mind remembers the bad relationship you had with the other person in a previous lifetime, so you've been set up to have tremendous unconscious resistance to forgiving them in this lifetime. Plus, there's the resistance to giving up your personal identity that is always there, because the ego senses that if you practice forgiveness, then this is its end. *Everyone* has these past-life relationships, and the memories are unconscious. That's why it's so much harder to forgive your special hate relationships than your special love relationships.

YIR133 (Pursah)

Remember, everyone has preferences, and no one should feel guilty about them. This isn't about giving them up, because the *Course* isn't about behavior. At the same time, it's helpful to remember, when you can, that none of what you see with the body's eyes in this lifetime is true, and *everything* is for forgiveness. Many of the desires people have, as well as the relationship intricacies, both good and bad, are continuations of themes from past dream lifetimes.

DU199 (Pursah)

Never forget that the ego is a killer, so it wants you to think God is a killer and fear Him. The very best way to keep itself going is to suck you into reacting to the script so you'll make it real in your mind. The ego wants conflict, and if you react with any negative emotion, that's conflict. It's your judgment that keeps the ego system alive, but your forgiveness will free it.

DU113 (Pursah)

Insane actions such as genocide are a routine part of the story of man's inhumanity toward man; true forgiveness is the only way to break the pattern.

YIR188 & 201 (Gary)

The only viable way of functioning in the world is to be prepared to forgive no matter what happens, and then it won't *matter* what happens. The more you practice, the more natural forgiveness seems, and the less natural the world seems. This isn't your home but you can have a good time here, and go home at the same time by seeing the world differently.

Mikey's Note: I just wanted to close out this chapter with a summary on forgiveness, followed by a few quotes from the *Course* on true perception. Forgiveness is all about taking full responsibility for *all* of your experiences, because on the level of the unconscious mind, you made up what you are perceiving. So, when you forgive someone in the true sense of the word, you're really forgiving the symbolic contents of your own unconscious mind.

Now, I'm not saying that this forgiveness gig is easy, in fact, it's often hard,[12] because our egos love to suck us into being right or being a victim in some way, rather than just being happy and at peace. But the truth is we are never a victim in this world no matter what comes our way, and it's just a matter if you want to listen to the ego's interpretation of everything, or take responsibility for your dream and choose *true perception*.

As Gary humorously says in his workshops, 'Forgiveness isn't easy. In fact, it sucks, because they don't deserve it!' But seriously, this path *is* very doable[13] and well worth it! And as Pursah puts it, 'The more you practice, the better you'll get at it, and it *will* seem easier to you at times. The key is doing it and not giving up!'[14] So, you gotta hang tough!

'Knowledge is not the remedy for false perception since, being another level, they can never meet. The one correction possible for false perception must be *true perception*. It will not endure. But for the time it lasts it comes to heal. For true perception is a remedy with many names. Forgiveness, salvation, Atonement, true perception, all are one. They are the one beginning, with the end to lead to Oneness far beyond themselves. True perception is the means by which the world is saved from sin, for sin does not exist. And it is this that true perception sees.'[15]

'Salvation is nothing more than "right-mindedness," which is not the One-mindedness of the Holy Spirit, but which must be achieved before One-mindedness is restored. Right-mindedness leads to the next step automatically because right perception is uniformly without attack, and therefore wrong-mindedness is obliterated. The ego cannot survive without judgment, and is laid aside accordingly. The mind then has only one direction in which it can move. Its direction is always automatic, because it cannot but be dictated by the thought system to which it adheres.'[16]

'Forgiveness removes only the untrue, lifting the shadows from the world and carrying it, safe and sure within its gentleness, to the bright world of new and clean perception. There is your purpose *now*. And it is there that peace awaits you.'[17]

'This world of light, this circle of brightness is the real world, where guilt meets with forgiveness. Here the world outside is seen anew, without the shadow of guilt upon it. Here are you forgiven, for here you have forgiven everyone. Here is the new perception, where everything is bright and shining with innocence, washed in the waters of forgiveness, and cleansed of every evil thought you laid upon it.'[18]

Chapter 12

Unconscious Guilt: The Root of all Evil

Most people assume it's what they believe in their conscious mind that matters, when the truth is it's what they believe in their unconscious mind that makes all the difference.[1]

DU17 (Arten)

Your good times in this world are good only in comparison to the bad times. The comparison isn't a valid one, because both the seemingly good times and the bad times are *not* Heaven. You will eventually learn that it's all a trick, that your perception – something you value very highly – is simply lying to you. You wouldn't listen to your unconscious thought system if it didn't hide itself and lie to you, because it's so seemingly despicable, and listening to it is so painful, that you'd run away from it if you could really examine it. J can help you examine it. He can show you a way to make your unconscious mind conscious to a degree that Freud could not have imagined.

YIR11 (Arten)

Everybody's afraid of something in this world, and as difficult as it may be for people to believe, because it's unconscious to them, all fears that people have can be directly traced at the level of the unconscious mind to the fear of God that is a result of your seeming separation from Him and the unconscious guilt that resulted from it.

DU169 (Pursah)

The people who give you trouble, you *want* them to show up – they're your scapegoats. That's how you trick yourself into thinking you're not guilty, or at least not terribly guilty, so you can cope most of the time – for the guilt is somewhere else. If you could just remember that fact the next time some apparently real flamer pushes your buttons, then you could hold your tongue, think with the Holy Spirit and change your mind. As long as you're stuck in the maze, you can't see that the whole thing is unnecessary, because you were never really guilty in the first place. The whole maze is an illusion to defend yourself against an illusion.

Mikey's Note: If we choose to look at these 'scapegoats' with the Holy Spirit rather than with the ego, then we realize that they are our opportunities for practicing forgiveness – and we can't get Home without them. So, these people are actually doing us a big favor, even if they do feel like a big pain in the ass, or as 'The Wayner' once put it, '…they're like the turd that won't flush!' So, they just keep coming back in one form or another until the particular aspects they represent in our minds that need healing have been completely forgiven.

DU238 (Pursah)

Remember that others' call for love is your call for love. You should be grateful to them; you need them as much as they need you. Without those images you see and the miracle, you'd *never* be able to find the way out. These images are symbolic of what's in your unconscious mind and without them, your unconscious guilt would be forever hidden from you – there would be no escape.

DU159 (Pursah & Arten)

Your real life is in Heaven, but you can also achieve peace and joy during your temporary life here. Those are your motivations for quitting grievances. Sometimes these motivations won't seem like enough. What's going to happen is that when you try to forgive, sometimes you'll be able to. Yet if you're really trying to do the *Course*, then just as often you're going to come up against a lot of things that you *don't* want to forgive and you *don't* want to give up. That's how your resistance and your hidden, unconscious hatred shows up. Those are the things you're going to have to look at that you don't want to look at.

Mikey's Note: Often times on this spiritual path things may appear to get worse before they get better. That's because you're noticing things more. Undoing the ego, or cleaning out the mind is like cleaning out a closet packed full of junk. Things may appear to get messier before they get cleaner, but that's just part of the process.

DU143 (Arten)

To illustrate just how much the ego resists looking at the guilt in the mind, all you need to do is consider that despite the fact that *A Course in Miracles* is very much *about* the healing of this unconscious guilt, most of the teachers of the *Course* never even mention it.

DU159 & 160 (Arten)

The *Course* wants to help people realize what's in their unconscious – so they can get rid of it. Most people, especially nice, spiritual people, don't know about the murderous thought system that runs this universe, or the hatred that's underneath the surface of their mind. Nor do most of them want to know. Most people just want everything to be hunky-dory. You can't blame them for wanting peace, but *real* peace is found by undoing the ego, not by covering it over.

DU159 (Gary)

The things I won't want to forgive, or even look closely at, are 'the secret sins and hidden hates'[2] that the *Course* talks about, which are really symbolic of how I hate *myself*, except I've projected them, so they seem to be outside of me. The way to forgive myself and help the Holy Spirit take over my unconscious mind is to uncover and observe these things with Him, and keep on forgiving them.

DU16 (Arten)

Your unconscious mind, which you are completely oblivious to, or else it wouldn't *be* unconscious, is under the domination of a sick thought system that is shared on both a collective and individual level by everyone who comes to the false universe – or else they wouldn't have come here in the first place. This will remain the case until your thoughts are examined, correctly forgiven, released to the Holy Spirit, and replaced by His thinking instead. Until then, your *hidden* beliefs will continue to dominate and assert themselves in a predetermined way.

DU84 & 85 (Arten)

You have often thought you had to try harder to be a more loving person, so you could exemplify the love of J. That's not true. If you really want to be perfect Love like him and God, then what you need to do is learn how to remove, with the Holy Spirit's help, the barriers that you have placed *in between* yourself and God. Then you will naturally and inevitably become aware of what you really are.

DU92 & 93 (Pursah)

The *Course* is about the healing of your unconscious guilt by the Holy Spirit and your return to Heaven through the dynamic of forgiveness, which harnesses the tremendous power of your mind's ability to choose. As J puts it, 'This is a course in mind training.'[3] And, 'An untrained mind can accomplish nothing.'[4]

Mikey's Note: As I stated in the *Introduction* piece to this book, this is not a path for the squeamish nor the faint of heart. Well, it's also not a path for the lazy-minded.

DU248 (Pursah)

Any kind of an upset, from a mild discomfort to outright anger, is a warning sign. It tells you that your hidden guilt is rising up from the recesses of your unconscious mind and coming to the surface. Think of that discomfort as the guilt that needs to be released by forgiving the symbol you associate with it. The ego is trying to get you to see the guilt as being outside of you by projecting the reason for it onto an illusory image. The ego thought system is trying to put some distance in between yourself and the guilt, and any suitable object or person who comes along will suffice.

DU339 (Gary & Arten)

Forgiveness is what the individual can do about his or her world, and nobody can ever take that away once you know how to do it. And once you know how to do it, then you realize that you're never a victim, and what you are seeing are merely symbols of your own insanity pictured outside of yourself – except now you have a way to be free of it by releasing the other. Other people in turn will live in peace only after they are willing to look at their *own* dark side as seen in others and forgive it.

Mikey's Note: This reminds me of my second favorite movie of all time, *Antwone Fisher*, about a young man who has an anger problem, and has to look back on his past in order to take responsibility for his life so that he can heal, instead of remaining a victim of his childhood; he has to forgive in order to move forward with his life. It's a very inspiring film, I highly recommend it, though I should warn you that it does have some pretty intense scenes, so it's not something to watch with children.

DU181 (Arten)

As far as the ego's plan is concerned, your seemingly multiple problems show up in this world in an attempt to get you to *react* – to feel bad, guilty, mad, defeated, bored, scared, inferior, self-conscious, annoyed, lonely, or superior and condescending. It's all some kind of a judgment, regardless of the form. As soon as you make that judgment, you give validity to the ego's world and reinforce the seeming reality of the separation and everything that goes with it.

DU220 (Arten)

The ego has tricked you into thinking you're getting rid of your unconscious guilt when you project it onto others, by making them wrong, or condemning them or blaming certain circumstances for your problems or the world's problems, or whatever. Instead, what this really does is cause you to hang on to your unconscious guilt forever. Are you beginning to understand how important forgiveness is for you?

DU108 & 109 (Arten)

Your unconscious belief system is held in place by *not* looking at it.[5] The thought system of fear, which has been denied and projected outward[6], must be closely examined in your life if you are to be free of it. The solution to the problems of the world and its relationships will *never* be found at the level of the interaction between individual bodies.

DU197 & 198 (Arten)

The guilt in your unconscious is more terrible and even more acute than what you see or feel on the surface because of your *proximity* to it – it's in your unconscious. That was the reason for the whole miscreation of the universe in the first place – the need to escape your guilt and your terrible, misguided fear of God. Now you have a world of bodies where the contents of your mind, including the thought of separation and your own unconscious guilt, are seen symbolically as being outside of you, in the world and in other people. You get to be the innocent victim of the world rather than the maker of it. Thus the world and other bodies are the cause of your problems, and even if you feel guilty it's still not your fault. Not *really*. There's always an exterior reason or contributing factor to explain your condition.

Mikey's Note: The last four sentences of this passage are the thinking of the world in a nutshell: 'You get to be the innocent victim of the world rather than the maker of it. Thus the world and other bodies are the cause of your problems, and even if you feel guilty it's still not your fault. Not *really*. There's always an exterior reason or contributing factor to explain your condition.'

DU175 (Pursah)

The conscious projection you see all around you is an entire level removed from the unconscious mind. So while at times the universe you see can be horrible and frightening, it's nothing compared to the awful thought system it springs from. In fact, because the projection you see is a defense, you could say that the universe exists *because* it is tolerable to you *compared* to what's in your unconscious mind. The world may not always be tolerable to everyone – often resulting in murders and suicides – but it's still a walk in the park compared to the deep, vicious crap that's underneath the surface.

DU267 (Arten)

When you're enlightened, you will completely awaken from the dream. Even though you'll still appear to be in a body, you'll see what the *Course* refers to as the real world.[7] You will only 'see' it when you have completely forgiven the world, because the real world has no projections of unconscious guilt upon it. You'll see only innocence everywhere, because it's your own innocence – the innocence of Christ. That is what J saw, and what he teaches you now to see.

DU197 (Arten)

Everyone participates equally in the script and ends up with just as many so-called good lives and bad lives as everyone else. That's why we emphasize that how much money or success you get has absolutely nothing to do with how spiritually enlightened you are. There's a danger of thinking you're better than other people if you're doing well, even if your feeling of superiority is a subtle one – but that's just a form of the projection of your unconscious guilt. On the other hand, the people who are having the seemingly less successful lifetimes feel guilty because they're not doing better! Remember, guilt can be projected onto your self as well as onto others. In any case, the roles people play are reversed in different lifetimes.

Mikey's Note: Which is another reason why *nobody* is special, which really sucks, because I've always thought *I* was special, regardless of what my life's circumstances happened to be at any given time. Well, maybe I'm just the exception to the rule! (LOL) No, but seriously, J says in the *Course*, 'Forgiveness is the end of specialness.'[8] So Mikey is S.O.L.!

DU176 (Arten)

Those who commit suicide, in any manner, seek to end the intolerable psychological pain of their guilt and suffering. Since their unconscious guilt remains intact, they merely end up reincarnating and keeping the problem unresolved. Death is not a way out. True forgiveness is the way out. As the *Course* teaches, 'The world is not left by death but by truth.'[9]

YIR79 (Arten)

Suicide is the biggest problem in the world that the world is in total denial of. It's the dirty little secret of the ego. Sure, people know about suicide, but they have no idea how widespread it is. *More people die from suicide than are killed by all of the wars and all of the crime in the world combined.* Nobody wants to talk about it. Nobody wants to examine it. If someone is depressed, the system will put them on drugs and never look at the reasons. That's because the ego doesn't want to look at the issue of unconscious guilt, which is the real cause of suicide. The ego runs away from looking at it as fast as possible.

Mikey's Note: I would add to this that the unconscious guilt is the real cause of *all* the madness and the fears in this world. Without the unconscious guilt in the mind, none of the madness would exist. They are just the projected effects of a guilt-ridden mind. And minds can be healed.

DU193 (Pursah)

Never forget that your fear of losing your individual identity will cause resistance, sometimes serious resistance, to the practice of forgiveness. Sometimes it will prevent you from even wanting to look at the ego, either in the world or in yourself. You're secretly afraid of what's in your unconscious. That's why you have to be vigilant. There is hatred in your mind underneath the surface, but it can be released simply by noticing it when it does surface, and then taking the Holy Spirit's hand instead of the ego's.

DU211 (Arten)

The ego says others are guilty, because it secretly believes you're guilty. It uses anger and righteous indignation, or even laughing at others, to put distance between you and your guilt. You think only animals and children are innocent, because that's where you've chosen to see your own seemingly lost innocence. The ego has to put the idea of innocence *somewhere*. But the Holy Spirit says everyone is completely innocent, because He knows you're completely innocent.

DU248 (Pursah)

Projection always follows denial. People have to project their repressed guilt onto others, or correctly forgive it. Those are the only two choices that are available, no matter how complex the world may seem. If you want to outplay the ego and successfully turn the tables on it, you have to be alert for that warning sign of discomfort or anger, and then stop reacting and start forgiving.

YIR99 (Pursah)

Doing forgiveness most of the time isn't enough. Sure, you're better off in many ways, but the only real ticket out of here is through universal application. If you remember it's really your own secret beliefs you have about yourself in your unconscious mind that you choose to see in others as a way of escaping from them, then you can get that *you* are the one being freed through your forgiveness. As the *Course* asks, 'Would they be willing to accept the fact their savage purpose is directed against themselves?'[10]

DU217 (Pursah)

The ego tries to convince you that your problems are the problem, but the Holy Spirit knows it's the well-hidden, unconscious guilt that makes you need to dream a world of separation in the first place that's the problem. Of course, the world doesn't think that. The world doesn't even know about it! As the *Course* makes sure to remind you late in the *Text*, 'Of one thing you were sure: of all the many causes you perceived as bringing pain and suffering to you, your guilt was not among them.'[11]

DU169 & 170 (Pursah)

You believe you really are guilty on a much deeper level than you realize. You need your defense because the *alternative* is unthinkable to your ego – that you might actually look upon your own guilt – the horror of which is presently covered over by the world. The ego has you convinced that to look upon the hideousness of this guilt is the equivalent of death. To avoid the viciousness that goes along with the entire can of worms, you project it outward, forgetting that what goes around comes around – because it never really left in the first place.

DU161 (Arten)

You're unconsciously attracted to sin, guilt, fear, pain, and suffering. It doesn't make you any different than anyone else, except you'll be one of the people who is aware of it – so you can observe it, forgive it, and eventually be free of it.

DU255 (Pursah)

Remember, others' judgment of you is really your own self-judgment that is seen as being outside of you. They're not even there. Yes, it looks like they're really there and the judgment is outside of you, but it's not. When you forgive the other, you're really forgiving what's in your own mind. Their call for love really is *your* call for love.

DU108 & YIR75 (Arten & Pursah)

The meaning of love cannot be taught or learned. Love will take care of Itself. *Your* job, as the *Introduction* to the *Course* says, is to learn how to remove, along with the Holy Spirit, the blocks to the awareness of the inheritance that you seemingly threw away. The blocks are those walls of guilt in the mind that keep you from your awareness of what you really are. Every act of forgiveness undoes the ego, and the Holy Spirit removes the blocks to the awareness of God, or spirit's presence. The opposite of God and His Kingdom is anything that is not God and His Kingdom, but what is all-encompassing – God – cannot *have* an opposite.

DU386 & 387 (Arten)

You fear death consciously and are attracted to it unconsciously, it's like a moth to the flame. The attraction of death is the third of what the *Course* describes as the four major obstacles to peace,[12] and your fear of death is subordinate only to your erroneous fear of God. You could say the fear of death is symbolic of the fear of God, and without guilt in your unconscious mind it would be impossible for you to fear either. J wasn't afraid of death, and he certainly wasn't afraid of God. There's no more need for you to fear your Father than there was for him to.

YIR195 (Gary & Arten)

There's no getting away from the fact that it's always about freeing yourselves from the unconscious guilt, which frees you from *everything*. And sooner or later, in order to do that, it always comes back to the forgiveness of relationships. As the *Course* puts it, 'The Holy Spirit teaches that you always meet yourself, and the encounter is holy because you are. The ego teaches that you always encounter your past, and because your dreams were not holy, the future cannot be, and the present is without meaning.'[13]

YIR215 (Pursah)

When your forgiveness lessons are complete, then not one trace of guilt will remain in your unconscious mind. At that point, you will break the cycle of birth and death, and never dream of going into a body again. That is the end of reincarnation.

YIR117 (Arten)

J says in the *Course*, 'When you forgive the world your guilt, you will be free of it.'[14] And without one, you have no need for the other. Your guilt, which is now unconscious, is the reason for the world.

Your job is to undo it. That's how to break the cycle of birth and death.

Mikey's Note: I just want to close out this chapter with a quote from the *Course,* 'Only illusions can be forgiven, and then they disappear. Forgiveness is release from all illusions, and that is why it is impossible but partly to forgive. No one who clings to one illusion can see himself as sinless, for he holds one error to himself as lovely still. And so he calls it "unforgivable," and makes it sin. How can he then give his forgiveness wholly, when he would not receive it for himself? For it is sure he would receive it wholly the instant that he gave it so. And thus his secret guilt would disappear, forgiven by himself.'[15]

Chapter 13

Definitive Statements

**A definitive statement is an idea in the *Course* that's
so clear it defines what the *Course* is teaching, and
it encapsulates what the *Course* is saying.[1]**

DU212 & YIR101 (Arten & Pursah)

As outrageous as it may seem to your ego, J says this in the
Workbook, 'There is no world! This is the central thought the course
attempts to teach. Not everyone is ready to accept it, and each one
must go as far as he can let himself be led along the road to truth. He
will return and go still farther, or perhaps step back a while and then
return again. But healing is the gift of those who are prepared to learn
there is no world, and can accept the lesson now. Their readiness will
bring the lesson to them in some form which they can understand and
recognize.'[2]

If there is no world, then there's nothing to forgive, and
recognizing that fact in the events, situations, and people you see *is*
advanced forgiveness, because now you're not forgiving other
people for something they've really done, you're recognizing that
they haven't really done anything. So you're actually forgiving
yourself for dreaming them. That distinction is vital. Without it,
you're doing the old-fashioned kind of forgiveness, which can't
undo the ego.

Mikey's Note: Another way of stating this would be that the world
is just a dream, an illusion, a projection, a movie, or whatever you want to
call it. It's all about taking full responsibility for what you are perceiving,
because on the unconscious level, you made it all up! So, we still act
responsibly in the world while we appear to be here, while doing our
necessary forgiveness work which will eventually *free* us from the world.

Another quote from the *Course* related to this, 'The world you see is but a judgment on yourself. It is not there at all. Yet judgment lays a sentence on it, justifies it and makes it real. Such is the world you see; a judgment on yourself, and made by you. This sickly picture of yourself is carefully preserved by the ego, whose image it is and which it loves, and placed outside you in the world. And to this world must you adjust as long as you believe this picture is outside, and has you at its mercy.'[3]

YIR101 (Arten)

Another definitive statement in the *Course* would be the idea that anger is *never* justified.[4] If you made the whole thing up, then who is there to be angry at? And a related definitive idea would be, 'The secret of salvation is but this: That you are doing this unto yourself.'[5] The two ideas fit together like a hand in a glove, and once you really *get* them then there's no getting away *from* them.

Mikey's Note: J goes on to say in the same section about the secret of salvation, '...No matter what the form of the attack, this still is true. Whoever takes the role of enemy and of attacker, still is this the truth. Whatever seems to be the cause of any pain and suffering you feel, this is still true. For you would not react at all to figures in a dream you knew that you were dreaming. Let them be as hateful and as vicious as they may, they could have no effect on you unless you failed to recognize it is your dream.'[6]

DU9 (Pursah)

God did not create duality and He did *not* create the world. If He did, He would be the author of 'a tale told by an idiot.' But God is not an idiot. He can only be one of two things. He is either perfect Love, as the Bible says when it momentarily stumbles upon the truth, or He's an idiot. You can't have it both ways.

Mikey's Note: If God really created the world and the universe of bodies, why the hell would God create parts that are used for both sexual pleasure as well as for disposing of wastes? Damn, talk about God being an idiot! As it was put in the movie *Forgetting Sarah Marshall*, '...if God was a city planner, he would not put a playground next to a sewage system!'

DU126 (Arten)

The idea of separation, as well as your subsequent decisions, are things that God is totally unconcerned about. The events in a dream are of no consequence, simply because they are not really happening.

DU232 (Pursah)

An important component of your forgiveness is that you want to teach people, silently, that they are not bodies. That's how your mind learns for certain that *you* are not a body. As the *Course* puts it, 'I am not a body. I am free. For I am still as God created me.'[7] And, 'As you teach so shall you learn.'[8]

DU216 (Arten)

You don't have to establish your worth with God. That was done in God's mind when He created you. Nothing else that appears to happen in the universe of perception can change that – except in your mistaken dreams. As the *Course* helps you to remember, 'You dwell not here but in eternity. You travel but in dreams while safe at home.'[9] And, 'Whenever you are tempted to undertake a useless journey that would lead away from light, remember what you really want, and say: *The Holy Spirit leads me unto Christ, and where else would I go? What need have I but to awake in Him?*'[10]

DU98 (Arten)

Everyone wants their life to have meaning, but they're looking for it in the wrong place – in the world. People feel a deep emptiness somewhere, and then they try to fill in the hole with some accomplishment or relationship on the level of form. Yet all of these things, by definition, are transitory at best. Thus you need to realize, as J counsels very early in the *Text*, 'A sense of separation from God is the only lack you really need correct. This sense of separation would never have arisen if you had not distorted your perception of truth, and had thus perceived yourself as lacking.'[11]

Mikey's Note: This reminds me of a *Seinfeld* episode where Jerry and George have a conversation with each other, agreeing that they are kids and not real men because of the way they live their lives, breaking up with women for very shallow and superficial reasons. Then Jerry mentions this conversation to Kramer, and he's like, 'So I bet you asked yourselves, isn't there something more to life?' And Jerry says 'yes.' Then Kramer goes on to say, 'Well, let me clue you in on something. There isn't. What are you thinking of Jerry? Marriage? Family? They're *prisons* – man made *prisons;* you're doing *time!* You get up in the morning, she's *there!* You go to sleep at night, she's *there!*' Kramer goes on to mention about having to ask permission to use the bathroom and not being able to watch TV while eating dinner because you're supposed to talk about your day. (LOL)

DU298 (Arten)

Home is where the heart is. If your heart is with God, then you're already home. Renounce the world, not physically but mentally. As the *Course* says, 'This world you seem to live in is not home to you. And somewhere in your mind you know that this is true.'[12] That attitude will make it ten times easier to forgive. The next time the crap hits the fan, remember God and forgive – for if you forgive then you *will* remember God.

DU235 (Pursah)

With salvation, there is no one out there to blame for your one real problem, of which all the others are symbolic. The cause, which is the decision to believe in the separation from God, and the solution, which is the principle of the Atonement, are both in your mind – where you now have the power to choose the Holy Spirit's Answer.

DU125 (Arten)

God could not have created this world. It would not be in His nature. He is not cruel, and as J points out to you, 'If this were the real world, God *would* be cruel. For no Father could subject His children to this as the price of salvation and *be* loving.'[13]

Mikey's Note: A related quote from the *Course*, 'The world as you perceive it cannot have been created by the Father; for the world is not as you see it. God created only the eternal, and everything you see is perishable. Therefore, there must be another world that you do not see. The Bible speaks of a new Heaven and a new earth, yet this cannot be literally true, for the eternal are not re-created.'[14]

DU212 (Arten)

The ego attempts to convince you that you have a personal story that is obviously real. The attitude of the Holy Spirit though, can be summed up in just three words: *It never happened.*

DU169 (Pursah)

It's always a case where you took the hatred you have for yourself – for throwing away Heaven – and made up a world where the reason for this hatred, your guilt and lack of peace could now be seen outside yourself, almost always connected in some way to other beings. Now the guilt is not in you. It's not *you* who took the peace of God away from you, it's *them*. Of course, nobody can really take the peace of God away from you except by your own decision.

DU85 (Arten)

The seeming interaction between you and God is really an interaction within your own unconscious split mind – between the part of you that has forgotten your reality and the part of your mind where the Holy Spirit dwells. He has never left you. His voice is your memory of God – your memory of your true home. This voice represents your long-forgotten reality. Now you must choose between the Holy Spirit, who represents the real you, and the ego, which represents the false you.

DU343 (Arten)

Don't ever forget that the goal of the *Course* is the only thing worth having, and this world isn't. You think the universe is of value because you're used to it and it's all you remember. But as the *Course* asks you, 'Is it a sacrifice to give up pain? Does an adult resent the giving up of children's toys? Does one whose vision has already glimpsed the face of Christ look back with longing on a slaughter house? No one who has escaped the world and all its ills looks back on it with condemnation. Yet he must rejoice that he is free of all the sacrifice its values would demand of him.'[15]

DU111 (Pursah)

As far is wisdom is concerned, the world believes that wisdom is having good judgment and being right. That's not true. All being right will do is keep you stuck here forever.

DU213 (Arten & Gary)

Since the *Course* teaches that you have only two emotions, love and fear, then the Holy Spirit sees everything in the world as either an expression of love or a call for love. Now if someone's *expressing* love, the appropriate response is love. And if someone is *calling out* for love, the appropriate response is love. Under the Holy Spirit's thought system, the proper response to any situation is always love. When you think with the Holy Spirit, you're consistent in your attitude, which is love.

YIR184 & 185 (Pursah)

The people of the world will never live in peace until the people of the world have inner peace. If you want to have world peace, the only way to do it in a lasting and meaningful way is to bring about a condition of inner peace within the people who appear to be here. As J says in his *Course*, what you see is 'the outside picture of an inward condition.'[16] Any attempt to bring peace to the world *in* the world will have only a temporarily helpful impact at best, because you're trying to solve the problem where it isn't, instead of where it is.

DU125 (Arten)

In order to really accept God's helper, the Holy Spirit, you must begin to trust God. You cannot trust Him until you recognize that it is not Him, but *you*, who is responsible for your experiences. You will feel guilty until you understand that this world is not real, and that nothing has really happened. That doesn't mean you shouldn't act responsibly in the illusion. It means you must understand certain things in order to apply the true forgiveness that enables the Holy Spirit to help you the most.

DU40, 41, & 294 (Arten)

You've got to be willing to surrender the idea of Authorship to God if you want to be able to share in your real power. Humility is the way – not a false humility that says you are inadequate, but a real humility that simply says God is your only Source. You will realize that except for His Love you need nothing, and he who needs nothing can be trusted with everything. J had the kind of humility that said, 'God, I just want *you*.' How many people are ready to say that and mean it? Are *you* ready to go for the end-game?

DU214 (Arten)

The ego calls for sacrifice. In contrast, the Holy Spirit says there is no need for sacrifice of any kind. The ego says, 'The Lord giveth and the Lord taketh away.' The Holy Spirit knows that God only gives, and *never* takes away. The ego reverently proclaims death is real. The Holy Spirit says nobody is dead, and no one can ever really die. The ego judges something as good or bad; the Holy Spirit says it is neither, because it isn't true. Thus all things on the level of form are equally untrue because of their illusory nature.

DU267 & 268 (Arten)

The *Course* says, 'A universal theology is impossible, but a universal experience is not only possible but necessary. It is this experience toward which the course is directed.'[17] That universal experience is the Love of God. While the *Course* is *directed* toward experience, it takes the wise intellectual choices of a trained mind to bring about that experience.

DU79 (Pursah)

The awareness of your oneness with the Presence of God is yours because God gave it to you. You have forgotten it. Yet it is still there, buried in your mind.[18] There is a way to remember. And by remembering, you will reclaim what you really are and where you really belong.

YIR112 (Pursah)

It's not *what* you do in the world, it's whom you do it *with*, the ego or the Holy Spirit. Each choice leads to a totally different experience. People may think they can judge others by what they do, but that's not always the case. Somebody may have a job where they have to do things that may not appear to be spiritual to the world. Yet *anything* can be spiritual if you choose the Holy Spirit to guide you. So no job is really any more spiritual than any other job.

Mikey's Note: Yes, what we do in the world while we appear to be here is not important, it's irrelevant. But we're all going to be doing something while we appear to be here; I don't think any of us are going to be staring at a wall until they attain their enlightenment. The point is we must do our forgiveness work while we go about doing whatever it is we do in this world. Our healing is dependent on what's going on in our minds, *not* about what action we take in the world. It's about living at cause, which is in the mind, and not screwing around with effects. Forgiveness is our *real* job, and *anything* we appear to be doing in the world is just a cover job.[19]

YIR99 (Pursah)

Every forgiving thought is an expression of love; every unforgiving thought is a murder. It doesn't matter if there isn't a corpse. Each day the earth turns is a day full of murders without corpses – people thinking unforgiving thoughts toward one another. As J says in no uncertain terms, 'What is not love is murder. What is not loving must be an attack.'[20]

DU402 (Pursah)

J says that you shouldn't feel any pressure. He says salvation will come to each mind when it's supposed to. He advises you to just give people your love, your forgiveness, and your experience – and let the Holy Spirit take care of the rest.

Mikey's Note: What a breath of fresh air this was to hear for the first time, 'no pressure.' After several years of reading books on the topic of ascension, which came with its subtle guilt trips and sense of urgency, reading this felt like a heavy weight had been taken off my shoulders. Thank you J-Dog!

Chapter 14

The Crucifixion, Resurrection, the Second Coming of Christ, and Oneness

**J is outside the door of the asylum, calling you to come out and join him, and you keep trying to drag him back in.[1]
Here's J, challenging people to come up to his level, and they keep bringing him down to their own.[2]**

Gary talks about going to see the movie *The Passion of the Christ* on the third disc of his audio program *Secrets of the Immortal* as well as in chapter four of *Your Immortal Reality – Murders without Corpses*. Gary describes the scene of people lined up around the block to get tickets to see this bloody, horrific movie that he says is so violent that it should have been rated *NC-17* instead of *R*. So, he says people were like taking their nine and ten year old kids to go see this thing. And after the movie was done, Gary describes the look on the parents' faces as they were coming out of the movie theatre as if they were saying to their kids:

'There, you see? You see what Jesus did for *you*? You see how he suffered and sacrificed himself for *you*? You guilty little bastids! Now what are you going to do for *him*? Well, you're gonna be a Christian, right?' Gary goes on to say in the program, 'And there you have the makings of a very successful religion. Because, if you want to get people to do something in this world, then you make them feel guilty – that's what makes the world go round. That's why Christianity is such a successful religion and has over a billion members because they make people feel guilty about the death of Jesus and they are indoctrinated at a very young age.'

DU246 (Pursah)

The message of the crucifixion has been interpreted by the world as a message of sacrifice. That is not the lesson J intended it to be. His lesson was one of resurrection rather than crucifixion. J says there is no death, and that the body is nothing. The church has confused the manner of his death as a call to sacrifice and suffer for God. That is incorrect.

It is not necessary for you to repeat the example of the crucifixion. As J tells you in the *Course,* 'You are not asked to be crucified, which was part of my own teaching contribution. You are merely asked to follow my example in the face of much less extreme temptations to misperceive, and not to accept them as false justifications for anger.'[3] Remembering that, all you need to do is understand the real lesson of it and apply it, through your forgiveness attitude, to your own body and your own personal life's circumstances. Here is part of what J says in the *Course* in the section titled *The Message of the Crucifixion.* You will never find a more striking example of refusing to compromise on the truth.

'Assault can ultimately be made only on the body. There is little doubt that one body can assault another, and can even destroy it. Yet if destruction itself is impossible, anything that is destructible cannot be real. Its destruction, therefore, does not justify anger. To the extent to which you believe that it does, you are accepting false premises and teaching them to others. The message the crucifixion was intended to teach was that it is not necessary to perceive any form of assault in persecution, because you cannot *be* persecuted. If you respond with anger, you must be equating yourself with the destructible, and are therefore regarding yourself insanely.'[4]

He then goes on to say in that same section, 'The message of the crucifixion is perfectly clear: *Teach only love, for that is what you are.* If you interpret the crucifixion in any other way, you are using it as a weapon for assault rather than as the call for peace for which it was intended.'[5]

DU111 & YIR106 (Gary, Arten, & Pursah)

Even though it appeared to be a terrible attack, the crucifixion was really nothing to J, because he was so totally identified with the invulnerable Love of God, which he knew he really was, instead of illusions like the body. The fact that the crucifixion and J's supposed suffering for others on the cross are central ideas to Christianity is just an indication of how much his message was misunderstood and distorted.

But don't expect to attain the same non-suffering level of accomplishment as J in your first year doing the *Course*. It's an ideal that can only come with a great deal of experience. The time will eventually come when you will never suffer. That is one of the long term payoffs of this spiritual path. Even while you still appear to be in your body, it's possible for you to attain psychological invulnerability.

As the *Course* says, 'The guiltless mind cannot suffer.'[6] It blows the whole idea of glorifying sacrifice right out of the water. Because pain is not a physical process, it's a mental process, and if you healed all the unconscious guilt in the mind, then you couldn't feel any pain. That changes the message of the Crucifixion from the idea of worshiping suffering and sacrifice to a demonstration that if you were healed, then it would be *impossible* for you to feel any pain or to suffer. But suffering, like people now believe J did, is a hallmark of the religion that he had nothing to do with, but that was founded in his name.

YIR154 & 155 (Pursah)

J's whole point was to teach the *meaninglessness* of the body, not glorify it. The focus should always be on doing your forgiveness lessons and going home, not on the level of form and the body, which *cannot* be spiritualized. People are always looking for vicarious salvation. They want to be enlightened by following an enlightened one and having it bestowed on them. It doesn't work that way. In addition, there are so many people out there presenting themselves as some kind of a master and saying they're going to teach you 'mastery,' that it's comical. If you drove a nail through the wrist of these people, it would hurt like hell. J really *was* a master, and he could feel no pain because the guiltless mind cannot suffer.

DU245 & 246 (Pursah)

The law of forgiveness is this, 'Fear binds the world, forgiveness sets it free.'[7] The world feels solid to you because fear binds it. It didn't feel solid to J because he had forgiven the world. That's why the nails didn't hurt him as they were being driven into his flesh. Being guiltless, his mind could not suffer – and someday you will attain the condition where *you* cannot suffer. That is the destiny the Holy Spirit holds out to you when you forgive the episodic fantasies of your bodily addicted ego.

DU269 & 270 (Arten)

Here are a few passages from the *Manual for Teachers* on the resurrection. 'Very simply the resurrection is the overcoming or surmounting of death. It is a reawakening or a rebirth; a change of mind about the meaning of the world. It is the acceptance of the Holy Spirit's interpretation of the world's purpose; the acceptance of the Atonement for oneself.'[8] It goes on to say, 'The resurrection is the denial of death, being the assertion of life. Thus is all the thinking of the world reversed entirely. Life is now recognized as salvation, and pain and misery of any kind perceived as hell. Love is no longer feared, but gladly welcomed.'[9]

When you have completely awakened from the dream of death and attained your resurrection, 'Christ's face is seen in every living thing, and nothing is held in darkness, apart from the light of forgiveness.'[10] Once you have seen the face of Christ, 'Here the curriculum ends. From here on, no directions are needed. Vision is wholly corrected and all mistakes undone. Attack is meaningless and peace has come. The goal of the curriculum has been achieved. Thoughts turn to Heaven and away from hell. All longings are satisfied, for what remains unanswered or incomplete?'[11]

The time will come when each seemingly separated mind has attained its enlightenment or resurrection. When everyone – not every*body*, mind you – but every mind that has dreamed thousands of lifetimes has reached this state of awakening from the dream, *that* is the Second Coming of Christ. As the *Course* teaches, 'The Second Coming is the one event in time which time itself can not affect. For every one who ever came to die, or yet will come or who is present now, is equally released from what he made. In this equality is Christ restored as one Identity, in which the Sons of God acknowledge that they all are one. And God the Father smiles upon His son, His one creation and His only joy.'[12]

DU392 (Pursah)

J calls you to be with him, and join him where life *really* is! 'The First Coming of Christ is merely another name for the creation, for Christ is the Son of God. The Second Coming of Christ means nothing more than the end of the ego's rule and the healing of the mind. I was created like you in the First, and I have called you to join with me in the Second.'[13]

DU109 (Gary)

Resurrection is something that takes place in your mind even though you still appear to be in your body, and it actually has nothing to do with the body at all. The ideas of physical resurrection and physical immortality are not only fantasies, but totally unnecessary.

DU270 (Gary & Arten)

You left as one and you'll return to Heaven as one. Of course, you never *really* left, because you can't help but be safe in God no matter *what* you're dreaming. When the entire Sonship is ready, then God will give His Last Judgment. As J informs you, 'This is God's Final Judgment: You are still My holy Son, forever innocent, forever loving, and forever loved, as limitless as your Creator, and completely changeless and forever pure. Therefore awaken and return to Me. I am your Father and you are My Son.'[14]

Mikey's Note: This reminds me of another quote from the *Course* I'd like to share here, 'You who are sometimes sad and sometimes angry; who sometimes feel your just due is not given you, and your best efforts meet with lack of appreciation and even contempt; give up these foolish thoughts! They are too small and meaningless to occupy your holy mind an instant longer. God's Judgment waits for you to set you free.'[15]

DU271 & 272 (Pursah)

Heaven is *real* oneness, unlike the idea of being one with the universe, or even one with the mind that is outside of time and space that made the universe. Those ideas are still seemingly outside of God. With true oneness there is *only* God, and there cannot ever *be* anything else. The *Course's* idea of God is as lofty as it can possibly be, because it is the truth. Oneness cannot be perfect if there is anything else to be aware of. As J puts it in the *Course*, 'Heaven is not a place nor a condition. It is merely an awareness of perfect Oneness, and the knowledge that there is nothing else; nothing outside this Oneness, and nothing else within.'[16]

DU266, 272 & 273 (Arten)

The *Course* is directed toward the experience of true oneness which can be summed up in just two words – two words that do indeed express the absolute truth. Keep your mind on the goal as you forgive the world, and always remember what the *Course* is leading you to, 'God is, and in Him all created things must be eternal. Do you not see that otherwise He has an opposite, and fear would be as real as love?'[17] And, 'Oneness is simply the idea God is. And in His Being, He encompasses all things. No mind holds anything but Him. We say "God is," and then we cease to speak, for in that knowledge words are meaningless. There are no lips to speak them, and no part of mind sufficiently distinct to feel that it is now aware of something not itself. It has united with its Source. And like its Source Itself, it merely is.'[18]

Chapter 15

The Unreality of the Body

Everything is in your mind, including your own body.[1]
The body is a mental experience and not a physical one.[2]
At no single instant does the body exist at all.[3]

DU44 (Arten)

The number one reason why the thinking of the world and the thinking of J are mutually exclusive is because J's reality was not the body, and the world's thinking is completely based upon an identification with the body as your reality. Even those of you who glance past the body still maintain the idea of an individual existence, which is actually little different than having a body. In fact, it is with this idea of separation, and all that arises from it, that you sentence yourself to continue in the universe of bodies.

DU109 (Arten)

Reality and love are natural and abstract; bodies and fear are unnatural and specific. As the *Course* teaches, 'Complete abstraction is the natural condition of the mind.'[4]

DU7 (Pursah)

The physical act of sex doesn't even come close to the incredible bliss of Heaven. It's just a poor, made-up imitation of union with God. It's a false idol made to fix your attention on the body and the world with just enough of a payoff to keep you coming back for more. It's very similar to a narcotic. Heaven, on the other hand, is a perfect, indescribable ecstasy that never ceases; the very peak of a perfect sexual orgasm, except this orgasm never stops. It keeps going on forever with no decrease in its powerful and flawless intensity.

Mikey's Note: Coming back for more? No pun intended, right Pursah? Yeah, right, and the Pope is Jewish! Anyway, this sounds pretty damn cool to me – what the hell are we waiting for?

DU179 (Pursah)

You must forgive yourself as surely as you must forgive others, or else you're not really getting the insignificance of the body. Your body is no more real or more important than any other body.

DU214 (Arten)

The ego says you're a body. The Holy Spirit says you are not a body; you are not a person, you are not a human being – you are like Him. The ego says your thoughts are quite important. On this level, the *Course* considers the thoughts you think with the Holy Spirit to be your real thoughts. Moreover, it could be said that the Holy Spirit *is* the only truth on the level of the world.

DU385 (Pursah)

Death is symbolic of your illusory separation from God. What happens when someone you love appears to die? All of a sudden you're separate. You appear to lose them just like you appeared to lose God. But it's not true. You can't really lose them any more than you can lose God. You are inseparable. You cry when a body you love appears to die, but as the *Course* teaches you, it's really your experience of God and Heaven that you miss, 'And who could weep but for his innocence?'[5]

YIR51 & 52 (Pursah)

The purpose of the body is to make the illusion seem real. But since the body is part of the illusion, it can hardly be counted on to tell you of the illusion's unreality. It was given form by the same decision to be separate through projection, which is what made the entire illusion in the first place. You wanted the separation so the guilt would be in other bodies and not yours, and thus outside of you and in them. But because projection made the perception of everything, the cause of it all is still right there in your mind, and minds can be changed.

YIR133 (Pursah)

The next time you get upset with someone's behavior, think of their body as being a wind-up toy. If you really *knew* that the body was just a wind-up toy, then it couldn't upset you, no matter *what* it said or did. If you really understood that what you were seeing wasn't true, then it wouldn't bother you at all. That's the way you should be with people who give you a difficult time.

Mikey's Note: The only problem with this quote is that some people may be tempted to pick up the wind up toy and chuck it against the wall! (LOL)

DU112 & 167 (Gary & Pursah)

How can a man like Hitler be innocent? That's a typical question, and the answer doesn't have anything to do with Hitler. The reason he, the Nazis, skinheads, and the KKK are all innocent has nothing to do with the level of form. Hitler, and everyone else in the world, including you, are equally innocent because *what you are seeing is not true*.[6] This is *your* dream. As the *Course* teaches, the dream is not being dreamed by somebody else.[7] How can what you're seeing be true if the separation from God never occurred? If the separation never occurred, then how can what you are seeing have any more of an affect on you than it had on J?

Mikey's Note: I just wanted to add this quote from the *Preface* of the *Course* where '…what you are seeing is not true' was taken from, followed by another quote from the *Course* about innocence:

'The world we see merely reflects our own internal frame of reference – the dominant ideas, wishes, and emotions in our minds. "Projection makes perception."[8] We look inside first, decide the kind of world we want to see, and then project that world outside, making it the truth *as we see it*. We make it true by our interpretations of what it is we are seeing. If we are using perception to justify our own mistakes – our anger, our impulses to attack, our lack of love in whatever form it may take – we will see a world of evil, destruction, malice, envy, and despair. All this we must learn to forgive, not because we are being "good" and "charitable," but because what we are seeing is not true. We have distorted the world by our twisted defenses, and are therefore seeing what is not there. As we learn to recognize our perceptual errors, we also learn to look past them or "forgive." At the same time we are forgiving ourselves, looking past our distorted self-concepts to the Self That God created in us and as us.'[9]

'Innocence is not a partial attribute. It is not real *until* it is total. The partly innocent are apt to be quite foolish at times. It is not until their innocence becomes a viewpoint with universal application that it becomes wisdom. Innocent or true perception means that you never misperceive and always see truly. More simply, it means that you never see what does not exist, and always see what does.'[10]

DU182 & 183 (Pursah)

The Holy Spirit's love says that bodies cannot keep you apart. Rejoin with yourself through forgiveness, that you and your brothers and sisters may be one and unlimited. Then, if you should choose to join with bodies on the level of form after that, you are simply doing what you're supposed to do – the same things you would have done anyway. Now you do them with forgiveness, and the Holy Spirit is with you.

Mikey's Note: The ironic thing about this spiritual path is that even though it is all about undoing the idea of separation in the mind and returning to Oneness, on the level of form, however, you may be guided to separate as you practice forgiveness; separate from your spouse, your job, your place of residence, your friends, or what have you. Once certain forgiveness lessons have been learned, sometimes you'll feel guided to move on, and there's certainly nothing wrong with that. You may very well find you have outgrown the need for particular relationships and circumstances in your life due to your practice of true forgiveness.

As J says in the *Course*, 'Forgiving dreams have little need to last. They are not made to separate the mind from what it thinks. They do not seek to prove the dream is being dreamed by someone else.'[11] That statement would apply to certain aspects of your dream as well. And as Gary's teachers state, 'If you want unity, it is to be found in the goal. The goal *is* the same.'[12]

DU397 & 398 (Pursah)

Always remember that your state of mind and the resulting goal you will achieve are in your own hands, because there are really only two things you can do – judge as an expression of fear, or forgive as an expression of love. One perception leads to the peace of God and the other perception leads to war. As the *Course* teaches, 'You see the flesh or recognize the spirit. There is no compromise between the two. If one is real the other must be false, for what is real denies its opposite. There is no choice in vision but this one.'[13]

Mikey's Note: Here is a good place to share this quote from the *Course,* 'You have no idea of the tremendous release and deep peace that comes from meeting yourself and your brothers totally without judgment. When you recognize what you are and what your brothers are, you will realize that judging them in any way is without meaning. In fact, their meaning is lost to you precisely *because* you are judging them.'[14]

DU349 (Pursah)

When you have a deep desire for anything then you must think you're a body, or separate from God in some way. What else could want something? If you're spirit, or joined with God, then you need nothing. If you remember that you're *not* a body then you can step back and see that what you desire is valueless. We're not talking about giving up everything physically; we're talking about the way you look at it.

YIR107 & DU295 (Arten)

J's real message is the *opposite* of making the body real. In fact, if you want to be like J, then you want to eventually experience that the body is meaningless. Instead of believing in the body, you want to get to the point where you *can't* believe it. It doesn't matter whether your body is healthy or not. *It's not you.* How can it matter unless it *is* you? Health and sickness are two sides of the same illusory coin. Neither one is true.

DU291 (Arten)

When you are apparently awake during the day and you have your eyes open, it's not really the body's eyes you are seeing with any more than when you're asleep at night dreaming. It's *always* your mind that is seeing. It's *always* your mind that is hearing and feeling and doing the other things you give the body's senses credit for. There is no exception to this. The body itself is just a part of your projection.

Mikey's Note: I remember having a dream while asleep in bed one night where a dog bit me on the ass – it hurt!

DU188 (Arten)

The only *real* freedom you have is to choose to return to God by listening to the Voice for Him, instead of continuing indefinitely within a fixed system that has nothing to do with Him. Your brain isn't hard wired to know God; your mind tells your brain what to do! Be glad the universe and your brain have nothing to do with God, and that there's a way to return to *His* Universe.

Mikey's Note: Since the last two quotes were about the eyes and the brain, I thought this would be a good place to share this idea from the *Course*:

'You do not think of light in terms of strength, and darkness in terms of weakness. That is because your idea of what seeing means is tied up with the body and its eyes and brain. Thus you believe that you can change what you see by putting little bits of glass before your eyes. This is among the many magical beliefs that come from the conviction you are a body, and the body's eyes can see.

You also believe the body's brain can think. If you but understood the nature of thought, you could but laugh at this insane idea. It is as if you thought you held the match that lights the sun and gives it all its warmth; or that you held the world within your hand, securely bound until you let it go. Yet this is no more foolish to believe the body's eyes can see; the brain can think.'[15]

DU217 (Arten)

When the *Course* says you cannot be hurt, it means that practicing the kind of forgiveness that knows you cannot really be hurt will eventually result in the same ability as J had, not to suffer or feel pain. How significant will your problems be then? As the *Course* says, 'The guiltless mind cannot suffer.'[16]

DU392 (Arten)

The body, the universe, and everything in it are just pictures in your mind, parts of a virtual reality game. Perhaps at times it's a rather convincing forgery of life but it's a fake. Don't look there for your salvation. Always look where the Answer *really* is – in the mind where the Holy Spirit abides – and you'll find it. Remember, we say God is, and then we cease to speak because there *is* nothing else.

YIR17 (Gary)

The key to enlightenment lies in a secret that very few people have ever known, but which J knew well. The way you will experience and feel about yourself is not determined by how other people look at and think about you. The way that you will experience and feel about yourself is actually determined by how *you* look at and think about *them*. Ultimately, this determines your identity. You will identify yourself either as a body or as perfect spirit, as either divided or whole, depending on how you see others. And once you understand that, I would think you'd want to get pretty damn careful how you think about other people!

Mikey's Note: Yes, definitely still working on this. We cannot hear these right-minded ideas too many times to remind us what this is all about. Projection sucks! Seeing only innocence is much more satisfying and rewarding. Projection may give one a state of instant gratification of feeling right, or better than, but that gratification doesn't last because the unconscious guilt associated with it remains in place.

DU376 & 377 (Arten)

Not only is it your task to forgive what you see on television or read on the Internet, but it is *especially* vital for you to forgive the bodies your eyes see as the relationships in your every day life. These people are there for a reason. As J says, 'Salvation does not ask that you behold the spirit and perceive the body not. It merely asks that this should be your choice. For you can see the body without help, but do not understand how to behold a world apart from it. It is your world salvation will undo, and let you see another world your eyes could never find.'[17] Or you can continue to worship your idols. But how wise would that be? As the *Course* also counsels you, 'Seek not outside yourself. For it will fail, and you will weep each time an idol falls. Heaven cannot be found where it is not, and there can be no peace excepting there.'[18]

YIR107 & 108 (Arten)

J says in the *Course* about the body, 'Why should the body be anything to you? Certainly what it is made of is not precious. And just as certainly it has no feeling. It transmits to you the feelings that you want. Like any communication medium, the body receives and sends the messages that it is given. It has no feeling for them. All of the feeling with which they are invested is given by the sender and the receiver. The ego and the Holy Spirit both recognize this, and both also recognize that here the sender and receiver are the same. The Holy Spirit tells you this with joy. The ego hides it, for it would keep you unaware of it. Who would send messages of hatred and attack if he but understood he sends them to himself? Who would accuse, make guilty, and condemn himself?'[19]

DU291 (Arten)

As you attain mastery, you really understand the whole idea of the world being *your* movie, and that what you're watching is *all* your projection; it's not coming from someone else's mind because there *is* only one mind. That's why all judgment is folly. Yes, the projection you call the universe is coming from a different, split-off *level* than the one you are currently experiencing. That's why it *seems* real if you let it *be* real. On this level, the body *appears* to be experiencing something outside itself, but what *appears* to be outside you is merely a *macro* view that is being projected by your own mind, and your experience of it here is merely a *micro* view that is being projected by your own mind! It's absolutely true to say that only your interpretation of it – your judgment or forgiveness – makes it real or unreal.

Mikey's Note: I just wanted to wrap up this chapter with three quotes from the *Course* in regards to the body:

'Child of God, you were created to create the good, the beautiful, and the holy. Do not forget this. The Love of God, for a little while, must still be expressed through one body to another, because vision is still so dim. You can use your body best to help you enlarge your perception so you can achieve real vision, of which the physical eye is incapable. Learning to do this is the body's only true usefulness.'[20]

'A world forgiven cannot last. It was the home of bodies. But forgiveness looks past bodies. This is its holiness; this is how it heals. The world of bodies is the world of sin, for only if there were a body is sin possible. From sin comes guilt as surely as forgiveness takes all guilt away. And once all guilt is gone, what more remains to keep a separated world in place? For place has gone as well, along with time. Only the body makes the world seem real, for being separate it could not remain where separation is impossible.'[21]

'God did not make the body, because it is destructible, and therefore not of the Kingdom. The body is the symbol of what you think you are. It is clearly a separation device, and therefore does not exist. The Holy Spirit, as always, takes what you have made and translates it into a learning device. Again as always, He reinterprets what the ego uses as an argument for separation into a demonstration against it. If the mind can heal the body, but the body cannot heal the mind, then the mind must be stronger than the body. Every miracle demonstrates this.'[22]

Chapter 16

The Illusory Nature of the Universe

**All your lifetimes have been just one big,
gigantic mind trip going nowhere.**[1]

DU13 (Arten)

This isn't about trying to save a world that isn't really out there. You save the world by concentrating on your *own* forgiveness lessons. If everybody concentrated on their own lessons instead of somebody else's, the collective, prodigal Son would be home in a New York minute.

DU110 (Arten)

One way the Holy Spirit will awaken you is to teach you that what you *think* is happening is *not* happening. Reality is invisible and *anything* that can be perceived or observed in *any* way, even measured scientifically, is an illusion – just the opposite of what the world thinks.

DU327 (Arten)

The ego's script is like a carrot and a stick. It tries to suck you into thinking you have freedom *within* the script, when the only real freedom you will ever find is completely outside the whole mess.

DU47 (Arten)

J had forgiven the world – his mind had been returned to the Holy Spirit where it belonged. That's where your mind belongs. You took it, and you have to give it back.[2] And I've got a message for you: You'll never really be happy until you do. No matter what you imagine you have accomplished in any lifetime, there will always be a part of you that feels like something is missing – because in your illusions something *is* missing.

DU107 (Arten)

When J told you to make the world meaningless to you, he was talking about giving up the *value* that you have given it, and accepting the Holy Spirit's meaning for it instead. For example, he says in the *Text*, 'To learn this course requires willingness to question every value that you hold.'[3]

Mikey's Note: I had mentioned earlier that I was already questioning every value that I had well before I knew anything about *A Course in Miracles* and before Gary was even a published author. However, I didn't realize that I didn't have to give these things up physically, only my psychological attachment to them, until I read Gary's books. That makes more sense.

DU215 (Pursah & Arten)

The Holy Spirit knows that with the exception of forgiveness, it doesn't matter what you do. The ego wants *what* you do to be important. As a way of intruding on your spirituality and delaying the truth, it tries to make what you do in the world important and special. Yet, to the Holy Spirit, what you do for Jesus or for God is not important. How can anything that occurs in an illusion be important if you actually understand it's not real? Only forgiveness and your healing matter. True, that kind of a teaching may not be the basis for a popular religion that takes over the world and tells everybody else how they should be living their lives – but it is definitely the truth.

Mikey's Note: Yes, it doesn't matter *what* you do in the world whether you're a peace activist, an environmental activist, a doctor, a lawyer, a janitor, an accountant, a politician, an organic farmer, a spiritual author, a brick layer, a minister, a nurse, a school teacher, a musician, a psychiatrist, a plumber, a cashier, a bookie, or a prostitute. They are equally unimportant because none of them are true. The only thing that matters is *where are you coming from* while you're doing it? Are you doing it with the Holy Spirit by your side, or the ego? Are you doing it with forgiveness? At the same time, keep in mind what I quoted Pursah as saying earlier, 'What you do is the result of what you think.'

YIR95 & DU 115 (Pursah & Gary)

No matter how much it looks like you're right, and on the level of form you may certainly be right, it won't bring you peace. It's all a set-up; it's a classic case of the ego laying its trap. And if you watch carefully, you can see that most of the judgments people have don't really make them happy anyway. In fact, the *Course* asks you at one point, 'Do you prefer that you be right or happy?'[4]

Mikey's Note: When I was sixteen, back in my days as a smart ass teenager, I was watching a television show, I think it was *Doogie Howser M.D.*, and the episode had to do with a man who couldn't decide if he should forgive his father or not for abandoning him when he was a little boy. He had to make a decision about whether or not to forgive his father and let him back into his life, or stay angry at him and *not* let him into his life. Well, he decided not to let him back into his life. I then said out loud, 'I probably wouldn't forgive him either.' And then my mom asked me, 'Would you rather be right, or would you rather be happy?' And my response was, 'Well, I'm happy when I'm right, damn it!' (LOL)

Another thing about being right is that it's so easy to want to be right because it can give you that sense of instant gratification, whereas forgiveness doesn't always do that. But with the practice of true forgiveness, if you don't experience gratification immediately you will eventually, in the form of just feeling very peaceful for no apparent reason. Whereas with being right, all you do is keep your unconscious guilt intact, and those situations that push your buttons and drives you to want to be right will continue to stay unhealed within your own unconscious mind.

DU104 (Arten)

The Bible *begins* by telling you, 'In the beginning, God created the heavens and the earth.' He didn't! If you're going to understand what J is telling you, then you cannot compromise on these words from the *Course,* 'The world you see is an illusion of a world. God did not create it, for what He creates must be eternal as Himself. Yet there is nothing in the world you see that will endure forever. Some things will last in time a little while longer than others. But the time will come when all things visible will have an end.'[5]

DU144 (Arten)

In order to really work with J or the Holy Spirit, you must be able to *observe* the ego's thought system in action – which is the same thought system you've subscribed to for eons without being aware of it. You have to be willing to *look* at it with the Holy Spirit or J as your teacher. As J puts it in the *Course*, 'No one can escape from illusions unless he looks at them, for not looking is the way they are protected.'[6]

Mikey's Note: Just like I started questioning every value that I held in my pre-*Course* days, I started looking at all my fears as well. I was tired of being in denial. It was time for me to *grow up* and 'be a man!' Forgiving illusions will put hair on your chest! Some of you ladies who may still be a little too serious, remember to take the previous sentence as metaphor. (LOL)

YIR43 (Arten)

As far as the idea of separation from God goes, because your idea is not of God, He does *not* respond to it. To respond to it would be to give it reality. If God himself were to acknowledge anything *except* the idea of perfect oneness, there would no longer *be* perfect oneness. There would no longer be a perfect state of Heaven for you to return *to*. You never really left anyway. You're still there, but you have entered into a nightmare state of illusion.

DU79 & 80 (Pursah)

The saying in the *Gospel of Thomas,* 'Be passersby,' is not to be applied at the level of the physical, it's about not being *mentally* attached to things. It has nothing to do with physically giving up anything. If you believe that you have to give something up, then you are making it just as real as if you covet it.

DU260 (Gary)

The simplicity of seeing the universe as a dream, and forgiving the images your body's eyes are apparently showing you, is well summed up in one of the *Workbook's* explanations of forgiveness, 'Forgiveness recognizes what you thought your brother did to you has not occurred. It does not pardon sins and make them real. It sees there was no sin. And in that view are all your sins forgiven.'[7]

Mikey's Note: Another related quote from the *Course,* 'No one forgives unless he has believed in sin, and still believes that he has much to be forgiven. Forgiveness thus becomes the means by which he learns he has done nothing to forgive. Forgiveness always rests upon the one who offers it, until he sees himself as needing it no more.'[8]

DU289 (Arten)

When it comes to what seems to be a terrible tragedy, it's *very* easy to get drawn into it. Yes, you have to forgive, but you also need to be aware of a couple of things in such a situation. First, choosing to recognize the unreality of the dream doesn't mean you shouldn't be sensitive to the needs and the feelings of people who are going through something such as the death of a loved one. You can't expect bereaved people to do anything except grieve. Always allow the feelings and beliefs of others. Second, it would be equally insipid to tell people at a time like that it's all a script they chose to experience. Let people learn the truth when they're pursuing the truth, not when they're grieving for their friends or relatives.

DU78 (Pursah)

What is in front of your face is illusion, and God's Kingdom – which appears to be hidden – will be revealed to those who learn from the Holy Spirit the unique way of forgiving whatever is in front of them the way J did. Eventually you will be one with him, and there will be nothing left but your true joy in the Kingdom of Heaven.

DU342 (Arten)

When J said, 'Renounce the world and the ways of the world; make them meaningless to you,' he meant that what you are seeing doesn't exist. It's nothing because it's not really there. How can nothing mean anything? If you make it mean something, good or bad, then you're trying to change nothing into something. The only thing you should make it is meaningless.

DU224 (Arten)

Most of the universe is dark, or hidden from you. Not only is it correlating to the unconscious, it's also set up that way so you can continue to make discoveries about it and look for answers in the universe instead of in the mind, where the answer *really* is.

YIR10 (Pursah)

It's only through disciplined application that the practitioner can enter the glorious phase of *experience*. And I guarantee you, dear brother, that experience is the only thing that will ever make you happy. Words will never do it; intellectual concepts, theology, philosophical speculation – forget it. As J says in the *Course*, '...words are but symbols of symbols. They are thus twice removed from reality.'[9] And when you think about it, how is a symbol of a symbol ever going to make you happy? No. The only thing that will make you happy is the experience of what you really are. What will truly satisfy you is *not* a symbol of reality, but an *experience* of reality.

YIR127 (Arten)

It's only after the ego is sufficiently undone that you can look back and see how crazy your ego thought system was. That's why J says this, 'You cannot evaluate an insane belief system from within it. Its range precludes this. You can only go beyond it, look back from a point where sanity exists and *see the contrast*. Only by this contrast can insanity be judged as insane.'[10]

YIR52 (Gary)

So it may look like all these things and people are out there, but they're not. They're not real people; it just looks that way. I made what I'm seeing, then I forgot. And I wanted it to be the way it is so what I secretly believed to be true about myself, what the *Course* calls 'the secret sins and hidden hates'[11] that I have buried in my mind about me over the original separation are now seen to be in others and in the world. And what holds the whole thing in place is my judgment and condemnation of others.

YIR44 (Arten)

The universe of time and space is meant to cover over the one and only problem, which is the seeming separation from God, and especially the one and only solution, which is to go home through forgiveness. As the *Course* says, and this is very important, 'A sense of separation from God is the only lack you really need correct.'[12] If that's the *only* lack, then all the others are simply symbolic of the first and only lack.

DU319 (Arten & Gary)

Once you really understand that the great projection of time and space is just like a movie, then the question becomes who are you going to watch the movie *with?* You can watch it with the ego and listen to its interpretation, or you can watch it with the Holy Spirit and listen to *Its* interpretation.

DU188 (Arten)

You think your universe is impressive because it's all you can remember. You think it's big, but it's not. What you've done is make yourself look and feel small, like one little piece of the puzzle. You're like a child with little toys you don't want to give up. Yet what you *really* are cannot even be contained by your universe.

DU249 & 250 (Pursah)

You've got to understand that if the *Course* is teaching there is no hierarchy of illusions, and if a miracle is a shift in perception where you switch over to the Holy Spirit's script, then one miracle is no less important than another. So, it's just as important to forgive a cold as it is to forgive a physical assault, and just as important to forgive a subtle insult as it is to forgive the death of a loved one. What is perceived as a tragedy can be forgiven just as quickly as you're willing to recognize that the separation from God never occurred, so it's only a dream and nobody's guilty – including you.

DU42 & 43 (Arten)

The universe doesn't really want to wake up. The universe wants candy to make it feel better, but the candy is designed to bind you to the universe.

DU392 (Pursah)

Remember what the *Course* says about your seeming life and death in this world, 'In any state apart from Heaven life is illusion. At best it seems like life; at worst, like death. Yet both are judgments on what is not life, equal in their inaccuracy and lack of meaning. Life not in Heaven is impossible, and what is not in Heaven is not anywhere.'[13]

DU81 (Pursah)

You dream of a desert, where mirages are your rulers and tormentors, yet these images come from you. Father did not make the desert, and your home is still with Him. To return, forgive your brother, for only then do you forgive yourself.

Mikey's Note: This quote here is Pursah quoting J from her lifetime as Thomas. According to Pursah, these were the three 'secret' sayings given to Thomas. Thomas was told not to repeat them for his own protection,[14] as to say in public at the time that God did not create the world could have been fatal.[15] And eventually it was.[16]

DU193 (Arten)

In the illusion there are beings who live on other planets, and some of them do visit Earth. And yes, they do have their own forgiveness lessons to learn. But they are not *really* out there, because the universe is in your mind. To believe that beings are necessarily more spiritually advanced than you just because they are more technically advanced would not always be true. What is important is that whether they are compassionate or not.

YIR51 (Arten & Gary)

There isn't *really* anything out there, but it looks that way. It's an optical illusion. As the *Course* says, 'Projection makes perception. The world you see is what you gave it, nothing more than that. But though it is no more than that, it is not less. Therefore, to you it is important. It is the witness to your state of mind, the outside picture of an inward condition.'[17] So, it may *look* like you've escaped from those things by projecting them outside of you, but it's just an illusion, and they're still in your mind. It just doesn't seem that way because it's been denied and you're oblivious to it. So it looks like it's outside of you, and you've forgotten that when you joined with the ego, you made it. You *made* what you are seeing.

DU213 & 214 (Pursah)

If the *Course* is saying there is no world, then there are not really any people out there who are smarter or more gifted than you. There are not really any people out there who are richer than you, or any who are more famous than you, or getting more sex than you, or doing whatever is necessary to make you feel angry, inferior, or guilty. There's not really anyone coming after you for whatever reason. There are no problems or threats that can harm what you really are in any way. It's only a dream, and it's actually possible for you to have the kind of peace of mind and lack of fear that would accompany the conviction of that truth.

As J asks you so pointedly in the *Text*, 'What if you recognized this world is an hallucination? What if you really understood you made it up? What if you realized that those who seem to walk about in it, to sin and die, attack and murder and destroy themselves, are wholly unreal?'[18]

Mikey's Note: J goes on to say in that same section of the *Course*, 'Hallucinations disappear when they are recognized for what they are. This is the healing and the remedy. Believe them not and they are gone. And all you need to do is recognize that *you* did this. Once you accept this simple fact and take unto yourself the power you gave them, you are released from them. One thing is sure; hallucinations serve a purpose, and when that purpose is no longer held they disappear. Therefore, the question never is whether you want them, but always, do you want the purpose that they serve?'[19]

DU395 (Gary)

No matter what appears to happen, always remember that this world isn't God's world, and no one in their right mind would come here – except to teach others how to leave. But you *can* have a happy dream of forgiveness here; the dream that leads to the real world.

Mikey's Note: I just want to close out this chapter with a quote from the *Course*, 'Life has no opposite, for it is God. Life and death seem to be opposites because you have decided death ends life. Forgive the world, and you will understand that everything that God created cannot have an end, and nothing He did not create is real. In this one sentence is our course explained. In this one sentence is our practicing given its one direction. And in this one sentence is the Holy Spirit's whole curriculum specified exactly as it is.'[20]

Chapter 17

Spiritual Healing

**Every single disease you know of, and each one
to come, is made by the mind.[1]**

DU301 & 302 (Pursah)

Every location of time and space that you behold is projected by the mind that is outside of time and space. It's possible to get in touch with that mind. The best way to do it is to eliminate the barriers that block your awareness. All aspects of healing contribute to removing those barriers.

DU302 (Arten & Gary)

Here is the number one rule of all time when it comes to spiritual healing: *It's not about the patient.* All healing is a result of some kind of forgiveness, and all forgiveness leads to self-healing. So even when it comes to healing the sick it's really about forgiving your own dream, and forgiving yourself for dreaming it.

Mikey's Note: As J says in the *Manual For Teachers*, 'To forgive is to heal.'[2] And early in the *Text*, 'Miracles enable you to heal the sick and raise the dead because you made sickness and death yourself, and can therefore abolish both.'[3]

Also, this reminds me of a quote from the *Course* about true empathy, 'To empathize does not mean to join in suffering, for that is what you must *refuse* to understand. That is the ego's interpretation of empathy, and is always used to form a special relationship in which the suffering is shared. The capacity to empathize is very useful to the Holy Spirit, provided you let Him use it in His way. His way is very different. He does not understand suffering, and would have you teach it is not understandable. When He relates through you, He does not relate through your ego to another ego. He does not join in pain, understanding that healing pain is not accomplished by delusional attempts to enter into it, and lighten it by sharing the delusion.'[4]

DU305 (Pursah)

Here is the second biggest rule of all time when it comes to spiritual healing: *Pain is not a physical process; it is a mental process.* Healing requires a shift in perception, and as the *Course* asks and answers for you, 'What is the single requisite for this shift in perception? It is simply this; the recognition that sickness is of the mind, and has nothing to do with the body. What does this recognition "cost?" It costs the whole world you see, for the world will never again appear to rule the mind. For with this recognition is responsibility placed where it belongs; not with the world, but on him who looks on the world and sees it as it is not.'[5]

Mikey's Note: In the past, when I would bang my elbow or knee against something, very often, and just as my mom does, I would shout out in semi-anger, 'asshole!' Now, most of the time I can stop myself from saying 'asshole' when that happens, and remember the pain is in my mind and not in my elbow or knee. The pain seems to subside much quicker, although it feels like I'm making that up. But then again, that's the whole point!

DU263 & 310 (Pursah)

Now here's the third biggest all-time, perhaps hard to believe yet absolutely true rule, when it comes to spiritual healing: *Ultimately, the universe itself is a symptom that will disappear.* When you really wake up, what appeared to be real before is now *recognized* as the idle dream that it is. Then it is forgotten, or at least rendered meaningless. Your present lifetime and all of the others will disappear, and when everyone reaches the same state of enlightenment, the universe will disappear – leaving only God's universe of Heaven.

Mikey's Note: To borrow a line from the movie *The Shawshank Redemption*, the universe will 'vanish like a fart in the wind.' The universe will disappear because there will be no need for it any longer. Once there is no need to project unconscious guilt, there will be no need for a universe of time and space. The universe of time and space exists in its unreality as a hiding spot from our unconscious guilt; it's a symptom of separation from God and the *projection* of unconscious guilt.

We created this universe, or better yet, mis-created it. God certainly did not create this mess, nor has anything to do with it, no matter how beautiful it may seem at times. So our guilt can now be seen as being outside of ourselves, rather than within, and we go on to judge and condemn others. But when we judge and condemn others, what we are really doing is judging and condemning ourselves, as the 'others' we perceive as being out there are really just symbols of what's in our own unconscious minds. But once we stop reacting with condemnation, and start forgiving and seeing everyone as totally innocent, which in reality we all are, then all of the guilt will eventually be removed, and we will then simply return our awareness to our natural and original condition of being one with God.

As J puts it in the *Course*, 'The world is false perception. It is born of error, and it has not left its source. It will remain no longer than the thought that gave it birth is cherished. When the thought of separation has been changed to one of true forgiveness, will the world be seen in quite another light; and one which leads to truth, where all the world must disappear and all its errors vanish. Now its source has gone, and its effects are gone as well.'[6]

DU308 & 309 (Arten)

These four statements from the *Course* are like cornerstones of J's entire attitude about healing:

1 - 'Only salvation can be said to cure.'[7]

2 - 'Atonement does not heal the sick, for that is not a cure. It takes away the guilt that makes the sickness possible. And that is cure indeed.'[8]

3 - 'Being sane, the mind heals the body because *it* has been healed. The sane mind cannot conceive of illness because it cannot conceive of attacking anyone or anything.'[9]

4 - 'The ego believes that by punishing itself it will mitigate the punishment of God. Yet even in this it is arrogant. It attributes to God a punishing intent, and then takes this intent as its own prerogative.'[10]

DU304 (Arten)

When it comes to healing, sooner or later, it always comes down to some kind of forgiveness and how willing you are to do it. How willing are you to accept that it's all *your* dream? How willing are you to release your dream and choose God? You know, J plays a little trick on you in the *Course*. Most of the time he says it takes a little willingness. But that's not for advanced students. In the *Manual for Teachers*, he says it takes a*bundant* willingness.[11]

Mikey's Note: Yes, J uses 'the little willingness' most of the time in the *Course* to encourage you in the beginning. But it'll only get you so far. You got to really want this! You have to be willing to do whatever it takes to achieve the goal of the *Course*, and that *doing* would be to open up 'a can of whoop ass' on the ego by forgiving the *hell* out of everything!

YIR55 (Pursah)

You perceive yourself as being in a body, and then the body tells you what to feel. But you should be the one who tells the body what to feel. You are not in the body; the body is in your mind. When you put the mind in its proper perspective, then you're taking charge of the cause instead of being at the mercy of the effect. Then you can choose the Holy Spirit and His answer instead of the ego's questions. Thus will you be returned to wholeness. Because of that, how you experience things will change on this level, and the Holy Spirit will take care of the job on the larger, metaphysical scale.

DU310 (Pursah)

Never forget, *all* healing is spiritual, not physical. *A Course in Miracles* is always done at the level of the mind, with some form of forgiveness always being the Holy Spirit's tool. What you do is think right-minded thoughts with the patient or even yourself, if you're the one who's hurting, and sometimes the symptoms will disappear. You can get better and better at making pain disappear.

DU292 (Arten)

Whatever appears to be causing your pain, whether it's a circumstance or a relationship or both, may or may *not* disappear when you practice forgiveness. The ego's script doesn't always appear to change when you want it to. But it *is* possible to end all the suffering that's called for by the ego's script and have peace instead of fear. *That's* the Holy Spirit's script.

DU391 (Pursah)

There are people who have all the physical reasons to have heart disease and Alzheimer's disease, whose arteries are all clogged up or have unlucky family history, yet they show no symptoms of the diseases whatsoever. It's always the mind that decides whether or not to get sick – and whether or not to get well.

DU301 (Pursah)

Sickness isn't personal. Sickness is not made by you at *this* level. That's just another reason why no one should feel bad about it if they get sick. You don't choose cancer on this level any more than a baby chose to be deformed on this level. Illness was made by your mind at a larger level, and is being acted out here in a predetermined way. You *can* get in touch with your power to choose and thus have an enormous influence on whether or not you feel pain, and sometimes lessen or eliminate your physical symptoms.

DU303 (Gary & Arten)

You should see another person's illness as your own call for help. You have a chance to be healed in your mind by forgiving that person. It may *seem* selfish to use another person's difficulties as your way to get home, but it's actually selfless. Ultimately, forgiveness is saying that *neither* you nor the person who appears to be sick really exists separately from God. Thus are you *both* free. Furthermore, it's the *only* way for *you* to be free! It's all right to want freedom, and the way out is to see both of you as guiltless.

DU111 (Arten)

The time will eventually come when you will never suffer. That is one of the long-term payoffs of this spiritual path. Even while you still appear to be in your body, it's possible for you to attain psychological invulnerability. As the *Course* says, 'The guiltless mind cannot suffer.'[12] But it takes the illusion of time for you to learn your forgiveness lessons and get to your goal.

YIR85 (Arten)

If you're sick and your symptoms change through choosing forgiveness, then consider that to be a fringe benefit. That's not what the *Course* is about though. The real goal is Heaven, but the short term goal is peace, and the end of all pain and suffering. It's absolutely within your means to learn to end all pain and suffering, despite anything that appears to be happening in the world and regardless of what your symptoms appear to be. That's the Holy Spirit's answer to the ego's script of guilt, pain, suffering, and death.

DU291 & 292 (Arten)

As you become accomplished in the application of forgiveness, your pain and your discomfort will lessen and sometimes disappear. Notice I didn't say that the *apparent* cause of the pain and discomfort would disappear. It would be theoretically possible for a master to die of cancer, or be murdered like J, and not feel the pain associated with such events. If your pain is gone, and your suffering along with it, then does it really matter if the illusory cause of the pain still *appears* to be there?

YIR117 (Pursah)

The more you forgive, the less you're taken in by the ego's tricks. As J says late in the *Course* about God's teachers, 'Awareness of dreaming is the real function of God's teachers. They watch the dream figures come and go, shift and change, suffer and die. Yet they are not deceived by what they see. They recognize that to behold a dream figure as sick and separate is no more real than to regard it as healthy and beautiful.'[13] So bodies, sick or healthy, are really all the same, because none of them are true.

Mikey's Note: I just want to close this chapter with a quote from the *Course* on sickness and healing, followed by my summary and example.

'The acceptance of sickness as a decision of the mind, for a purpose for which it would use the body, is the basis of healing. And this is so for healing in all forms. A patient decides that this is so, and he recovers. If he decides against recovery, he will not be healed. Who is the physician? Only the mind of the patient himself. The outcome is what he decides that it is. Special agents seem to be ministering to him, yet they but give form to his own choice. He chooses them in order to bring tangible form to his desires. And it is this they do, and nothing else. They are not actually needed at all. The patient could merely rise up without their aid and say, "I have no use for this." There is no form of sickness that would not be cured at once.'[14]

So, most folks couldn't handle a spontaneous healing without freaking out, so we need these 'special agents' to support our decision to get well, whether it be medicine, herbs, a change in diet, more exercise, a chiropractor, acupuncture treatment, fasting, or whatever other healing modality that is acceptable to your mind; one that you can accept without fear in order to make you feel better.

For example, maybe you're always feeling sluggish, lazy, and out of shape, and you live a very sedentary lifestyle, spending a lot of time on the computer or eating donuts and ice cream all day in front of the television. Now, it could be theoretically possible to end the sluggish and uncomfortable feelings associated with this passive lifestyle just by practicing forgiveness. But for those whose minds that this approach would be acceptable to, I'm quite certain are very few and far between, so I don't recommend that. Being a person whose priority in my adult life has been eating organic and natural foods, it certainly wouldn't be acceptable to *my* mind I can tell you *that!*

So, to bring tangible form to the healing of this circumstance, perhaps you decide to go walk or run every day, or start going to the gym, and perhaps start eating less junk food and more fruits and vegetables. Gary would call this 'throwing the ego a bone.'[15] What matters is that you forgive, because if you just administered the 'special agents' without the forgiveness process, then they won't work, or at least not in a permanent way. Or you may very well find yourself reverting back to your old habits because the unconscious guilt associated with this particular aspect of your mind that's driving you to indulge in your bad habits has not been healed. The application of true forgiveness is the only way to heal pain and suffering of any kind in a permanent way.

Chapter 18

It's About Time

Time heals not all wounds, but forgiveness will heal all time.[1]

DU103 (Arten)

The *Course* says that the miracle can progress you much farther and faster along your spiritual path than would have otherwise been possible. For example, the *Text* says, 'The miracle is the only device at your immediate disposal for controlling time.'[2] And, 'The miracle substitutes for learning that might have taken thousands of years.'[3]

YIR84 & 85 (Arten)

The only real power you have here is the power to choose between the ego and the Holy Spirit. In the process, if you happen to change dimensions of time through the Holy Spirit's collapsing of time and thus have a different scenario play itself out within the fixed script, then you should consider that to be a fringe benefit. That's not what the *Course* is about though. The real goal is Heaven, but the short term goal is peace, and the end of all pain and suffering. As for the collapsing of time, remember that only the Holy Spirit knows what's best for everyone. Put Him in charge of time and space. Put the one in charge who knows everything.

DU248 & 249 (Pursah)

The *Course* turns you on to the fact that this is only a dream, and asks, 'Yet where are dreams but in a mind asleep? And can a dream succeed in making real the picture it projects outside itself? Save time, my brother; learn what time is for.'[4] The purpose of time is to forgive. That is the only viable answer to life. Act accordingly, child of God.

DU192 (Arten)

If you choose forgiveness instead of the ego, then J has made the following promise to you, 'When you perform a miracle, I will arrange both time and space to adjust to it.'[5] He's not talking about changing time here, so much as taking out the parts you don't need in your future anymore, because you've already learned those particular forgiveness lessons. He says, 'The miracle shortens time by collapsing it, thus eliminating certain intervals within it.'[6]

DU327 (Arten & Pursah)

The Holy Spirit's script is the forgiveness of all the people in your life – no matter where you appear to be. That's how time disappears. One of the best ways to get the distinction between the ego's time and the Holy Spirit's timelessness is to remember that the Holy Spirit's lessons of true forgiveness lead to the *undoing* of time by rendering it unnecessary. This undoing is accomplished at the level of the mind – outside of time – and instead of changing time, collapses it.

DU390 & YIR109 (Gary & Arten)

The real world is what you'll see – not with your body's eyes but with your attitude – when you've completely forgiven the world so you're no longer projecting any unconscious guilt onto it. That would also have to mean that *you're* completely forgiven, and that perception and time are coming to an end for you. As the *Course* puts it, 'The real world is the symbol that the dream of sin and guilt is over, and God's Son no longer sleeps. His waking eyes perceive the sure reflection of his Father's Love; the certain promise that he is redeemed. The real world signifies the end of time, for its perception makes time purposeless.'[7]

DU331 (Arten)

Don't take the tricks of time seriously. What you think of as the past is an illusory happening that is taking place right *now*. The future is happening right *now,* but your mind has divided these images up to make them look like time. Yet the whole thing happened all at once and is already over. The *Course* asks you to relinquish your judgment. 'And where is time, when dreams of judgment have been put away?'[8]

DU230 & YIR133 & 134 (Pursah)

When you forgive in one lifetime, you help the Holy Spirit heal all of them. Practicing true forgiveness has an effect on you in other dimensions of time. You can choose to forgive anything in *any* lifetime because time isn't linear, but holographic. For that reason, there's *no* difference between choosing the Holy Spirit right now and choosing the Holy Spirit at the exact instant of the separation! People don't realize that history is happening right now, and so is the future, and the *only* thing that matters is choosing forgiveness now. Don't be concerned about your past lifetimes. It's *always* about now, and it's *always* about forgiveness. It's this lifetime that matters, always, and then you learn that every instant is really always the same instant anyway.

DU323 (Pursah)

No matter how many dimensions of time there are, or alternate universes with their own dimensions, there is still that same simplicity that you can never really escape: Your salvation always comes down to a decision you are making right *now*. There's no getting away from that. No matter what appears to be going on for you, the choice is really very simple and immediate. Whenever you remember that, you'll know which interpretation of the dream you should listen to.

DU271 (Arten)

Once you attain your enlightenment and lay your body aside, then you're awake and *outside* the dream – which means that you're actually outside time and space. While it may appear to others that many, many years are passing, for *you* the end of time has already occurred, and the 'waiting' for when everybody 'else' is enlightened is only an instant.

DU330 (Arten)

To sum up our discussion on the topic of time, the *Course* teaches you, 'Time and eternity are both in your mind, and will conflict until you perceive time solely as a means to regain eternity. You cannot do this as long as you believe that anything happening to you is caused by factors outside yourself. You must learn that time is solely at your disposal, and that nothing in the world can take this responsibility from you.'[9]

Chapter 19

The Tools

There is a way in which escape is possible. It can be learned and taught, but it requires patience and abundant willingness.[1]

Here are four tools designed to help undo the idea of separation from God, while helping you to not take the University of Hell, aka 'Psycho Planet,'[2] so damn seriously. These tools will help you to awaken from where you *think* you are, while helping you to remember *where* you really are, and *what* you really are. And remember, this spiritual path is all about taking full responsibility for your dream and never being a victim of it. Utilizing these tools will empower you to do just that.

Tool #1 Putting the Holy Spirit or J in charge

<u>YIR76 (Pursah & Gary)</u>

This section from early in the *Course* invites the Holy Spirit to be in charge and it works very well:

You can do much on behalf of your own healing and that of others if, in a situation calling for help, you think of it this way:

I am here only to be truly helpful.

I am here to represent Him Who sent me.

I do not have to worry about what to say or what to do, because He Who sent me will direct me.

I am content to be wherever he wishes, knowing He goes there with me.

I will be healed as I let Him teach me to heal.[3]

Mikey's Note: I find this particular tool helpful when I find myself in a situation where I feel a bit awkward and/or shy and have no idea as to what to say or do – usually when I find myself around non-*Course* people. (LOL) It helps to relax me, as well as prevents me from saying something stupid – when I remember to use it, that is! I've always been more of an introvert and a private person, and I suck at small talk, so making conversation with 'regular' people is not always an easy thing for me. However, for some strange reason, I really do like talking about the weather.

Another thing I find useful from the *Course,* if you are in need of some guidance as to what to say or do about a particular situation, try this:

> *What would You have me do?*
> *Where would You have me go?*
> *What would You have me say, and to whom?*[4]

And here is another piece from the *Course* that may be helpful to you for bringing in the Holy Spirit:

I loose the world from all I thought it was.

I who remain as God created me would loose the world from all I thought it was. For I am real because the world is not, and I would know my own reality.[5]

Tool #2 True Prayer

YIR26 & DU351 (Pursah)

The best form of meditation is the one described in *The Song of Prayer.* That kind of meditation actually reflects the original form of prayer, which was silent and really about joining with God. By putting God first, and acknowledging Him as your one true Source, it not only helps to undo the separation in your mind, but can also result in the aftereffect of inspiration.

'The secret of true prayer is to forget the things you think you need. To ask for the specific, is much the same as to look on sin and then forgive it. Also in the same way, in prayer you overlook your specific needs as you see them, and let them go into God's Hands. There they become your gifts to Him, for they tell Him that you would have no gods before Him; no Love but His.'[6]

'The form of the answer, if given by God, will suit your need as you see it. This is merely an echo of the reply of His Voice. The real sound is always a song of thanksgiving and of Love. You cannot, then, ask for the echo. It is the song that is the gift. Along with it come the overtones, the harmonics, the echoes, but these are secondary. In true prayer you hear only the song. All the rest is merely added. You have sought first the Kingdom of Heaven, and all else has indeed been given you.'[7]

As one example, when you meditate, you might visualize yourself taking J's or the Holy Spirit's hand and going to God. Then you might think of yourself as laying your problems and goals and idols on the altar before Him as gifts. Maybe you'll tell God how much you love Him and how grateful you are to be completely taken care of by Him – forever safe and totally provided for. Then you become *silent*. You have the attitude that God created you to be just like Him and to be with Him forever. Now you can let go of everything, join with God's Love, and lose yourself in joyful Communion with Him.

That's the key: joining with God in love and gratitude. You forget everything else and get lost in His Love. *That's* what it is to be filled with the spirit. That's the *Song of Prayer*. The echo is a fringe benefit, but that's not the purpose of the prayer. It just happens naturally when you join with God and love Him.

Mikey's Note: Here is a section from the *Course* that may be helpful to use as a preamble to the *True Prayer* meditation. That is followed by another section from the *Text* called *The Forgotten Song*, which may be helpful to use as a visualization during your meditation as a way of undoing the unconscious fear of God we all have, and making God more approachable:

A Course in Miracles version of The Lord's Prayer:

Forgive us our illusions, Father, and help us to accept our true relationship with You, in which there are no illusions, and where none can ever enter. Our holiness is Yours. What can there be in us that needs forgiveness when Yours is perfect? The sleep of forgetfulness is only the unwillingness to remember Your forgiveness and Your Love. Let us not wander into temptation, for the temptation of the Son of God is not Your Will. And let us receive only what You have given, and accept but this into the minds which You created and which You love. Amen.[8]

The Forgotten Song

'Beyond the body, beyond the sun and stars, past everything you see and yet somehow familiar, is an arc of golden light that stretches as you look into a great and shining circle. And all the circle fills with light before your eyes. The edges of the circle disappear, and what is in it is no longer contained at all. The light expands and covers everything, extending to infinity forever shining and with no break or limit anywhere. Within it everything is joined in perfect continuity. Nor is it possible to imagine that anything could be outside, for there is nowhere that this light is not. This is the vision of the Son of God, whom you know well. Here is the sight of him who knows his Father. Here is the memory of what you are; a part of this, with all of it within, and joined to all as surely as all is joined in you.'[9]

DU349, 350, 352, & 353 (Pursah & Arten)

If you need something – and you would have to lack it to need it – then you can remember that it's just a substitute for God, and that a sense of separation from Him is the only real problem. If you need something then you're coming from weakness, but if you need nothing then you can come from the strength of Christ. When you are coming from a position of strength rather than weakness, you may find yourself being more patient and relaxed in your endeavors, and thus more effective. By emptying your mind of your perceived desires when you go to God, you can experience His Love. Upon returning to the world where you *think* you are, you can remember more regularly where you *really* are – with God. At times you will see, very naturally and very clearly, what you should do in this world to solve your problems – or if you are faced with an important decision, exactly what that decision should be. The most striking evidence of this approach's validity will be that it works.

Mikey's Note: Speaking of song, I know for me when I'm out doing my daily walk with my iPod in tow, I can sometimes get lost in this peaceful, joyful state where at the moment I don't need anything else, I'm just so into the music. It doesn't happen all the time, but most of the time it does, and to me that's another form of true prayer. In that moment, I get so lost in the music that I'm not thinking about what's missing, because at that moment nothing *is* missing – I feel totally joined in Spirit. And as a result of that, sometimes I'll receive an inspired idea.

I have to tell you that I struggle to do the *True Prayer* meditation without my mind wandering, so doing my walk, coupled with some loud rock n roll, works just as well. Of course, for somebody else, it could be singing, painting, knitting, playing a musical instrument, or some other activity where you get so lost in it that you don't think about what you feel is missing – you're just 'in the zone!' Anyway, as far as I'm concerned, rock n roll is the *one* thing that the ego got right!

YIR26 (Pursah)

Remember something, though: There is no substitute for practicing forgiveness, and that's the spiritual 'life in the fast lane' that our brother J was teaching by both word and example 2,000 years ago.

Tool #3 True Forgiveness

Yes, I have to totally agree with Arten and Pursah, that from my experience, there is no substitute for the practice of true forgiveness. Of course, what is there that Arten and Pursah have to say that I *don't* agree with? For those who may be still lacking faith in the validity of true forgiveness, keep working at it, I assure you that it does work.

DU256 (Pursah)

In this forgiveness thought process, the words *you* and *you're* can apply to any person, situation or event. It's all right to improvise while maintaining the basic ideas. Also, please note that the Holy Spirit will remember to remove the unconscious guilt from your mind and perform His healing of the universe when you forgive, regardless of whether you remember to ask Him. That's His job and He's pretty good at it. You have to remember to do *your* job – if not immediately, then later on. If you completely forget, then you can be confident that the ego's script will eventually provide you with a similar opportunity that will do just as well.

True Forgiveness: A thought process example

You're not really there. If I think you are guilty or the cause of the problem, and if I made you up, then the imagined guilt and fear must be in me. Since the separation from God never occurred, I forgive 'both' of us for what we haven't really done. Now there is only innocence, and I join with the Holy Spirit in peace.

Mikey's Note: Here are couple of other forgiveness thought processes from the *Course* that may be helpful to you in facilitating your forgiveness practice, while helping you to remember to take full responsibility for your dream. That is followed by a couple of forgiveness thought process from Arten and Pursah.

A Course in Miracles Forgiveness thought process #1

This is the only thing that you need do for vision, happiness, release from pain and the complete escape from sin, all to be given you. Say only this, but mean it with no reservations, for here the power of salvation lies:

I am responsible for what I see.

I choose the feelings I experience, and I decide

upon the goal I would achieve.

And everything that seems to happen to me

I ask for, and receive as I have asked.

Deceive yourself no longer that you are helpless in the face of what is done to you. Acknowledge but that you have been mistaken, and all effects of your mistakes will disappear.[10]

A Course in Miracles Forgiveness thought process #2

Say this to yourself as sincerely as you can, remembering that the Holy Spirit will respond fully to your slightest invitation:

I must have decided wrongly, because I am not at peace.

I made the decision myself, but I can also decide otherwise.

I want to decide otherwise, because I want to be at peace.

I do not feel guilty, because the Holy Spirit will undo all the consequences of my wrong decision if I will let Him.

I choose to let Him, by allowing Him to decide for God for me.[11]

YIR78 (Arten)

People typically have a tendency to project their unconscious guilt onto other people and make them wrong. But everybody has times when they blame themselves. This is for those times. When you're beating yourself up, remember this forgiveness thought process:

I am immortal spirit.

This body is just an image.

It has nothing to do with what I am.

YIR80, 81, & DU307 (Arten)

This is how you should always think of another person. Say it in your mind to others when it's appropriate. Obviously there will be times when you're carrying on a conversation with someone. Don't stop and think of this and then say it to them in your mind. Carry on a normal conversation. Always be appropriate. Don't be weird. When you don't have to talk, and you have a chance to send these words in your mind to another mind, think of the following:

You are Spirit.
Whole and innocent.
All is forgiven and released.

Remember, the words aren't important; it's the attitude. I used to think as I looked at a patient, 'You are Christ, pure and innocent. We are forgiven now.' You'll think whatever feels right for you after you ask the Holy Spirit for guidance. Saying those words in your mind to another is a way to have it be true about yourself in your own unconscious mind, and it allows the Holy Spirit to heal and release the unconscious guilt that binds you to the universe of form. The secret of reawakening to your immortality is in mastering not the *things* of this world, but the way you *look at* this world.

Mikey's Note: Here is a good place to insert these quotes from the *Course:*

'When you meet anyone, remember it is a holy encounter. As you see him you will see yourself. As you treat him you will treat yourself. As you think of him you will think of yourself. Never forget this, for in him you will find yourself or lose yourself.'[12]

'Forgiveness is the means by which we will remember God. Through forgiveness the thinking of the world is reversed. The forgiven world becomes the gate of Heaven, because by its mercy we can at last forgive ourselves. Holding no one prisoner to guilt, we become free. Acknowledging Christ in all our brothers, we recognize His Presence in ourselves.'[13]

'All that must be forgiven are the illusions you have held against your brothers. Their reality has no past, and only illusions can be forgiven. God holds nothing against anyone, for He is incapable of illusions of any kind. Release your brothers from the slavery of their illusions by forgiving them for the illusions you perceive in them. Thus will you learn that you have been forgiven.'[14]

DU240 (Pursah)

This is the way to remember God, a companion to the *Course's* formula of forgiveness, 'You are not trapped in the world you see because its cause can be changed. This change requires, first, that the cause be identified, and then let go, so that it can be replaced. The first two steps in this process require your cooperation. The final one does not. Your images have already been replaced. By taking the first two steps, you will see that this is so.'[15]

The Holy Spirit's part (the final step) is not your responsibility. That's why we say you have to *trust* Him. Still, it's helpful to think of yourself as choosing His strength, because ultimately you are exactly the same as Him and Christ. Through true forgiveness, you are becoming aware that you are the same as J and the Holy Spirit – One with God and Christ.

DU237 & 238 (Pursah)

Your job is to forgive, not to beg for the agreement of those seemingly separated minds you are forgiving. As another way of looking at this component of forgiveness, remember this paragraph from the *Workbook*, 'There is a very simple way to find the door to true forgiveness, and perceive it open wide and welcome. When you feel that you are tempted to accuse someone of sin in any form, do not allow your mind to dwell on what you think he did, for that is self-deception. Ask instead, "Would I accuse myself of doing this?" Thus you will see alternatives for choice in terms that render choosing meaningful, and keep your mind as free of guilt and pain as God himself intended it to be, and as it is in truth.'[16]

Mikey's Note: Just so this is clear, there is a *world* of difference between blaming and accusing yourself, and taking responsibility for your experiences. If you accuse yourself, then you would just be projecting blame/guilt onto *your* own body and making yourself guilty. There's really no difference between blaming or accusing yourself and blaming or accusing someone else – they're both projections of your unconscious guilt; it doesn't matter who the 'projectee' is.[17] By taking full responsibility for your experience by seeing a particular situation with the Holy Spirit, instead of playing the ego's game of placing guilt onto yourself or someone else, then that is *true* forgiveness, which *will* undo the unconscious guilt in the mind.

YIR43 & 44 (Pursah)

Sometimes after you forgive, you may feel you are being guided in some way by the Holy Spirit as to what you should do or not do. That's inspiration, which comes as an aftereffect of forgiveness in much the same way as it comes as an aftereffect of true prayer.

DU232 & 233 (Pursah)

Forgiveness is an attitude. Everything you learn becomes incorporated into that attitude until forgiveness happens automatically. For most people, especially during the first few years, forgiveness requires that you think about it. You become a master by having *forgiving thought processes*. These right-minded thoughts eventually dominate your mind instead of the ego. Using your understanding of the *Course's* entire thought system contributes to and strengthens your attitude of forgiveness.

DU256 (Pursah)

Remember that it helps to be on the lookout for the ego's surprises. It takes a sharp mind if you're going to do what the *Course* says and be vigilant only for God and his Kingdom.[18] As the *Course* informs you, 'Miracles arise from a miraculous state of mind, or a state of miracle-readiness.'[19]

YIR53 & 54 (Arten)

We've never said that true forgiveness is easy. But the truth *is* simple. It's what the ego made that's complicated. And that's what needs to be undone by your forgiveness. The more the ego is undone, the easier it will get for you.

Mikey's Note: How I see it, Gary's books are for those who can handle simple, whereas the *Course* is those for who aren't ready for simple, and need it complicated. Now, that's certainly not a putdown. I once complicated the hell out of my spirituality too. But I didn't know any better until I read *The Disappearance of the Universe* for the first time – I was finally ready for simple! All the answers are right in there as clear as can be. Anyway, as I quoted J earlier, 'Simplicity is very difficult for twisted minds.'[20] Glad my mind isn't as twisted as it used to be!

Here is a little passage from *The Song of Prayer* to wrap up this section on *true* forgiveness:

'As prayer is always for yourself, so is forgiveness always given you. It is impossible to forgive another, for it is only your sins you see in him. You want to see them there, and not in you. That is why forgiveness of another is an illusion. Yet it is the only happy dream in all the world; the only one that does not lead to death. Only in someone else can you forgive yourself, for you have called him guilty of your sins, and in him must your innocence now be found. Who but the sinful need to be forgiven? And do not ever think you can see sin in anyone except yourself.'[21]

Tool #4 Laughing

The movie *Patch Adams* starring Robin Williams is a great demonstration on the power of laughter. If we take everything so seriously all the time, then we're making this illusion of time and space psychologically real for ourselves. There's like this endless list of things that people take so personally and that society takes so seriously – this is all *so* unnecessary!

Of course, I'm not suggesting we go about living our daily lives in an irresponsible and insensitive fashion, but rather change the way we look at everything. I mean, we all need to freakin' lighten up. Even if you're not a *Course* student and have no intention of being one, it's just a much more freeing, healthier, less stressful way of being. There's really no need to take ourselves, and the world we appear to live in, so seriously – so cheer up and laugh, *damn it!*

DU348 & YIR13 (Pursah)

One of the Holy Spirit's finest tools is laughter, my brother. If you take the world too seriously, it will take you. It's important to remember to laugh. Remember what J says in the *Text*, 'Into eternity where all is one, there crept a tiny, mad idea, at which the Son of God remembered not to laugh.'[22]

Mikey's Note: Here's another great quote from the *Course* on laughter that I would like to share, 'You can indeed afford to laugh at fear thoughts, remembering that God goes with you wherever you go.'[23]

Yes, so rent some comedy movies, or watch reruns of *Seinfeld*, take up laughter yoga, hang out with funny people, go to a comedy club, or you could even join a *Course* group and piss everybody off by laughing all the time for no apparent reason. I'm just kidding on that last idea by the way, well, sort of – I've done it many times myself with mixed reactions. (LOL) Anyway, the point is, stop taking yourself *so damn seriously!* It's ok – Mikey gives you permission to lighten up, laugh, and have fun!

Love Holds No Grievances

DU157 & 158 (Arten)

When things happen fast in the world, almost everybody allows themselves to get away with condemning others, including experienced *Course* students. So we have a question for you. What if you refused to compromise on what you learned from the *Course,* not just how you talk about it with others, but in the way that you practice it? What would it look like if you actually followed lesson #68 in the *Workbook* to the letter, and applied its principles every day the way J did when he appeared to be in a body? Think of what it would do for your peace of mind and your psychological strength if you always did it.

'You who were created by Love like Itself can hold no grievances and know your Self. To hold a grievance is to forget who you are. To hold a grievance is to see yourself as a body. To hold a grievance is to let the ego rule your mind and to condemn the body to death. Perhaps you do not yet fully realize just what holding grievances does to your mind. It seems to split you off from your Source and make you unlike Him. It makes you believe that He is like what you think you have become, for no one can conceive of his Creator as unlike himself.

Shut off from your Self, which remains aware of Its likeness to Its Creator, your Self seems to sleep, while the part of your mind that weaves illusions in its sleep appears to be awake. Can all this arise from holding grievances? Oh, yes! For he who holds grievances denies he was created by Love, and his Creator has become fearful to him in his dream of hate. Who can dream of hatred and not fear God?

It is as sure that those who hold grievances will redefine God in their own image, as it is certain that God created them like Himself, and defined them as part of Him. It is as sure that those who hold grievances will suffer guilt, as it is certain that those who forgive will find peace. It is as sure that those who hold grievances will forget who they are, as it is certain that those who forgive will remember.

Would you not be willing to relinquish your grievances if you believed all this were so? Perhaps you do not think you can let your grievances go. That, however, is simply a mater of motivation.'[24]

Special Relationships

DU294 & 295 (Arten)

Just as the world confuses pain with pleasure, it also confuses sacrifice with love. Yet what is sacrifice in the final analysis but a call for pain? Is that what you really want for the ones you love? Your special loves are simply idols in which you seek to get what you feel is lacking in yourself. Romance is a vain attempt to fill an imagined emptiness – a hole that doesn't really exist, but that you experience as a result of the separation. That sense of lack can really only be healed by the Atonement and salvation, leading you to the wholeness of your oneness with God.

Mikey's Note: Certainly nothing wrong with being in a romantic relationship, or having any other type of special love relationship. Even Jesus had special love relationships, as Arten and Pursah inform us that he was married to Mary Mag'dalene.[25] So, it's not about *giving up* special love relationships, it's all about forgiving any psychological attachment you may have to your special love relationships. So if you find yourself demanding, what Arten refers to as, 'the fulfillment of special love bargains'[26] then that's the red flag that there is something that needs to be forgiven. Also, any feelings of abandonment and resentment when the special love relationship comes to an end will obviously need to be forgiven as well.

DU296 (Arten)

I give you this humble bit of counseling when it comes to all of your relationships in this world, whether they were founded on special love *or* special hate: Why don't you stop worrying about whether or not people love you and just love them? Then it doesn't matter what they think about *you*. You can just *be* love. It's so simple! And guess what? It will ultimately determine how you feel about yourself!

Mikey's Note: Gary adds this quote from his teachers on his *Fearless Love* CD, 'You don't have to go looking for love if that is where you are coming from.'

How long does it take to become a master?

DU93 (Arten)

Everybody asks how long does it take to become a master, and nobody likes the answer at first. The answer is it happens when it happens. Still, the time comes *before* that when you're so happy that the question doesn't really matter anymore!

Final Thoughts

DU386 (Gary & Pursah)

Once you know and understand the truth, it can still be very hard to remember it when shit happens, especially when it has to do with something that's important to you. Vigilance can be difficult, yet it's mandatory. You need to recommit yourself once in a while to being even more vigilant. It's your happiness that's delayed when you fail to remember the truth the Holy Spirit holds out to you. As the *Course* asks, 'What is a miracle but this remembering? And who is there in whom this memory lies not?'[27]

DU189, 190, & 198 (Arten)

When it comes to hearing right-minded ideas, not only is repetition perfectly all right, it's mandatory. It's very necessary to hear these ideas repeated in order for them to sink in. That's the only way you can possibly learn a thought system, have it become a part of you and get to the point where you apply it automatically – eventually without even thinking about it. That's why it's called *practicing* forgiveness. You practice over and over, until it becomes second nature.

DU254 & 255 (Pursah)

The *Course* is a *process*. It's that way for everyone, unless you're a spiritual genius who is practically enlightened already. The bad news is that for everyone else, this is a process that takes time and work. It's a life long spiritual path. There are numerous rewards along the way, some of them beautiful and quite unexpected. But they happen within a difficult process. In the *Manual for Teachers*, the *Course* talks about a period of unsettling, 'And now he must attain a state that may remain impossible to reach for a long, long time. He must learn to lay all judgment aside, and ask only what he really wants in every circumstance.'[28]

DU377 (Gary & Arten)

You can still live your life, pursue your goals and forgive at the same time. It's all about giving up psychological attachment. However, you may find that your goals will change as a result of the inspiration and guidance you receive from practicing true prayer and forgiveness.

YIR77 (Pursah)

The more you do your forgiveness homework, the freer your mind will become from the blocks to hearing spirit. And the more you practice joining with God in the silent form of true prayer, the clearer you'll be to listen to spirit. And then there's the conscious act of joining with spirit whenever it's appropriate in order to help yourself or others in a situation that calls for it.

DU284 (Pursah)

Be mindful of your goal. Heaven is permanent, and nothing you seem to do outside of Heaven is permanent. How can it be important? You want to keep things in perspective. As you practice forgiveness your awareness increases, and as the *Manual* says of any such student, 'As his awareness increases, he may well develop abilities that seem quite startling to him. Yet nothing he can do can compare even in the slightest with the glorious surprise of remembering Who he is. Let all his learning and all his efforts be directed toward this one great final surprise, and he will not be content to be delayed by the little ones that may come to him on the way.'[29]

Keep in mind that there is only one of two things you can do – make something real or forgive it – then any new abilities that come your way should be given to the Holy Spirit and used under His direction. The *Manual* says, 'God gives no special favors, and no one has any powers that are not available to everyone.'[30] The Holy Spirit would certainly remind you that you're not special, and you shouldn't try to convince yourself or others that you are.

YIR213 (Arten)

So, to make it short and sweet, you fell asleep and started dreaming, and when you're ready to wake up by listening to your memory of God, the Holy Spirit, instead of listening to the ego, then you'll wake up. It's *your* dream, so only *you* can wake yourself up. The Holy Spirit is actually your own Higher Self. But remember, God did not send the Holy Spirit. He was always with you, because even though you could deny the truth, you could never lose it. Once again, if the dream was created by God and He could wake you up from it, it would be real. It would be a reality that was done *to* you by an outside force. But it's not. God is still perfect Love, and your job is to wake up and return your awareness to where you really are.

Mikey's Note: Yes, the Holy Spirit is really your own Higher Self – H.S. either way, just be sure not to confuse it with *Holy Shit.*

Chapter 20

The Funnies

**We are reverent only to God and spirit, and
perhaps that will help you cut to the chase.**[1]

I had to throw in this bonus chapter of stuff that I found to be
funny from Gary's books. Gary tells us in his workshops for us to be
normal and not to be weird – well, too late for *me!* So, if you don't
have much of a sense of humor, or are very easily offended, you may
want to bypass this chapter. Or better yet, read through it anyway, and
use it as an opportunity to practice forgiveness. As for the rest of you
who are as sick and twisted, and as easily amused as I am, enjoy!

DU10

Gary: So rather than resisting the world, I should look for ways I
can use it as a chance to get home?

Pursah: Exactly. Good boy.

DU12 & 13

Gary: The world, nature, and the human body all seem pretty
awesome to me. I'm not exactly what you'd call a cock-
eyed optimist, but there's a lot of beauty, order, and
intricacy that would appear to me to have the touch of
God. If I told people that God didn't create the world, I
have a feeling it would probably go over about as big as a
fart in an elevator.

DU20

Gary: Why come to me? Why not some guy with a fire in his
belly who wants to be a prophet? My main ambitions are to

move to Hawaii, commune with nature, and drink beer, not necessarily in that order.

DU22

Pursah: How would you feel if someone who you knew beyond a doubt was as dead as a doornail stopped by to have a chat with you, and even let you touch him so you could know he was legit?

Gary: I wouldn't know whether to take a crap or go blind.

DU23

Gary: Although I wasn't a Catholic, I had agreed to go along with the friend I had stopped suing and participate in a three-day spiritual experience called the Cursillo, which was held at a Catholic church in Massachusetts. The event emphasized laughter, song, love, and forgiveness, and came as a big surprise to me, because I didn't know there were Catholic people who were happy.

DU28

Pursah: Some in your generation think the Mayans vibrated off the planet in a state of spiritual enlightenment. What makes you think they were enlightened? They practiced human sacrifice. How enlightened do you think that was? They were just people: like the Essenes, like the Europeans, like the American Indians, and like you. Accept that and move on.

Gary: So I shouldn't be too impressed by that ancient spiritual book I want to read to help me with my trading – the one about the art of war?

Pursah: War isn't art, it's psychosis. But why shouldn't you try to spiritualize it? You try to spiritualize everything else.

DU28

Pursah: As just one example of spiritualizing objects, you romanticize the South American rainforest by thinking it's one of the holiest spots on earth. If you could observe in accelerated motion what goes on underneath the ground there, you would see that the roots of the trees actually compete with each other for the water, just as all the creatures of the rainforest fight for survival.

Gary: Boy, it's a tree-eat-tree world out there. Sorry.

DU43

Pursah: Do you really believe, as it says in various verses of Leviticus, Chapter 20, that God told Moses that adulterers, wizards, mediums, and homosexuals should be put to death?

Gary: That does seem a little extreme. I've always liked mediums.

DU44

Arten: Why do you think the master, unlike the other people of his time, treated all men and women equally?

Gary: You tell me. I assume there's more to it than the fact that he wasn't trying to get the babes into the sack.

DU55

Pursah: You don't like to speak in front of a crowd, do you?

Gary: I'd rather stick broken pieces of glass up my butt.

Pursah: I don't think *that* will be necessary.

DU56

Gary: I feel a little uncomfortable not telling Karen about this. Would she be able to see you two if she were here?

Pursah: Sure. The bodies we project are just as dense as yours, although our brains aren't.

DU67

Pursah: The Bible pretty much snubs people like me and Thaddaeus, but we were privileged to share J's teachings as spoken directly to us.

Gary: Quite an honor. Were you ordained?

Pursah: I was pre-ordained.

Gary: Did you get crucified?

Pursah: No. I got my head cut off in India. When you're in a body, you just never know what kind of a day it's going to be.

DU72

Gary: I'm sorry, but I'm bursting with one more question I have to ask.

Pursah: Careful, kid. Too many interruptions and we may have to cook up Dante's *Inferno* for you.

DU91

Arten: You've had an eventful few weeks. Did you read it?

Gary: You mean the *Course?*

Arten: Yes.

Gary: No. I'm waiting for the movie.

Arten: God help us all.

DU96

Gary: You say the *Course* is being translated into other languages?

Pursah: Yes. You're not bilingual, are you?

Gary: I have enough to handle with English.

DU112 & 113

Pursah: You were born in Salem. You know the story. How many people died during the Salem witch trials?

Gary: Around nineteen or twenty.

Pursah: Yes. That was a classic example of the projection of unconscious guilt. Do you know how many people were killed during the witch trials that preceded that event in Europe?

Gary: I don't know. Hundreds?

Pursah: Try forty thousand.

Gary: Forty thousand! Wow, that would make the news – unless there was a big sex sandal somewhere.

DU128 & 129

Arten: You've started writing our book?

Gary: Not really. I'm still trying to think of a title for it.

Arten: Any ideas?

Gary: So far, it's between *Love Is Letting Go of Beer* and *A Return to Beer.*

DU132

Arten: Much of the *Course* is presented in Shakespearean blank verse, or iambic pentameter. Do you know why?

Gary: I have not a freakin' idea.

DU136 & 137

Arten: Right now, the world has its head planted firmly up its butt looking for the light. There isn't any light up there, Gary.

DU144

Gary: So I keep reincarnating because of this unconscious guilt and fear that's in my mind. You're saying if the guilt was healed, and I didn't have this hidden fear, then I wouldn't have any need for a body, the world, or even the universe?

Arten: Excellent. I knew you weren't a dumb bastard. I tried to tell J, but he wouldn't listen.

DU166

Pursah: You said a mouthful accurately, my brother. We should get a gold star for your forehead.

Gary: Would the star have five points or six?

Arten: Knock it off. Religious jokes are our job.

DU173

Pursah: If what the *Course* is saying is true – that everyone who comes to this world is delusional or else they wouldn't think they were here in the first place – then if you have a hit book, all it means is that you are admired by a large group of disturbed people.

Gary: That *was* a joke, right?

Pursah: Yes. Don't worry about the reactions of people who take jokes like that seriously – *whoever* they may be. Don't be defensive and walk on eggshells. Just put it out there. If somebody doesn't like you because of it, forgive them.

Gary: There was a time, in the very recent past, when I would have used another *f* word.

Pursah: Now you have the new *f* word. Forgive them.

DU181

Gary: It's like The Poet said, 'We are symbols, and inhabit symbols.'

Arten: Why, yes. I believe that's from *Essays: Second Series (1844),* The Poet. You know you're very sophisticated, considering your immaturity.

Gary: Thank you. I'll put that on my résumé.

DU187

Gary: You know, I was driving the other day, and this guy was right on my ass. I mean, he was practically touching my bumper. That really pisses me off. I was just about to give this asshole the finger, when I thought about the *Course.* So I didn't do anything, and then he made a left turn a few blocks later, and that was the end of it.

Arten: Remember that your brother in that car was symbolic of what's in *your* mind, including the impatience that you exhibit in other areas of your life, symbolized by his impatience. You and your brother are impatient because you've made the separation real, and you think you have to strive to get somewhere so you can overcome God and prove yourself right.

Gary: I guess I shouldn't have thought of him as an asshole, though?

Arten: That's correct, your assholiness. As J counsels you in the *Course,* 'As you see him you will see yourself.'[2]

DU195

Arten: People might not know from the words you've spoken so far that you actually have a good attitude toward women. In fact, haven't you always considered them to be more intelligent than men?

Gary: I think it's pretty clear they are. They're less violent, more nurturing, and they vote more intelligently. A lot of us men are just macho dick brains.

Pursah:	You're not – entirely.
Gary:	That's right. I stand as a glorious and inspiring example for all of the world to emulate.
Arten:	We've created a monster!

DU195

Arten:	You'll soon be entering a phase of your earthly life where you'll begin to be a little less concerned with bodily adventures and a little more concerned with accomplishments – in your case, spiritual accomplishments. Many men are preoccupied with physical pleasures in the earlier part of their lives, but as they begin to get a little older, their pursuit of sex is replaced by something else.
Gary:	Erectile dysfunction?
Arten:	No. It's something called maturity.

DU213

Arten:	Since the *Course* teaches that you have only two emotions, love and fear, then the Holy Spirit sees everything in the world as either an *expression* of love or a call for love. Now if someone's expressing love, what would be an appropriate response from you?
Gary:	Love, of course.
Arten:	Excellent, Gary. That high school diploma is finally starting to pay off.

DU216

Gary:	I *am* Christ in reality, and so is everybody else, and we're all one. On this level we all see the same dream, but from a different point of view. I think Freud said everybody in your dreams at night is really you, so day or night it's always a symbol of me over there who's seeing my own dream from a different vantage point. My job is to rejoin with myself through forgiveness and become whole again.
Pursah:	Not bad for a male of the species.

DU218

Arten: It's what you think that will either keep you dreaming or help get you home, not what you do.

Gary: You mean J never said to you, 'Go therefore and make believers of all nations?'

Arten: I'm glad you're kidding.

Pursah: Speaking of nations, remember that they're not important either. What you really are is eternal. The United States isn't.

Gary: Blasphemy!

DU222

Gary: I always forget to ask the questions I want to until after you leave, so do you mind if I ask you something while I'm thinking about it?

Pursah: What do you think, Arten?

Arten: I won't say anything. I promised him I'd stop being a smart ass if he would.

DU230

Pursah: Hey teacher of God. What's up?

Gary: If I told you, you'd slap my face.

Pursah: Did we forget to take our anti-smart ass pill this morning?

DU243

Gary: Say, I was wondering. J let you touch him so you could know he was real when he came to you after the crucifixion, right? So I was wondering, can I touch you just to see if you're real?

Pursah: Yeah, right. Where would you like to touch me, Gary?

Gary: Are you flirting or is it me?

Pursah: It's you.

DU247

Pursah: Remember, J is calling for teachers, not for martyrs. I did not seek for my death as Thomas consciously, nor did I have much time to think about it when I was killed in India.

Gary: Your old alma martyr.
Pursah: Cute.

DU260 & 261

Pursah: Hey forgiveness guy, how's the world holding up?
Gary: It's holding, but no thanks to me. I've been busy trying to free it.
Pursah: You remember Arten, who was more than your equal in the domain of smart-ass enlightenment.
Gary: I thought you looked familiar. Did you help the Holy Spirit heal my mind in another dimension?
Arten: We tried, but the damage was just too much.

DU268

Gary: The happy dream is necessary because if the rug of time and space got pulled out from under me suddenly, it would be too much for me to handle. The dream of separation seems too real for me to wake up suddenly without crapping a brick.

DU269

Gary: If you put enough holy instants together, in the happy dream of forgiveness, then you can't help but get your ass saved, or at least the mind that made it.

DU283

Gary: I have felt peaceful and joyous at times. They don't all have to be peak experiences, I guess. Just feeling good is fun.
Arten: Oh, you mean like last summer, when you were circling around on your riding lawnmower within earshot of your conservative neighbors and screaming at the top of your lungs, 'The Son of God is free! The Son of God is free!'
Gary: Yeah, that was me.

DU285

Gary: By the way, I've started writing a little, as I'm sure you know, and I was wondering if you have any advice for me on how to proceed?

Pursah: Of course. We knew you'd break down and write something eventually. You're slow, but you're not hopeless. Don't worry about the rules too much. Just between you and me, English is kind of a silly language anyway. But far be it for me to judge anything.

Gary: Yes. To do so might suggest you ain't got no culture.

Pursah: Perhaps – just as our book might suggest you don't speak no good English.

Gary: You're saying I shouldn't worry about what some English teacher might think about my writing style?

Pursah: Exactly. I'm glad I wasn't misconscrewed.

Gary: I love it when you talk dirty.

DU294

Arten: During my final lifetime, I was in my sixties by the time I met Pursah. It would be the final lifetime for both of us. Her husband had passed on a couple of years before that, and my wife had made her transition also. Pursah and I recognized quickly that we belonged together. Not only did we have the *Course* and our personal understanding of it in common, but we sensed we had known each other in previous lifetimes. In fact, we were able to help each other remember many events from previous incarnations. We lived together in that last lifetime but didn't marry. It was our way of honoring our spouses and yet having each other at the same time.

Gary: You rascal.

DU303 & 304

Arten: J really did heal that man as described in Mark. After he said, 'Your sins are forgiven,' he also said, 'that you may know the Son of man has authority on earth to forgive sins.' He didn't just mean that *he* had that authority, he meant that *you* also have that authority. Do you not appear to be a son of man on this level? Yet you are really Christ.

Of course, there really isn't any such thing as sin, and J did *not* pardon sins to make them real. His attitude was that everyone in the dream is equally innocent because it's just a dream.

Gary: Why didn't he just say there's no such thing as sin because this isn't real?

Pursah: You had to be there. People could only take so many blasphemies in one day.

DU304

Arten: Most of the time in the *Course* J says that it takes a little willingness. But that's not for advanced students. In the *Manual for Teachers*, he says it takes *abundant* willingness.[3]

Gary: The old bait and switch, huh?

Arten: Whatever it takes to get a lazy guy like you moving.

DU310 & 311

Pursah: People always do things, big and small, that they know will hurt them. Often they're even conscious of it. Like you. Why do you always eat those chocolate bars at the movies even though you know they'll make your face break out?

Gary: Because a man's gotta do what a man's gotta do.

Pursah: You're so butch.

Gary: Isn't that old-fashioned gay and lesbian language?

Pursah: Yes. You don't have anything against gays and lesbians, do you?

Gary: No. Most of my relatives are gays and lesbians.

Mikey's Note: I'll have more to say about gays and lesbians at the end of this book.

DU312

Gary: I've tried to heal people before and they haven't gotten well. Does that mean I suck?

Arten: Yes.

DU316

Gary: I was at the gas station and this guy blocked me in just as I was about to leave, and I was in a hurry. I asked him politely enough if he could let me out 'cause I was in a rush, and he just looked at me with this unbelievably condescending and disgusted look and said, 'Tough!' I couldn't believe it. There was a part of me that wanted to rearrange his face.

Pursah: What *is* it with men and cars? Anyway, you saw him as being really ignorant?

Gary: Oh, he was worse that that. People who talk at the movies are ignorant. This guy was the world-champion flamer. Mother Teresa would have been tempted to slap him.

DU323

Pursah: At some point, the *Course's* thought system becomes so much a part of you that you'll choose the strength of Christ even when you're asleep at night, which means you'll often choose that same strength automatically after you lay your body aside. That should be a comforting thought for you, not only because it will make you less fearful of death, but because it confirms that even if you died today you'd still take your learning with you – even though you're not a master.

Gary: Don't be so linear.

Mikey's Note: I recall a *Seinfeld* episode where Jerry says, 'I had a dream last night that a hamburger was eating *me!*'

DU325

Arten: People have already been brainwashed by the ego, and will remain so until they reclaim their minds. As the *Course* explains about the need for training, 'You are much too tolerant of mind wandering, and are passively condoning your mind's miscreations.'[4]

Gary: I'd never do that.

Mikey's Note: That quote from the *Course* reminds me of what Arnold Schwarzenegger aka 'The Governator' tells the five year olds in the movie *Kindergarten Cop*, 'Stop whining. You kids are soft. You lack discipline. Well, I got news for you – you are *mine* now! You belong to *me*! You're not gonna have your mommies right behind you anymore to wipe your little tooshies! Oh, no. It's time to turn this mush into muscles. No more complaining. No more, "Mr Kimble, I have to go to the bathroom." *Nothing! There is no bathroom!'*

DU326 & 327

Gary: The editing of movies and television in the last thirty years has speeded up so much it's almost laughable. They must seriously believe everybody has attention deficit disorder. Real conversations are becoming more and more rare. Everything is dumbed down. As far as the images are concerned, the philosophy sometimes is that if you can see it, it's too slow.

Arten: Yes; more and more style and less and less substance – like with your politics. Do you realize that Abraham Lincoln, the first great Republican president…

Gary: And the *last* great Republican President…

Arten: You give yourself away, but do you realize Lincoln could not be elected today? He didn't have a good speaking voice, and he actually took the time to think about the answer to a question. If you did that in a debate today, you'd be called stupid. Imagine having a thoughtful answer instead of a clever, pre-written sound byte?

DU327 & 328

Gary: …Like that day I was at the movies and I drove home at a different time because I no longer needed some particular forgiveness lessons – having already been practicing forgiveness?

Pursah: That's right, you lucky stiff. Oh, wait; I was going to save that particular description of you for the discussion about sex.

DU329

Pursah: Do you remember what the ten characteristics of a teacher of God are in the *Course*?

Gary:	Sure. A teacher of God is trustworthy, loyal, helpful, friendly, courteous, kind – oh, wait a minute. I used to be a Boy Scout.
Pursah:	You're certainly not one anymore.

DU341

Arten:	You've never fired a gun, have you?
Gary:	No. That's because a man who feels a need to fire a gun secretly feels inadequate about his penis. And a woman who feels a need to fire a gun is secretly jealous because she doesn't *have* a penis. That's just my opinion. Maybe I'm still upset about that woman near Waterville who was out in her yard with her children; a hunter mistook her for a deer and snuffed her.
Arten:	You're slipping, Gary. Forgiveness, remember?
Gary:	I'm taking the day off!

DU343

Gary:	I get the idea about the news being set up to make us react and see others as guilty, which is the same purpose as the rest of the illusion. I see it even in the regional news here.
Pursah:	Yes. For example, the local police might want to make it look like they're doing something, so they call up the town newspaper and then arrest the local call girls.
Gary:	There goes my social life.

DU357 & 358

Gary:	How do I live the normal life you said I could live, practice the *Course*, and still not feel bad about that body identification part of my dream life?
Arten:	By remembering what it is and forgiving it at an appropriate time. A dream is nothing, and sex is nothing. But I wouldn't recommend that you turn to your partner after making love and say, 'That was nothing.'
Gary:	I *knew* I was doing something wrong.

DU361

Arten: People have a lot of assumptions, but J didn't come to the world in order to start some religion so people could make other people wrong for having bodies and wanting to use them. He taught forgiveness, and still does, in order to teach people the total insignificance of the body.

Gary: So I can live and forgive simultaneously – and it's possible to have both an erection *and* a resurrection.

Arten: That's true – just not at the same time!

DU362

Arten: Speaking of associations, a man has a connection between Heaven and his mother's womb. That connection is also there for a woman, but it shows up more in the form of a man wanting to get inside of a woman, and sometimes a woman wanting to.

Gary: That would explain why a man is born through a woman's vagina, and then he spends the rest of his life trying to get back in there.

Arten: I'm glad *you* said it.

DU363

Gary: Hey, Pursah, do you have any advice for women about sex?

Pursah: Yes. Beware the one-eyed serpent.

Gary: Cute. Anything else?

Pursah: You don't have to worry about women and sex. They talk to each other about it; it's practically a cult.

DU378 & 379

Pursah: As J asks you in his *Course,* 'Would God have left the meaning of the world to your interpretation?'[5]

Gary: Him and his smart-ass rhetorical questions.

Pursah: Yes. It's not easy being humble when you know everything.

YIR9

Arten: You were just reading about that guy in Germany who killed somebody and then ate him. It's a big story there.

He's accused of cannibalism, and now they're putting him on trial.

Gary: Yeah. There's no such thing as a free lunch.

YIR18

Gary: I must say, you look more beautiful than ever. Tell me something, just between you and me. Would it be incest to make love to your future self?

Pursah: No, but it would be weird. Please proceed.

YIR23 & 24

Gary: It's funny how a spiritual document like the *Course* can use Christian terminology but incorporate so many Buddhist ideas into it. Maybe that's why some Christians are reluctant to embrace it.

Arten: Yes. Conservative Christians don't recognize the *Course*.

Gary: That's okay. They also don't recognize each other at Hooters.

YIR27

Arten: Remember what we said about teaching; there's nothing wrong with repetition. In fact, it's essential.

Gary: You already said that.

YIR36

Pursah: A minister in this lifetime may be a prostitute in the next, and vice versa. In fact, the prostitute J saved from being stoned to death had helped J in a lifetime previous to that. You're always switching roles. You may be a police officer in one of your dream lifetimes and then a criminal in the next.

Gary: Or worse, a politician.

YIR38

Gary: I remember reading about doctors doing a study of depressed people and their thoughts. The doctors assumed the patients were having all these bad thoughts because they were depressed. But what they found out was pretty startling. It turned out that the patients were depressed *because* they had been having all these bad thoughts!

Arten: Very good. You know, you're almost coherent at times.

Gary: That's the nicest thing you've ever said to me.

Arten: Don't tell anyone.

YIR45

Gary: After the publication of *The Disappearance of the Universe*, my first publisher, D. Patrick Miller, and I heard that there was some talk about the book on the Internet from other countries. One of them was Holland. We found a web page where someone was talking about the book and tried to have a computer program translate it. However, a computer program only knows how to give a literal translation, and simply provides the words that are the closest to those being translated. The computer can't translate the meaning. In describing how I said at the beginning of the book that I felt as though I had a relationship with Jesus, the translation came out, 'The writer bathed with Jesus.'

Pursah: That bathing-with-Jesus idea might go over in Holland.

Gary: I'd rather bathe with you.

Pursah: I'll be kind and overlook that.

YIR50

Arten: As J says in the *Course*, 'You do not realize the magnitude of that one error.'[6] He also says, 'Listening to the ego's voice means that you believe it is possible to attack God, and that a part of Him has been torn away by you. Fear of retaliation from without follows, because the severity of the guilt is so acute that it must be projected.'[7] Do you get the stunning implications of all this?

Gary: I can't believe I'm going to Australia.

YIR52

Pursah: From the moment you're born to the moment you die, it's all about the survival and success of your body, from attaining material comfort to receiving special love. It doesn't take too much power of observation to see that your society is crazed over bodies and the attainment of sex.

Gary: I can understand that. I had sex once, and it was one of the happiest minutes of my life.

YIR52

Pursah: The way J puts it about your life is, '...you but relive the single instant when the time of terror took the place of love.'[8]

Gary: I like that Jesus. He really sticks to the *Course.*

YIR58

Gary: My mother was a virgin. She just wasn't very good at it. All right, she wasn't a virgin. Of course, J's mother wasn't a virgin either, but it's a cute story.

YIR71 & 72

Arten: You've been doing really well on the road, by the way. I couldn't have done any better myself. Well, yes, I could, but I'm trying to make you feel good.

Gary: Funny, you least famous of the disciples.

YIR100

Gary: Adam and Eve are lying underneath a tree in the Garden of Eden. Adam looks at Eve and says, 'You know, I can't help but feel there's a book in this.'

Pursah: Cute. And you managed to work in an erotic touch.

Gary: Well, Pursah, speaking of erotic touches, when are you and I gonna hook up?

Pursah: Hmm...let me see. Does never work for you?

Gary: Still playing hard to get, huh?

Arten: You know, buddy, that *is* the image of my wife you're talking to there, even if she is you.

Gary: Sorry, I forgot. It's hard to keep track of everybody. It's a good thing there's really only one of us, huh? Say, Pursah, do you remember the last series of visits, when you came once all by yourself? You're not by chance gonna do that again are, are you?

Pursah:	Are you about ready to proceed?

YIR105

Arten:	You wanted to talk about the movie *The Passion of the Christ*. A lot of the time Jesus in the movies, or J, as we'll continue to call him –
Gary:	You could call him J dog.
Arten:	A lot of the time J has been portrayed……..

Mikey's Note: Gary got the *Seinfeld* treatment on the last two dialogue series. Sometimes George Constanza will say something, then Jerry and Elaine will carry on their conversation as if George never said anything.

YIR107

Arten:	J's real message is the *opposite* of making the body real. In fact, if you want to be like J, then you want to eventually experience that the body is meaningless. Instead of believing in the body, you want to get to the point where you *can't* believe it.
Gary:	I still can't believe the Sox traded Nomar.

YIR114

Gary:	I think if you get in touch with your innocence, everything is more enjoyable, because you're experiencing it with less guilt, and eventually with no guilt. Like how about sex? If you didn't have any guilt in your mind, wouldn't you enjoy sex more?
Pursah:	I take it that's a rhetorical question.
Gary:	It is as long as Arten's here.

YIR121

Pursah:	You've never been a vegetarian, have you?
Gary:	Nah, but I *do* believe there's a place for all of God's creatures – usually right next to the mashed potatoes.
Pursah:	That's all right, brother, as long as you don't make it real. Like anything else, if being a vegetarian is done from a place of love and as an expression of love, then it's a beautiful thing. If it's done to make other people wrong for

not being vegetarians, then it will imprison the mind. I say that because you're meeting a lot of people now who are vegetarians, and it might be good for you to help them keep things in perspective.

Mikey's Note: I didn't become a vegetarian/vegan back in 1994 for animal rights reasons. I also did not become one to make other people wrong for not being vegetarians, though, admittedly, I did do that at times during my first couple of years as a vegan, but I usually only did that to the people that made *me* wrong for being *one*. But I became a vegan for totally selfish reasons, because it was good for *me*, I just felt healthier and more energetic. I didn't care about saving the animals' lives. However, if I ever were to go back to eating animal products of any kind, I would definitely support the businesses that treat the animals much more humanely, where the animals aren't injected with all kinds of hormones and steroids and such, and are forced to live in unnatural and filthy conditions. Sorry, I didn't mean to get all serious and political sounding in what is supposed to be a 'funnies' chapter. (LOL)

Also, I once had a t-shirt I would often wear with drawings of three pieces of meat on it, with their faces shown, that read, 'Let's call them by their real names: Dead Chicken, Dead Cow, Dead Pig.' So, I certainly had my moments of being outspoken and obnoxious!

YIR138

Gary: An English teacher friend of mine from New Jersey told me that I'm the one who brought the *Course* into the vernacular. I'm gonna look that up.

Arten: Good boy.

YIR176

Arten: So have you thought of that title for our next book yet?

Gary: Yup.

Arten: All right, I'll bite. What is it?

Gary: I'm gonna call it *The Hidden Messages in Beer.*

YIR187

Gary: You know one of the good things about cell phones? I remember 15 or 20 years ago there used to be all these people walking around talking to themselves. Now they don't have to. They can walk around talking on their cell phones. Of course you know there are some of them walking around talking on their cell phones, and there's not really anybody on the other end.

YIR191

Gary: Arten, do you mind me asking who you are in this lifetime?

Arten: I don't mind you asking, if you don't mind me not answering.

Gary: Oh, come on. I haven't been able to figure it out. At least give me a hint!

Arten: Okay, my friend, I'll narrow it down for you. In the lifetime that appears to occur in this thread of time, I'm a woman.

Gary: All right. That helps. So you're a babe, huh?

Arten: It stands to reason I'd be female. The percentages alone would suggest it. I was a man 2,000 years ago, and I'm a man again the second half of this century and into the next one for our final lifetime. Do you expect me to be a man *all* the time? I'm a woman right now as we speak, and I might add that I'm fetching.

Gary: My dog Nupey used to do a lot of fetching, too.

Arten: You know, we *could* make an exception to that nobody's-going-to-hell idea.

YIR 205

Gary: These three guys are in hell, right? They've been there for quite some time, burning away, and after a while one of them figures that since they're gonna be there for eternity, maybe they should introduce themselves. So the guy says, 'Hi, my name's Arik, and I'm a rabbi. I'm here in hell because I cheated on my wife.' So the second man says, 'Hello, my name's John, and I'm a Catholic priest, and I'm here in hell because I *have* a wife.' Then finally the third guy says, 'Hi, my name's Alex, and I'm *A Course in Miracles* student, and I'm not here.'

Wrapping This Puppy Up

In an attempt to ease the minds of those who are new to this path and may be feeling a little overwhelmed, let me say this. If you're not ready to accept that the world is an illusion and that God has nothing to do with its creation, or better yet, its mis-creation, don't worry about that. The key thing you want to do on this spiritual path is to understand that you are *never* a victim. You want to start taking full responsibility for your life's experiences by examining what's in your mind. You're still responsible for the contents of your subconscious mind, as well as your experiences, whether you believe God created the world or not. As already stated earlier in the quotes section, 'Nobody can really take the peace of God away from you except by your own decision.'[1]

Even on the level of form, the level of energy, like energy attracts like energy, which means like unconscious mind attracts like unconscious mind. If there's somebody in your life who is pushing your buttons in some way, well, even on the level of the world you're still responsible for the experience. As I said, like unconscious mind attracts like unconscious mind, so they wouldn't be there pushing your buttons if there wasn't something in your unconscious mind that was attracting you to them, or them to you in the first place. So even from *that* linear point of view, you still have to recognize that they are the symbolic aspects of your own unconscious mind that need to be healed. So, the true forgiveness work still applies even at that level. You can forgive them, as well as yourself for 'attracting' them into your life.

Pursah tells Gary in *The Disappearance of the Universe*, 'Understanding the metaphysics of the *Course* is required in order to understand forgiveness, but it may be helpful to some people if you stress forgiveness first, then bring in the dreamlike nature of the world and other features of the truth gradually.'[2] So that would be my suggestion for a good starting point if you're feeling hesitant to accept that the world is an illusion or a dream, and that God has nothing to do with it and that you don't really exist separately from God. The ego always looks for ways to get out of taking responsibility for one's experiences; not being ready to accept all of the ideas in the *Course* is not really an excuse to not start trying to practice forgiveness. J, as well as Arten and Pursah, say that it is not necessary to accept all of the ideas of the *Course* right away.[3] But you got to start *somewhere!*

As for me, I have some moments where I just feel so totally peaceful where I feel like I'm very close to attaining the goal of the *Course.* And then I have other days where I feel like I'm doing a wretched job of practicing forgiveness; days when I feel so irritable and pissy, where it's like 'fogetaboutit – I'm not even close!' (LOL) But as my old man used to say to me as a kid, 'It's better to be pissed *off* than pissed *on!*' (LOL) Those days forgiveness can seem harder, but I always do the best I can to remember that it's all *my* dream. Also, when I do find myself in a state of uneasiness, I am always mindful as to not take it out on anyone. If you recall earlier, I mentioned that I have too much of an ego to put anybody up on a pedestal. Well, I also have too much of an ego to make myself look like a jerk, and even the ego part of me wants to represent the *Course* well.

Anyway, like I said earlier, I had no intention of becoming a spiritual person. It just sort of happened by 'accident' – I felt like I was *tricked* into it, actually. Thank God I was. I know I wouldn't have chosen this path voluntarily that's for sure. After nine years of Catholic school, I had no intention of having anything to do with God or Jesus – that was just a bunch of non-sense to me. But we all know what J says in the *Course,* 'There are no accidents in salvation.'[4]

Today, I love God and Jesus, and words can't express the gratitude I have for this particular spiritual path I'm on – I don't know where I would be in this world if it weren't for *it.* I have been studying metaphysics and spirituality since the age of twenty, but it wasn't until I read *The Disappearance of the Universe* that spirituality was something I *wanted* to do rather than feeling like something I *had* to do. Not that it was ever pushed on me. It was just an internal feeling I felt that it was something I was supposed to be doing, something I couldn't escape from. Knowing deep down it was leading me to something bigger is what kept me going – and still does.

I haven't had the experience of *revelation* that Gary describes as having in *The Disappearance of the Universe.* And I'm really not looking to have it. I don't need to have it in order to know that this is the right path for me. If it happens, so be it. If it doesn't that's fine too.

In fact, I don't think I want that experience right now, it might freak me out. (LOL) I know this path is working for me simply because I have a lot less buttons that can be pushed than I used to.

In the not so distant past, someone said to me, 'Mike, you seem to think *The Disappearance of the Universe* is the "be all and end all" of spirituality.' And my response was, 'Well, it is!' It's certainly not for everyone, but I had never had that attitude about anything else I had studied prior to Gary's books. Everything else I studied on spirituality always left me feeling like there was something missing, or made it too complicated. With Gary's books, I've got all the tools I need. Now it's just a matter of trying to master the forgiveness gig. Simple, but not easy. Anyway, here are three quotes from the *Course* I would like to share before I wrap this puppy up:

'Here does the dream of separation start to fade and disappear. For here the gap that is not there begins to be perceived without the toys of terror that you made. No more than this is asked. Be glad indeed salvation asks so little, not so much. It asks for nothing in reality. And even in illusions it but asks forgiveness be the substitute for fear. Such is the only rule for happy dreams.'[5]

'The world will end in joy, because it is a place of sorrow. When joy has come, the purpose of the world has gone. The world will end in peace, because it is a place of war. When peace has come, what is the purpose of the world? The world will end in laughter, because it is a place of tears. Where there is laughter, who can longer weep? And only complete forgiveness brings all this to bless the world.'[6]

'You do not have to seek far for salvation. Every minute and every second gives you a chance to save yourself. Do not lose these chances, not because they will not return, but because delay of joy is needless.'[7]

On a more personal note before I close, there is this episode of *Seinfeld* where people think Jerry is gay because of his being 'single, thin, and neat' and because he gets along well with women. Well, I am single, thin, and usually neat, not to mention that I have more female friends and acquaintances than male ones. Throw in being a vegan, a fan of Yanni, Enya, and Bon Jovi, and a spiritual person on top of that, and it makes me wonder if people think *I'm* gay – 'not that there's anything wrong with that!' (LOL)

Well, just for the record, it is true that Mikey isn't a 'real' man, but no, Mikey is *not* gay – Mikey digs women! Now, I have every intention of making this my final incarnation. However, if I do have to come back, and if I end up coming back as a woman, I'm gonna make sure that I'm a lesbian – I sure as hell don't want to be with some repulsive, sweaty and hairy dude, who burps and farts while sitting in front of the TV watching sports and drinking beer all day. Enough said – I am out!

Index of References

In the following Index, the first numerical listed is the footnote number, followed by the source code and page number. Majority of the footnotes come from *A Course in Miracles*, where I also list the exact location on the page the reference is located in the 3ʳᵈ Edition of the *Course*. Most of the quotes from Gary Renard's books used in this book already have the source listed, however, there were some other references made to Gary's books that weren't, so the source of those references is listed in this index. The list of reference codes are as follows:

References from *A Course in Miracles* 3ʳᵈ Edition
PR   Preface
T   Text
W   Workbook
M   Manual for Teachers
CL   Clarification of Terms
P   Psychotherapy
S   The Song of Prayer

References from Gary Renard's Material
DU   The Disappearance of the Universe
YIR   Your Immortal Reality
GRP   Gary Renard Podcast

Author's Note #1 1) T586 (27:VIII:6:2) **2)** DU40 & DU41
3) T177 (9:VII:8:4)

Author's Note #2 1) DU241 **2)** T272 (14:II:2:3)
3) DU210 **4)** T310 (15:IV:6:1-2) **5)** DU127 **6)** DU210
7) DU108 **8)** DU247 **9)** DU247 **10)** DU267 & 268 **11)** DU304
& 336; M46 (17:8:4) **12)** DU200 **13)** DU200 **14)** DU101
15) DU150 **16)** YIR149 **17)** DU29 **18)** W249 (134:7:4)
19) YIR139 **20)** DU117 & 266 **21)** DU305 **22)** DU256 **23)** T1
(Intro:1:7); DU108; and YIR75 **24)** DU113, 219, & 266; YIR54;
T13 (1:VI:1:1); W422 (256:1:1-2); & M37 (14:5:7) **25)** DU173
& 233 **26)** DU247 **27)** DU93

Author's Note #3 1) DU402 **2)** DU189 & 190; YIR12 & 27

Masshole Mike 1) DU175 **2)** DU159 **3)** YIR204 **4)** DU176
5) DU16 & 109 **6)** DU168 **7)** DU325 & YIR64 **8)** DU140
9) T668 (31:VIII:9:2) **10)** DU210 **11)** DU97 **12)** DU127
13) DU218 **14)** DU98 **15)** YIR1 **16)** DU87 **17)** DU229

Go West Young Man 1) DU13 **2)** YIR69 **3)** YIR1 & 12
4) DU155 **5)** DU94 **6)** DU262 **7)** YIR205 **8)** T116 (7:III:1:7-9)
9) DU323

Dude, Where's My Jesus Fish? 1) YIR163

Meeting Gary Renard 1) T434 (20:V:3:1) **2)** GRP24
3) GRP31 **4)** GRP32, 36, & 39 **5)** DU112 & T623 (29:IX:8:3)
6) DU390

Arten and Pursah's Keys to Understanding *A Course in Miracles*
1) DU147 **2)** T1 (1-2) **3)** T8 (1:II:6:1) **4)** T325 (15:X:4:2) **5)** T6
(1:I:48:1) **6)** T8 (1:II:6:7) **7)** T463 (21:VII:7:8) **8)** T445
(21:Intro:1:7) **9)** YIR61 **10)** T589 (28:I:1:1-4) **11)** T3 (1:I:5:1)
12) T349 (16:VII:6:3-6) **13)** T493 (23:II:19:1-2) **14)** T147
(8:V:2:8) **15)** T268 13:XI:7:1) **16)** M72 (29:8:2) **17)** DU45 &
46 **18)** DU30 **19)** DU46 **20)** DU53 **21)** DU319 & YIR2
22) T95 (6:I:16:3) **23)** T463 (21:VII:7:8) **24)** T19 (2:II:1:11-12)
25) CL83 (3:1:3-4) **26)** T74 (5:I:5:2-3) **27)** T98 (6:II:10:5-7)
28) W324 (169:10:1) **29)** CL77 (Intro:4:1-5) **30)** W298
(158:3:5-6) **31)** T25 & 26 (2:V:5:1)

32) M10 (4:I:A:3:3) **33)** M26 (9:1:7-9) **34)** DU127 & 237
35) T640 (30:VII:1:1) **36)** T145 (8:IV:6:3-5)

Arten and Pursah's Take on Other Teachings
1) DU17 **2)** GRP25 **3)** T267 (13:XI:6:3) **4)** T349 (16:VII:6:2)
5) T417 (19:IV:C:i:3:1-6) **6)** W119 (70 Title) **7)** T25 & 26
(2:V:5:1) **8)** T4 (1:I:24:3) **9)** T182 (10:I:2:1) **10)** T13
(1:V:5:1-3) **11)** T42 (3:IV:2:1-2) **12)** DU59 **13)** PRxi **14)** M61
(24:5:7-10) **15)** M60 (24:1:1-8) **16)** T25 (2:V:1:9-11) **17)** T388
(18:VII) **18)** DU48 & 109 **19)** DU262 **20)** T454
(21:IV:3:1-3) **21)** T660 (31:VI:2:1) **22)** T176 (9:VII:3:7-8)
23) GRP25 **24)** W243 (132:7:2) **25)** DU77, 85, 132, 162 &
YIR83

A Course in Miracles – **Teaching, Borrowing, and
Compromising 1)** DU107 **2)** DU18 **3)** T9 (1:III:1:6)
4) M1 (Intro:2:1) **5)** T217 (12:I:9:5)

Those Who Seek Controversy... 1) YIR165 **2)** DU69 **3)** YIR149 &
150 **4)** T25 & 26 (2:V:5:1) **5)** CL77 (Intro:2:1-3) **6)** YIR167

Jesus, Jeshua, Y'Shua or J or How 'Bout J-Dog?
1) DU13 **2)** T7 (1:II:3:10-13) **3)** T509 (24:V:3:1-4)
4) CL87 (5:2:5) **5)** T56 (4:I:13:10-11) **6)** CL87 (5:2:1-2)

Forgiveness as a Way of Life 1) DU317 **2)** W401 (1:1:1-4)
3) W214 (121:1:1-4) **4)** W217 (122:1:1-6) **5)** W217 (122:2:1-5)
6) W104 (62:1:1-5) **7)** T635 (30:V:1:1-3) **8)** M16 (4:X:2:12)
9) T13 (1:VI:1:1) **10)** W422 (256:1:1-2) **11)** W379 (198:4-6:1)
12) W401 (1:4:4) **13)** W119 (70 Title) **14)** W119 (70:1-2)
15) T346 (16:VI:8:8) **16)** W34 (23:2:3-7) **17)** M51 (20:4:8)
18) T19 (II:1:11) **19)** M70 (29:3:3) **20)** W363 (191:4:2-6)
21) T29 (2:VI:3:4-7) **22)** T668 (31:VIII:8:6) **23)** T6 (1:I:45:1-2)
24) T615 & 616 (29:VI:1:1-5) **25)** T353 (17:II:5:1-3) **26)** P6
(2:II:3:1-3)

Forgiving What Gets in Your Face 1) DU331 **2)** M7 (3:1:7-8)
3) T562 (26:IX:6:1) **4)** T651 (31:III:1:4-6) **5)** T594 (28:II:7:1-4)
6) DU232 **7)** T142 (8:III:4:2) **8)** T3 (1:I:1:3) **9)** W73 (46:1-2)
10) T373 (18:I:6:7-9 & 7:1) **11)** T634 (30:IV:6:1-2) **12)** DU252

& 253 **13)** DU34, 253, & 340 **14)** DU253 **15)** CL85 (4:3:1-9)
16) T59 (4:II:10:1-5) **17)** T396 (18:IX:14:3-5) **18)** T395
(18:IX:9:1-4)

Unconscious Guilt: The Root of all Evil 1) DU325 **2)** T668
(31:VIII:9:2) **3)** T16 (1:VII:4:1) **4)** W1 (Intro:1:3) **5)** T202
(11:V:1:1) **6)** T96 (6:II:2:1) **7)** W443 (8:4:1-3) **8)** T505
(24:III:1:1) **9)** T51 (3:VII:6:11) **10)** T496 (23:III:5:4) **11)** T583
(27:VII:7:4) **12)** T416 (19:IV:C) **13)** T246 (13:IV:6:9-10)
14) T588 (27:VIII:13:2) **15)** T505 (24:III:1:2-8)

Definitive Statements 1) YIR101 **2)** W243 (132:6:2-5 & 7:1-2)
3) T430 (20:III:5:2-7) **4)** T638 (30:VI:1:1) **5)** T587 (27:VIII:10:1)
6) T587 & 588 (27:VIII:2-6) **7)** W386 (VI:3:3-5)
8) T82 (5:IV:6:4) **9)** T257 (13:VII:17:6-7) **10)** T257
(13:VII:14:1-3) **11)** T14 (1:VI:2:1-2) **12)** W339 (182:1:1-2)
13) T236 (13:Intro:3:1-2) **14)** T210 (11:VII:1:1-4) **15)** M33
(13:4:2-6) **16)** T445 (21:Intro:1:5) **17)** CL77 (Intro:2:5-6)
18) W268 (139:8:2) **19)** DU85 & 86 **20)** T496 (23:IV:1:10-11)

**The Crucifixion, Resurrection, the Second Coming of Christ,
and Oneness 1)** DU17 **2)** DU28 **3)** T93 (6:I:6:6-7) **4)** T92
(6:I:4:1-7) **5)** T94 (6:I:13:1-2 & 14:1) **6)** T84 (5:V:5:1)
7) W468 (332 Title) **8)** M68 (28:1:1-3) **9)** M68 (28:2:1-4)
10) M68 (28:2:6) **11)** M68 (28:3:1-7) **12)** W449 (9:4:1-4)
13) T64 (4:IV:10:1-3) **14)** W455 (10:5:1-3) **15)** M38 (15:3:1-3)
16) T384 (18:VI:1:5-6) **17)** M67 (27:6:10-11) **18)** W323
(169:5:1-7)

The Unreality of the Body 1) DU36 **2)** DU389 **3)** T388
(18:VII:3:1) **4)** W304 (161:2:1) **5)** P9 (2:IV:1:7) **6)** PRxi
7) T623 (29:IX:8:3) **8)** T445 (21:Intro:1:1) **9)** PRxi **10)** T38
(3:II:2:1:6) **11)** T623 (29:IX:8:1-3) **12)** DU117 **13)** T660
(31:VI:1:1-4) **14)** T47 (3:VI:3:1-3) **15)** W159 (92:1:2-5 & 2:1-4)
16) T84 (5:V:5:1) **17)** T661 (31:VI:3:1-4) **18)** T617 (29:VII:1:1-3)
19) T415 (19:IV:B:i:14:1-12) **20)** T15 (1:VII:2:1-5) **21)** CL85
(4:5:1-9) **22)** T105 (6:V:A:2:1-7)

The Illusory Nature of the Universe 1) DU245 **2)** T89
(5:VII:2:6) **3)** T499 (24:Intro:2:1) **4)** T617 (29:VII:1:9)

5) CL85 (4:1:1-5) **6)** T202 (11:V:1:1) **7)** W401 (1:1:1-4)
8) T548 (26:IV:1:5-7) **9)** M53 (21:1:9-10) **10)** T176
(9:VII:6:1-4) **11)** T668 (31:VIII:9:2) **12)** T14 (1:VI:2:1)
13) T493 & 494 (23:II:19:3-6) **14)** DU81 **15)** DU82 **16)** DU24
& 67 **17)** T445 (21:Intro:1:1-5) **18)** T443 (20:VIII:7:3-5)
19) T443 (20:VIII:8:1-7) **20)** M52 (20:5:5-10)

Spiritual Healing 1) DU311 **2)** M55 (22:1:9) **3)** T4 (24:1)
4) T330 (16:I:1:1-7) **5)** M18 (5:II:3:1-5) **6)** W413 (3:1:1-5)
7) W270 (140 Title) **8)** W270 (140:4:4-6) **9)** T84 (5:V:5:2-3)
10) T84 & 85 (5:V:5:6-8) **11)** M46 (17:8:4) **12)** T84 (5:V:5:1)
13) M32 (12:6:6-9) **14)** M18 (5:II:2:1-13) **15)** GRP22 & 29

It's About Time 1) DU332 **2)** T6 (1:I:48:1) **3)** T8 (1:II::6:7)
4) T618 & 619 (29:VII:9:1-3) **5)** T27 (2:V::A:11:3) **6)** T8
(1:II:6:9) **7)** W443 (8:4:1-3) **8)** T624 (29:IX:8:7) **9)** T181
(10:Intro:1:2-4)

The Tools 1) M46 (17:8:3-4) **2)** DU45, 115, & 245
3) T28 (2:V:A:18:1-6) **4)** W122 (71:9:3-5) **5)** W244
(132:15:2-3) **6)** S2 (1:I:4:1-4) **7)** S2 (1:I:2:7-9 & 3:1-6) **8)** T350
(16:VII:12:1-7) **9)** T447 (21:I:8:1-6 & 9:1-3) **10)** T448
(21:II:2:1-7) **11)** T90 (5:VII:6:6-11) **12)** T142 (8:III:4:1-5)
13) PRxiii **14)** T349 (16:VII:9:2-6) **15)** W34 (23:5:1-6)
16) W249 (134:9:1-3 & 10:1) **17)** DU229 **18)** T109 (6:V:C:2:8)
19) T6 (1:I:43:1) **20)** T272 (14:II:2:3) **21)** S10 (2:I:4:1-8)
22) T586 (27:VIII:6:2) **23)** W64 (41:10:1) **24)** W115 (68:1-4)
25) DU360 & 361 **26)** DU295 **27)** T447 (21:I:10:4-5) **28)** M11
(4:I:A:7:7-8) **29)** M62 (25:1:4-6) **30)** M62 (25:3:7)

The Funnies 1) DU201 **2)** T142 (8:III:4:2) **3)** M46 (17:8:4)
4) T29 (2:VI:4:6) **5)** T640 (30:VII:1:1) **6)** T373 (18:I:5:2)
7) T84 (5:V:3:10-11) **8)** T552 (26:V:13:1)

Wrapping this Puppy Up 1) DU169 **2)** DU231 **3)** DU113 &
M61 (24:5:9) **4)** M7 (3:1:6) **5)** T635 (30:IV:8:1-7) **6)** M37
(14:5:1-7) **7)** T175 (9:VII:1:5-7)

Recommended Material:
All things Gary Renard

Books

The Disappearance of the Universe – Straight Talk about Illusions, Past Lives, Religion, Sex, Politics, and the Miracles of Forgiveness

Your Immortal Reality – How to Break the Cycle of Birth and Death

Love Has Forgotten No One – The Answer to Life

CDs

The Disappearance of the Universe (abridged) 6 Discs

The End of Reincarnation – Breaking the Cycle of Birth and Death 2 Discs

Secrets of the Immortal – Advanced Teachings from A Course in Miracles 6 Discs

Fearless Love – The Answer to the Problem of Human Existence 2 Discs

Gary Renard 2009 Workshop Audiobook 4 Discs

DVD

Beyond the Ego Workshop & *Reflections* 4 Discs

Other

Gary's free podcasts with Gene Bogart: www.forgiveness.tv

For more on Gary Renard including schedule of appearances, or to read excerpts of *The Disappearance of the Universe,* check out Gary's website: www.garyrenard.com

For a copy of *A Course in Miracles*, be sure to purchase the authentic version, the one published by Foundation for Inner Peace.

Links

Mikey's Website:
www.giddyupmikey.com

Mikey's Disappearance of the Universe blog:
www.giddyupmikey.blogspot.com

Mikey's DU Quote of the Day blog:
www.giddyupmikeyduquote.blogspot.com

Diary of a Mad Course Student blog by Dawn Sechrist Burkett:
www.diary-of-a-mad-course-student.blogspot.com

ACIM Blog by Bruce Rawles and company:
www.acimblog.com

On Course with Gene Bogart:
www.oncourse.genebogart.com

Foundation for Inner Peace:
www.acim.org

Foundation for A Course in Miracles
www.facim.org

Add Mikey as a friend on Facebook:
www.facebook.com/giddyupmikey